THE AGE OF IMPRESSIONISM AT THE ART INSTITUTE OF CHICAGO

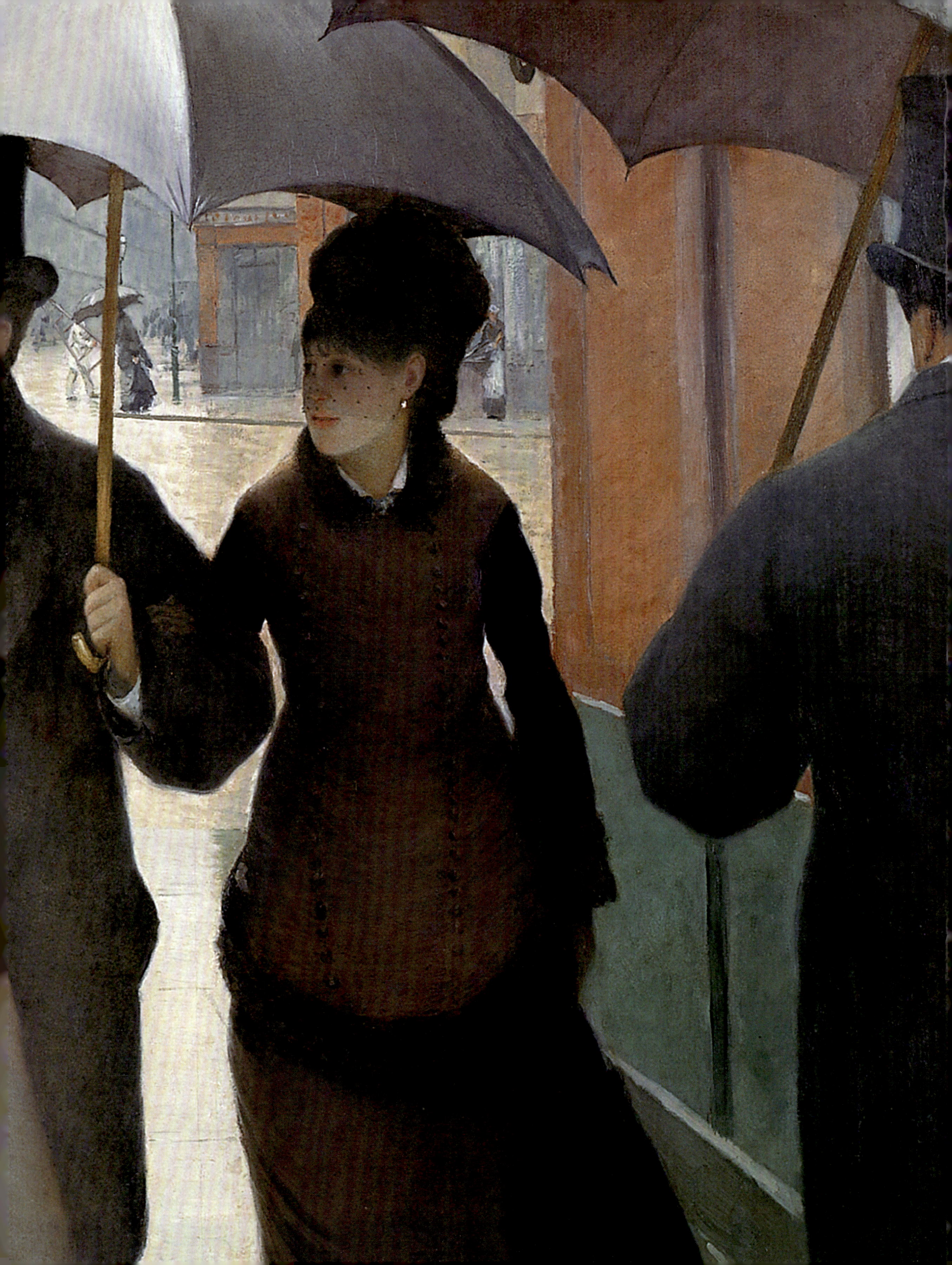

The Age of Impressionism at the Art Institute of Chicago

Gloria Groom and Douglas Druick

With the assistance of Dorota Chudzicka and Jill Shaw

The Art Institute of Chicago
Yale University Press, New Haven and London

First edition
Printed in Italy

Library of Congress Control Number: 2008922280
ISBN: 978-0-300-13678-4

Published by
The Art Institute of Chicago
111 South Michigan Avenue
Chicago, Illinois 60603-6404
www.artic.edu

Distributed by
Yale University Press
302 Temple Street
P.O. Box 209040
New Haven, Connecticut 06520-9040
www.yalebooks.com

Produced by the Publications Department of the Art Institute of Chicago, Susan F. Rossen, Executive Director

Edited by Susan E. Weidemeyer with Susan F. Rossen

Production by Sarah E. Guernsey, Associate Director, Carolyn Heidrich, Production Coordinator, and Kate Kotan, Production Assistant

Photography research by Joseph Mohan, Photography Editor

Designed and typeset by Joan Sommers Design, Chicago, Illinois

Separations by Professional Graphics, Rockford, Illinois

Printing and binding by Mondadori, Verona, Italy

DETAILS

Cover: *Lunch at the Restaurant Fournaise (The Rowers' Lunch)* (cat. 23).

Back flap: *The Plate of Apples* (cat. 34).

Frontispiece: *Paris Street; Rainy Day* (cat. 18).

Page 6: *Vétheuil* (cat. 82).

Page 8: *Fishing in Spring, the Pont de Clichy (Asnières)* (cat. 55).

Page 10: *Two Sisters (On the Terrace)* (cat. 28).

Page 27: *The Races at Longchamp* (cat. 7).

Page 45: *Woman at Her Toilette* (cat. 19).

Page 97: *At the Moulin Rouge* (cat. 62).

Page 153: *Waterloo Bridge, Sunlight Effect* (cat. 87).

Page 178: *Near the Lake* (cat. 27).

Page 182: *Self-Portrait* (cat. 57).

CONTENTS

FOREWORD

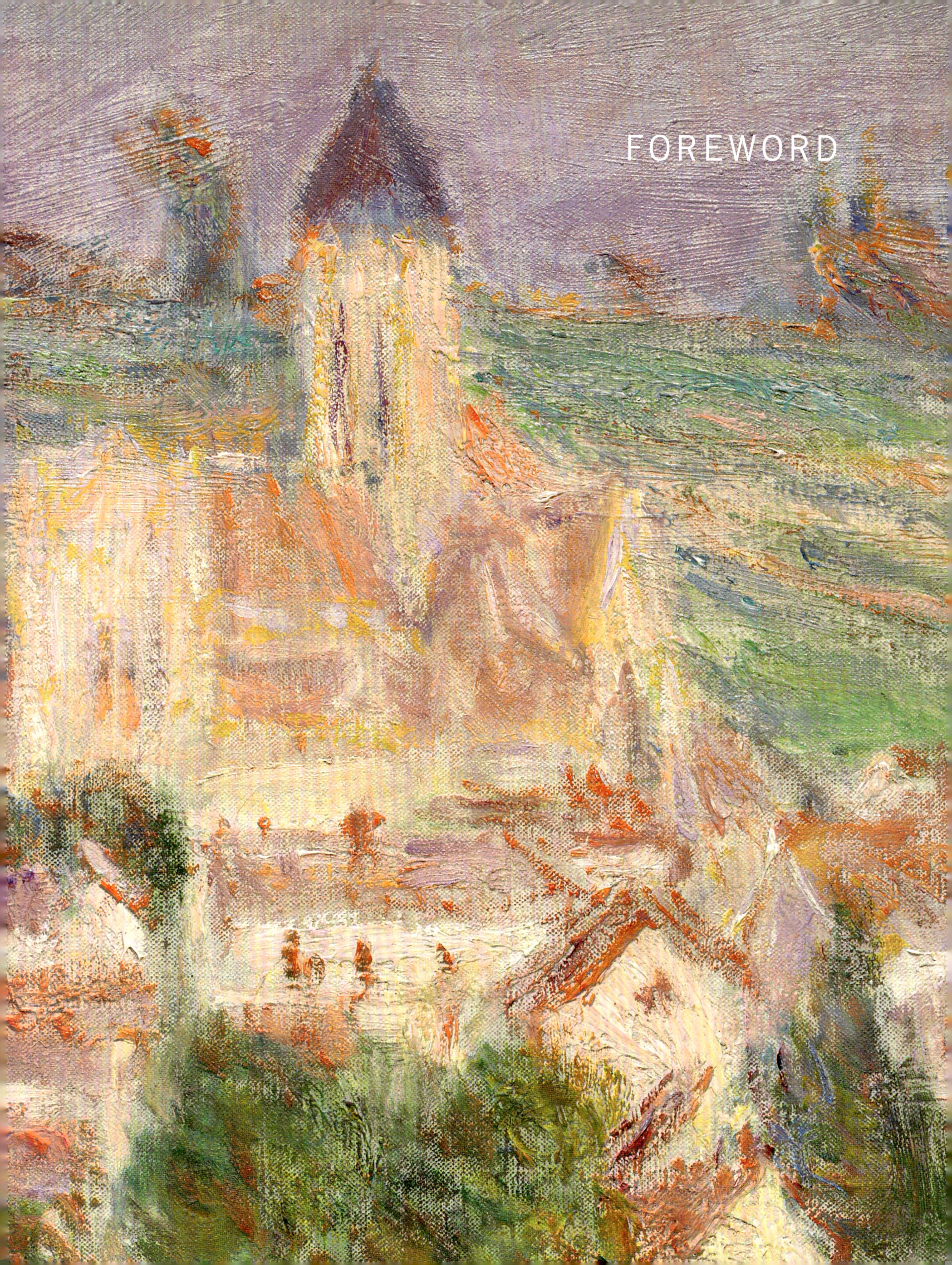

The Art Institute of Chicago's holdings of Impressionist and Post-Impressionist paintings are among the very finest outside of France. We take great pride in this collection, which is beloved by all who visit the Art Institute. Indeed, it plays a central role in the history of the museum and in that of the city as well. And it reminds us that the Art Institute has always been dedicated to the art of its time.

The history of Chicago is well known. It was virtually destroyed by a great fire in 1871 and, with the development of new technologies that allowed for tall, steel-frame structures, rebuilt itself into a thriving metropolis in time for the World's Columbian Exposition of 1893. In 1889 the Art Institute's first director and president, William M. R. French (1843–1914), traveled with a group of civic leaders to Paris to attend the Exposition Universelle, the highlight of which was Gustave Eiffel's great iron tower. They were intent on evaluating the fair in anticipation of Chicago's own upcoming exposition, and, while there, they also looked for recent works of art for the Art Institute's collection. Impressionist painting had been shown in increasingly popular exhibitions in Paris from 1874 to 1886. At the same time, commercial galleries were displaying contemporary art on a scale never before seen in the French capital. This art would be represented in an exhibition at the Columbian Exposition, thanks in particular to two of Chicago's earliest collectors of modern European art, Potter and Bertha Honoré Palmer. The generosity of the Palmers, and others whose names are included in the credit lines of the works that appear in this publication (among them, Frederic Clay Bartlett, Mrs. Lewis Larned Coburn, Mr. and Mrs. Martin A. Ryerson, and Charles H. and Mary F. S. Worcester), resulted in the Art Institute's encyclopedic representation of nineteenth-century French art.

As we prepare to open our Modern Wing in the spring of 2009—designed by the Pritzker Prize–winning architect Renzo Piano and dedicated to modern and contemporary art, architecture, and design—we have taken the opportunity to renovate and reinstall our historical galleries, including those that house our Impressionist and Post-Impressionist collections. These are being designed by the Chicago firm Vinci/Hamp Architects, Inc., long associated with the Art Institute and with the preservation of Chicago's landmark buildings. The resulting installation provides grander, more spacious galleries for our collection and integrates it more thoroughly into our earlier holdings.

To accompany this important reinstallation, we have elected to publish this book on the collection, accounting for its history and importance. This has been the task of Gloria Groom, David and Mary Winton Green Curator of Nineteenth-Century European Painting, and Douglas Druick, Searle Curator and Chair of Medieval through Modern European Painting and Sculpture and Prince Trust Curator and Chair of Prints and Drawings, who work most closely with the collection and have published and lectured widely on it. We are deeply grateful to them for their devotion to the project, which has brought new research to bear upon well-known and well-loved works. This is but a first step in an ambitious undertaking to publish a comprehensive scholarly catalogue, in several volumes, on the museum's nineteenth-century European paintings for the first time since our founders began to acquire them for the Art Institute and the citizens of Chicago and beyond.

James Cuno
President and Eloise W. Martin Director
The Art Institute of Chicago

ACKNOWLEDGMENTS

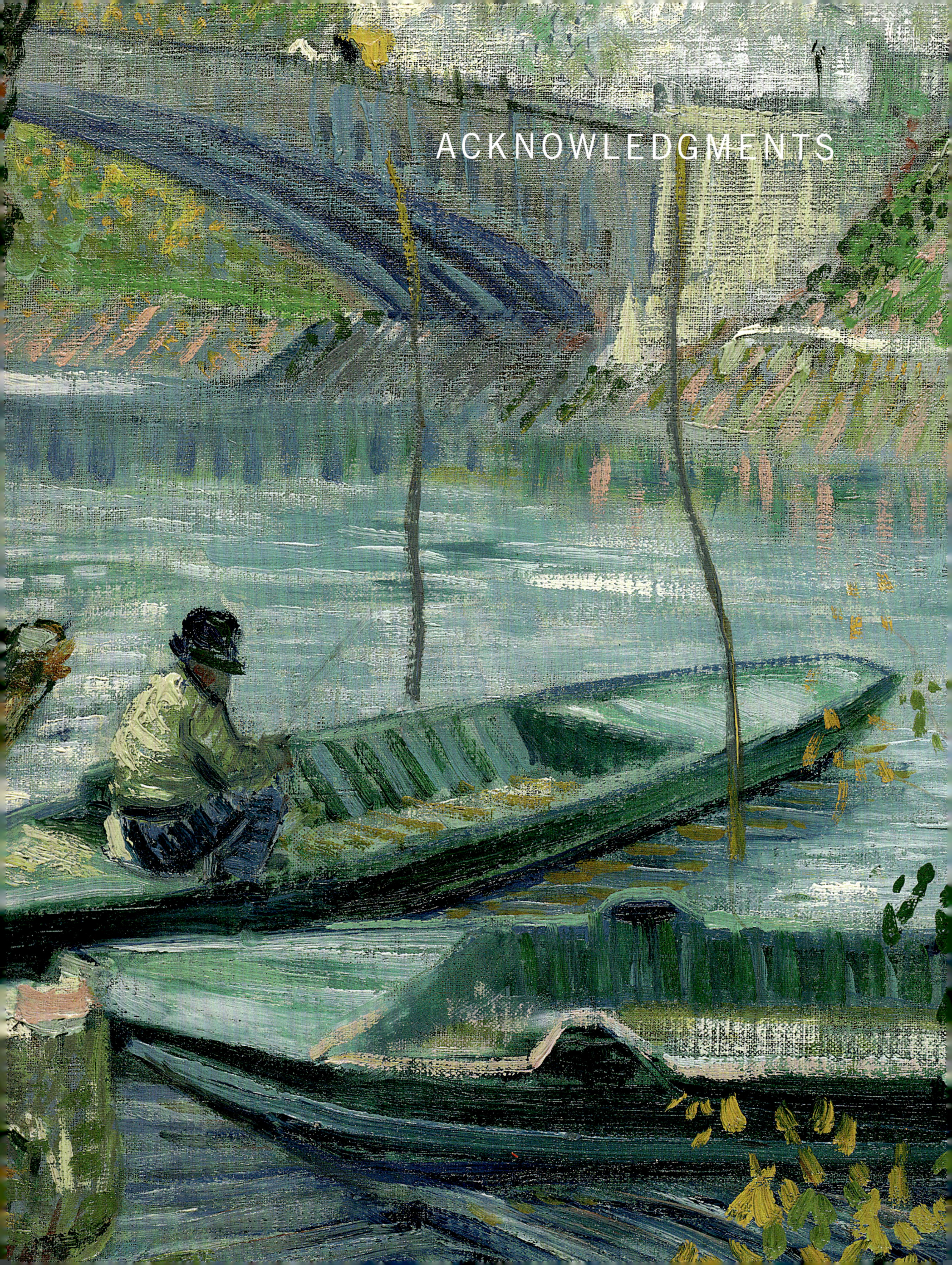

This project was conceived under the direction of James Cuno, President and Eloise W. Martin Director of the Art Institute of Chicago. We thank him, along with Meredith Mack, Deputy Director and Chief Operating Officer, and Dorothy Schroeder, Vice President for Exhibitions and Museum Administration, for their invaluable support.

Many other people in several departments in the museum are owed special thanks. The task of organizing and editing the text for this book was beautifully handled by Susan Weidemeyer, an editor in the Publications Department, assisted by Susan F. Rossen, Executive Director of Publications. Led by Sarah Guernsey, Associate Director for Production, Carolyn Heidrich, Kate Kotan, and Joseph Mohan were responsible for the book's visual elements and high production value. Photography was provided by the Department of Imaging: Associate Director Christopher Gallagher, along with Robert Hashimoto, Caroline Nutley, and Amy Zavaleta. The book owes its handsome design to Joan Sommers of Joan Sommers Design.

In the Art Institute's Archives, we owe particular thanks to Bart Ryckbosch for his assistance in unearthing important information on the museum's history for the illustrated chronology. We also thank Mary Woolever and Deborah Webb in that department. For their additional review of the chronology, we thank Jack Perry Brown, Director of Ryerson and Burnham Libraries, and Robert Sharp, Director of Publications. For their help with archival photography research, we acknowledge Mary Lou Perkins at the Woman's Board and Jane Allen, Paul Florian, and Randy White.

In the Department of Medieval through Modern European Painting and Sculpture, special thanks go to Dorota Chudzicka and Jill Shaw, without whom this book would not have been possible. We are also grateful to Geri Banik, Darren Burge, Robert Burnier, Stephanie D'Alessandro, Rachel Drescher, Adrienne Jeske, Jennifer Paoletti, and Martha Wolff, as well as to our interns Renee Inouye, Caroline Neely, and Anastasia Standa. In the Department of Conservation, Frank Zuccari, Executive Director of Conservation, and Kirk Vuillemot provided their expertise for the reframing of a number of featured paintings. We also acknowledge the efforts of Allison Langley, Kristin Lister, and Faye Wrubel, who, in addition to her diligent examination of the works, was always willing to share her knowledge of painting techniques with the authors. In the Department of Prints and Drawings, we want to acknowledge Rachel Freeman, Suzanne Folds McCullagh, Harriet Stratis, Emily Vokt, and Peter Zegers. We also wish to thank the following people: in Museum Registration, Darrell Green, Mary Solt, and John Molini and our art packers and handlers; in the Office of the General Counsel and Corporation Secretary, Julia E. Getzels and Maria Simon; in Museum Finance, Dawn Koster and Jeanne Ladd; in Marketing and Public Affairs, Carrie Heinonen, Erin Hogan, and Chai Lee; in Graphic Design, Lyn DelliQuadri; and in Protection Services, Michelle Lehrman-Jenness.

For this project, we have drawn upon the scholarship of authors who have previously published on the Art Institute's Impressionist and Post-Impressionist collection. We wish to acknowledge the work of Jean Sutherland Boggs, Richard Brettell, the late Andrew Forge, John Goodman, Sally Ruth May, Britt Salvesen, and Belinda Thomson. Research for this book went far beyond what is included in the Selected Bibliography. The important work of scholars we could not mention here will be fully credited in the upcoming scholarly catalogues on the Art Institute's collection of nineteenth-century European paintings.

Nonetheless, we would like to acknowledge the contribution of those individuals who helped us to address a number of questions still posed by these familiar works: Stephen Eisenman, Jodi Hauptman, Jean-François Heim, Robert Herbert, Joachim Pissarro, Susan Stein, Vérane Tesseau, Jayne Warman, and Mary Weaver Chapin. Special thanks go to Jill DeVonyar, an independent art historian, and Richard Kendall at the Sterling and Francine Clark Art Institute, Williamstown, Massachusetts; Aileen Ribeiro at the Courtauld Institute of Art, London; Richard Thomson at the University of Edinburgh; Louis van Tilborgh at the Van Gogh Museum, Amsterdam; and Juliet Wilson-Bareau, an independent art historian in London, all of whom generously shared their research and tirelessly responded to our inquiries. Finally, our thanks go to Jean Coyner, an independent art historian in Paris, for contributing her translation skills to the project.

This book is published on the occasion of a historic exhibition of the Art Institute's collection at the Kimbell Art Museum, Fort Worth. We thank our colleagues at the museum: Timothy Potts, former director; Malcolm Warner, Acting Director; and Wendy Gottlieb, Manager of Publications and Public Access.

Gloria Groom and Douglas Druick

IMPRESSIONISM AND POST-IMPRESSIONISM IN CHICAGO

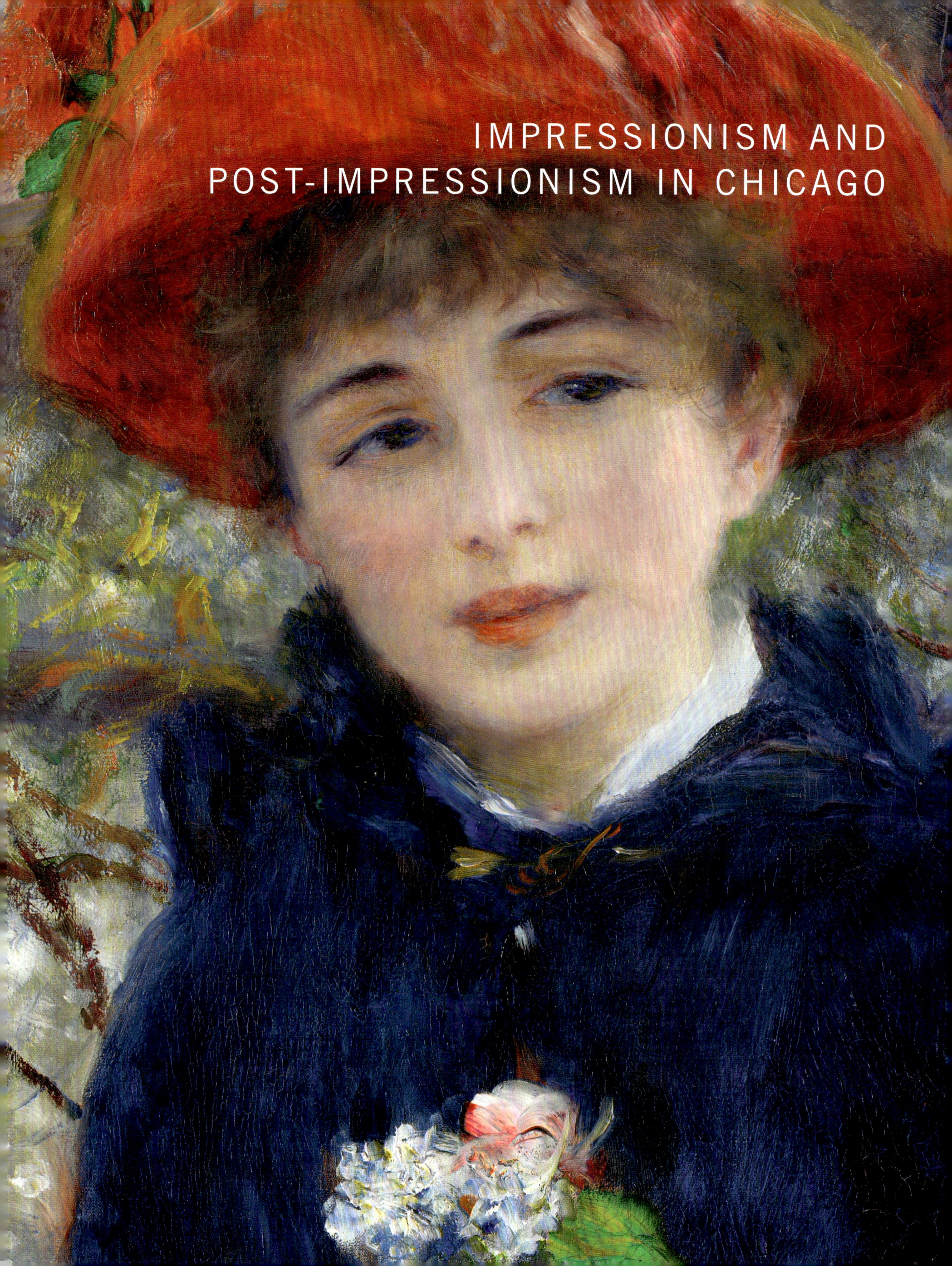

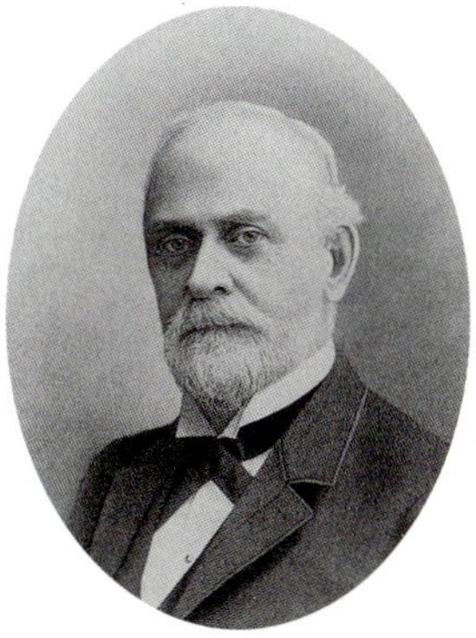

Potter Palmer (1826–1902).

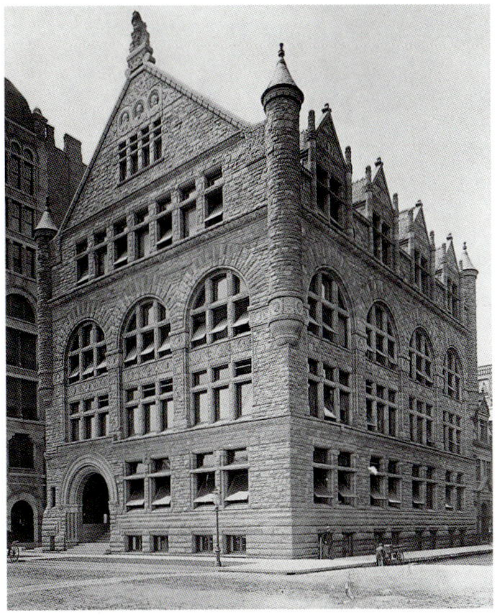

From 1887 to 1893, the Art Institute occupies a building designed by architects Burnham and Root. It is located at Michigan Avenue and Van Buren Street.

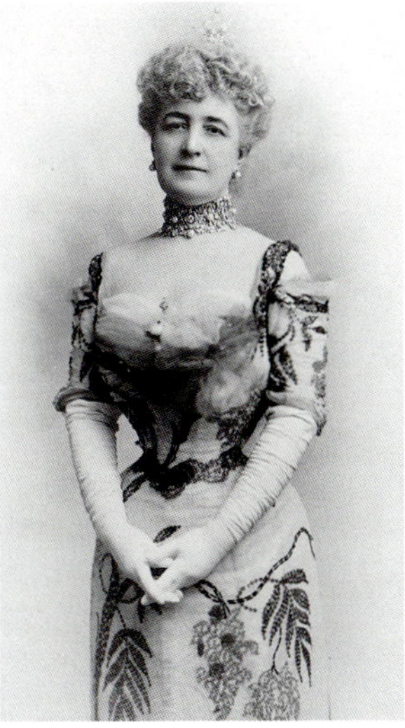

Bertha Honoré Palmer (1849–1918).

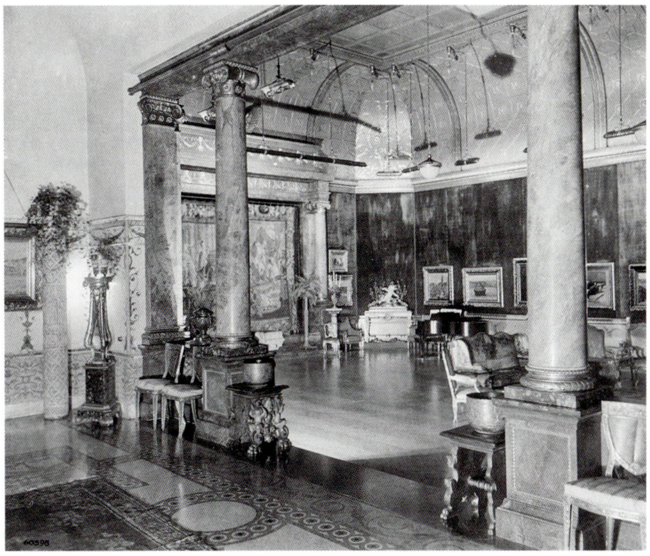

Interior of the Palmers' residence with paintings by Claude Monet, including *Stack of Wheat* (cat. 79), arranged along the far wall.

1879

On May 24, the Chicago Academy of Fine Arts is created from the Academy of Design, an institution established by a group of artists in 1866. In December 1882, the Academy will undergo a change in name, becoming the Art Institute of Chicago.

1888

In November the Thurber Gallery, Chicago, exhibits works by Claude Monet, Camille Pissarro, and Alfred Sisley. The exhibition is the earliest documented display of French Impressionist art in Chicago.

1889

Chicagoans Potter Palmer (1826–1902), a hotelier and real-estate developer, and his wife, Bertha Honoré Palmer (1849–1918), begin collecting works by Impressionist artists. Through their friendship with the artist Mary Cassatt and the art consultant Sara Tyson Halloway, the Palmers quickly become enthusiastic supporters of "the new painting." Among their first purchases is a pastel by Edgar Degas (*On the Stage*, 1876–77; Art Institute of Chicago), acquired from the dealer Paul Durand-Ruel in Paris.

1890

On September 3, the Inter-State Industrial Exposition of Chicago opens in a building located on the future site of the Art Institute. The exposition includes a fine-arts section with nearly five hundred oils, watercolors, and pastels gathered together by Sara Tyson Halloway, the secretary of its art department. Works by Eugène-Louis Boudin, Henri Fantin-Latour, Degas, Monet, Pissarro, Pierre-Auguste Renoir, and Sisley, among others, are exhibited.

1891

Martin A. Ryerson (1856–1932) makes his first purchase of Monet's work, probably *The "Red Road" near Menton* (1884; private collection), from the Durand-Ruel Gallery, New York. The painting will enter the Art Institute's collection with the Ryerson bequest in 1933 and will be deaccessioned in 1983. Ryerson, a trustee of the Art Institute from 1890 to 1924 and its vice president for many years, and his wife, Carrie Hutchinson Ryerson (1859–1937), will become the museum's greatest single donors.

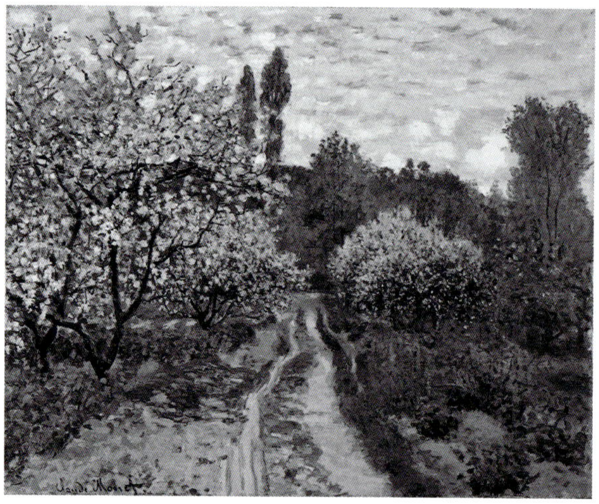

Claude Monet. *Pommiers en fleurs (Le Printemps)*, 1872. Collection of the Union League Club of Chicago. This work is shown in an 1895 Monet exhibition at the Art Institute.

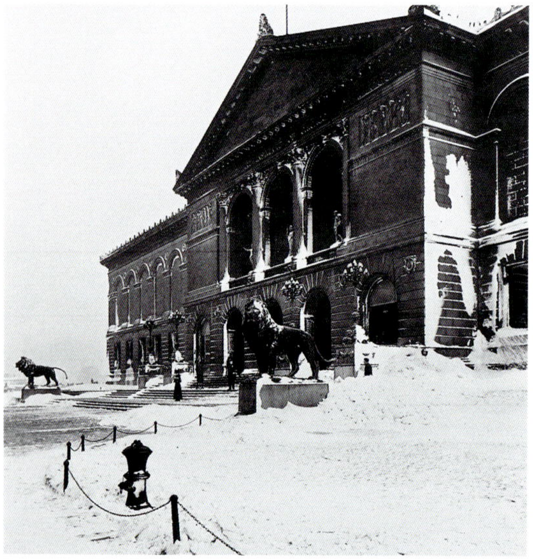

View of the Art Institute's new home on Michigan Avenue, c. 1894, after Mrs. Henry Field commissions and donates two bronze lions by Edward Kemeys to stand at the entrance.

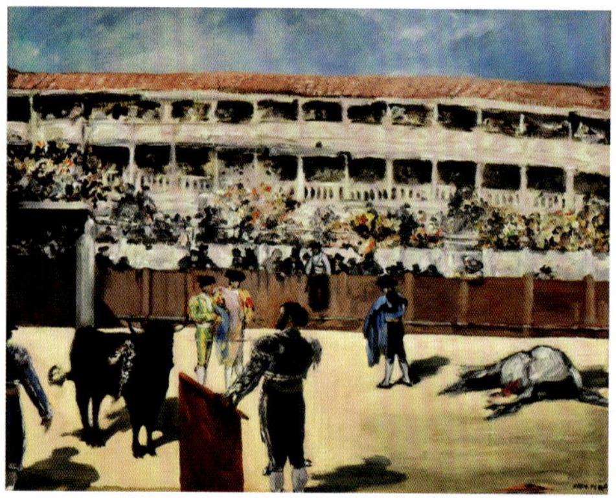

Édouard Manet. *Bullfight*, 1865/66 (cat. 8). This painting is included in an 1895 Manet exhibition and the 1913 Armory Show.

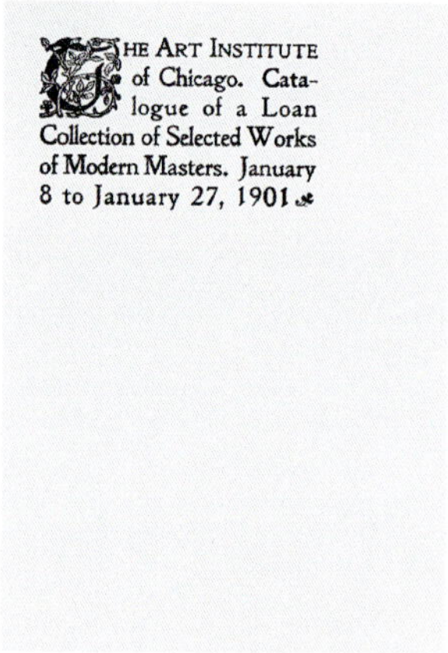

The Art Institute of Chicago. Catalogue of a Loan Collection of Selected Works of Modern Masters. January 8 to January 27, 1901

Catalogue cover for the 1901 exhibition *Loan Collection of Selected Works of Modern Masters*, on view at the Art Institute.

1892

In February construction begins on a new building on Michigan Avenue at Adams Street. Designed by the Boston architectural firm of Shepley, Rutan, and Coolidge and planned in cooperation with the 1893 World's Columbian Exposition, the Allerton Building, as it will later be named, is first occupied by the World's Congress Auxiliary of the Columbian Exposition. After the exposition closes, on October 31, 1893, the Art Institute takes possession of the building, which formally opens on December 8. Surrounded by later wings, it continues to serve as the main entrance to the museum.

In May the Palmers attend the opening of a Renoir exhibition at the Durand-Ruel Gallery, Paris. In the weeks before the show, they acquire ten Renoirs from the dealer. At the same exhibition, they see Monet, and by the end of 1892, they own a number of his works, including at least eight canvases from his series *Stacks of Wheat*. They display their collection prominently on the red velvet-covered walls of their residence at 1350 North Lake Shore Drive, Chicago.

1893

Bertha Honoré Palmer is the president of the Board of Lady Managers of the World's Columbian Exposition. Among its myriad displays is *Loan Collection: Foreign Masterpieces Owned in the United States*; most of the 126 works featured are by nineteenth-century French artists. The Palmers lend fifteen paintings, including canvases by Pissarro and Sisley.

1895

Between March 18 and March 28, the Art Institute hosts Monet's first-ever one-man exhibition held in a museum. Comprised of twenty paintings, it is one of a series of shows mounted this year by Durand-Ruel in order to introduce the artist's work to the American public. *Pommiers en fleurs (Le Printemps)* is purchased from the exhibition and enters the collection of the Union League Club of Chicago.

On May 29, *15 Works by Édouard Manet* opens at the Art Institute. A number of the featured paintings had been shown earlier this year at the Durand-Ruel Gallery, New York. Édouard Manet's *Bullfight* (cat. 8), exhibited at the New York venue, will be acquired from Durand-Ruel by Martin A. Ryerson in 1911 and later bequeathed to the Art Institute.

1901

Loan Collection of Selected Works of Modern Masters is held at the Art Institute from January 8 to January 27. It includes examples by a number of Impressionist artists—such as Boudin, Monet, Pissarro, and Sisley—lent by Durand-Ruel. Martin A. Ryerson loans a painting by Stanislas Lépine, a contemporary of the Impressionists, and Potter Palmer lends works by Jean-Charles Cazin to the exhibition.

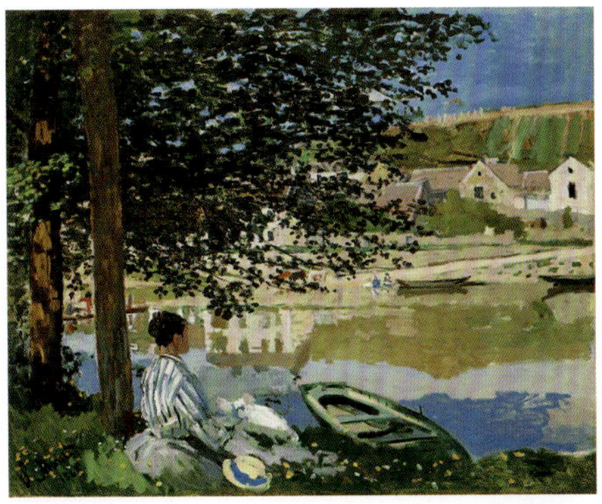

Claude Monet. *On the Bank of the Seine, Bennecourt*, 1868 (cat. 13). This painting is featured in a 1905 Boston show and a 1910 Chicago exhibition.

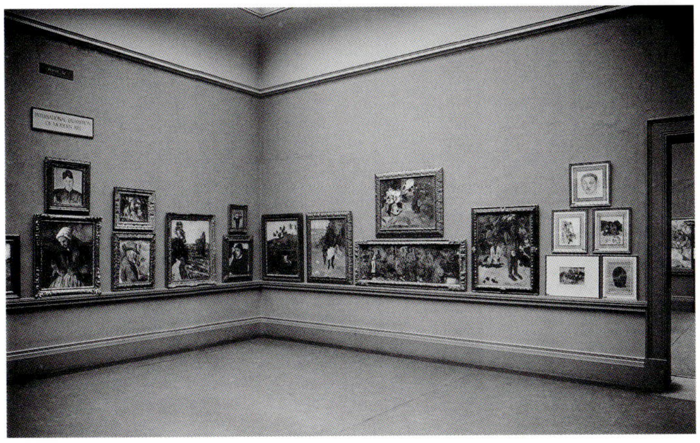

Room 52 of the Chicago installation of the 1913 Armory Show, including works by Paul Cézanne and Paul Gauguin. Four of Gauguin's drawings and watercolors (at right) will eventually enter the Art Institute's collection.

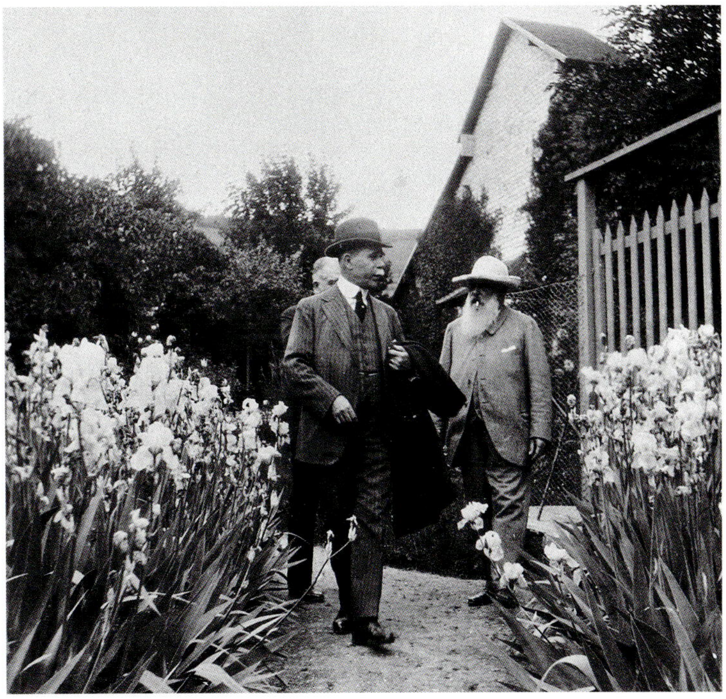

Martin A. Ryerson (1856–1932) with Monet (at right) and possibly Joseph Durand-Ruel at Giverny, France, June 1920.

1903

In February the Art Institute becomes the first American museum to acquire a work by Monet. It will deaccession the painting, *Pourville in Bad Weather* (1896; private collection), purchased from Durand-Ruel, in 1930.

1905

In March the Copley Society, Boston, hosts an exhibition of ninety-five paintings by Monet (along with eleven sculptures by Auguste Rodin) that is heralded as "the largest collection of works of the famous French Impressionist ever brought together in the United States." The greatest single lender is James F. Sutton of the American Art Association, but loans come from collectors throughout the country, including Chicagoans Mrs. John Jay Borland, the Palmers (who loan seven Monets, including *On the Bank of the Seine, Bennecourt* [cat. 13]), and Martin A. Ryerson.

1910

Paintings from the Collection of Mrs. Potter Palmer, on view at the Art Institute from May to August, features fifty-three works from this groundbreaking collection. Nine are by Monet, including *On the Bank of the Seine, Bennecourt* (cat. 13), *Stacks of Wheat (Sunset, Snow Effect)* (cat. 77), and *Bordighera* (cat. 47).

1913

From March 24 to April 16, the Art Institute hosts the controversial International Exhibition of Modern Art, better known as the Armory Show. Exhibited the previous month at the 69th Regiment Armory, New York, it is the most comprehensive assemblage of European modern art held in the United States to date and attracts 188,650 visitors in Chicago. Manet's *Bullfight* (cat. 8) is lent by Martin A. Ryerson to the New York exhibition.

1920

On June 4, Joseph Durand-Ruel, the Ryersons, and Mrs. Charles (Frances) Hutchinson (1857–1936), the wife of the president of the Art Institute's Board of Trustees, visit Monet at Giverny. They travel there in order to see the artist's recent *Water Lilies* murals and buy them for the Art Institute. Although this transaction is not realized, the Ryersons have acquired seventeen Monets by this time.

The Art Institute stages an exhibition of work by Degas from March 9 to April 1. It includes four paintings, fifteen pastels, and twenty-three drawings.

Pierre-Auguste Renoir. *Acrobats at the Cirque Fernando (Francisca and Angelina Wartenberg)*, 1879 (cat. 26).

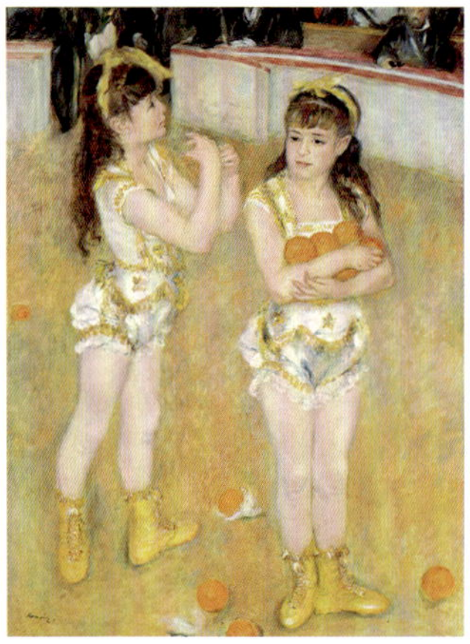

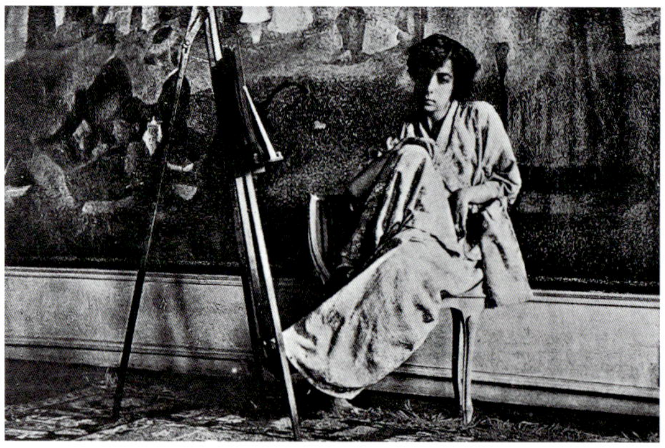

Lucie Bru Cousturier in front of *La Grande Jatte*, early 1920s. Frederic Clay Bartlett buys the painting from her in 1924.

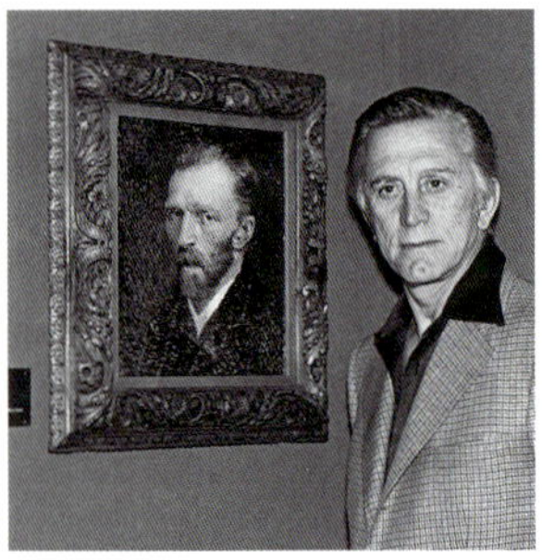

The actor Kirk Douglas next to the Art Institute's *Self-Portrait* (cat. 57) by Vincent van Gogh, a work in the Joseph Winterbotham Collection. Douglas will play the role of Van Gogh in the 1956 film *Lust for Life*.

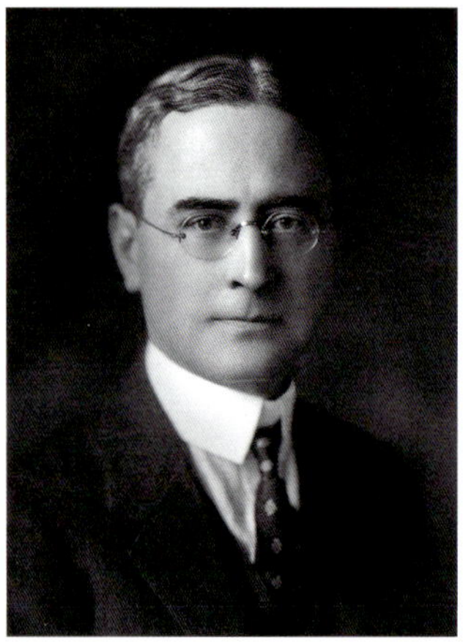

Potter Palmer II (1875–1943).

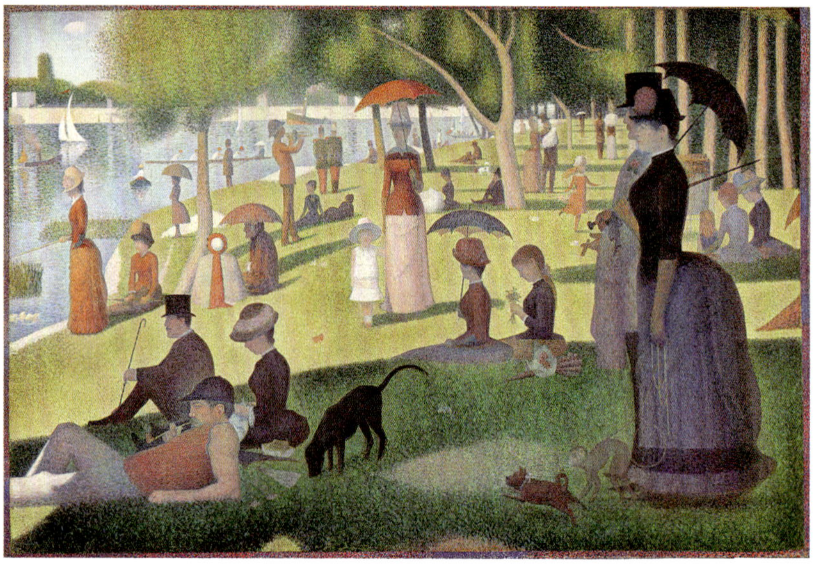

Georges Seurat. *A Sunday on La Grande Jatte—1884*, 1884–86. The Art Institute of Chicago, Helen Birch Bartlett Memorial Collection, 1926.224.

1921

Joseph Winterbotham (1852–1925) makes an initial gift of $50,000 to the Art Institute with an unusual stipulation: the money will be invested and the museum will use the interest to build a collection of thirty-five European paintings. Once the first group of thirty-five is assembled, any of these can be sold or exchanged to insure that "the purchase of paintings, as time goes on, is toward superior works of art and of greater merit and continuous improvement." Paintings such as Paul Gauguin's *Woman in Front of a Still Life by Cézanne* (cat. 65), Vincent van Gogh's *Self-Portrait* (cat. 57), and Henri de Toulouse-Lautrec's *Equestrienne (At the Cirque Fernando)* (cat. 60) will all become part of the Joseph Winterbotham Collection at the Art Institute.

1922

Four years after Bertha Honoré Palmer's death, her sons, Honoré (1874–1964) and Potter II (1875–1943), together with Robert Harshe, the Art Institute's director from 1921 to 1938, and several trustees, select works from her collection and acquire them with money bequeathed to the museum in her will. At the same time, Honoré and Potter II present the Art Institute with additional works that they have inherited from their mother. Along with examples by French Romantic and Barbizon artists, the Palmer gift brings the first major group of French Impressionist art to the museum's collection. Of these works, Renoir's *Acrobats at the Cirque Fernando (Francisca and Angelina Wartenberg)* (cat. 26) was Mrs. Palmer's favorite; she took it with her on her European trips and visits to the East Coast. Potter II will serve as the museum's president from 1925 to 1943.

1924

In June Robert Harshe receives news from the artist and trustee Frederic Clay Bartlett (1873–1953) that he has acquired "almost by a miracle . . . the finest modern picture in France." He acquires Georges Seurat's *A Sunday on La Grande Jatte—1884* from the artist Lucie Bru Cousturier, whose father had purchased it in 1900.

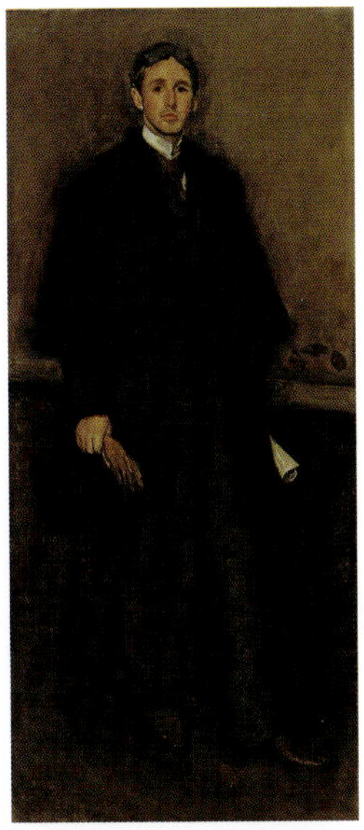

James McNeill Whistler (American, 1834–1903). *Arrangement in Flesh Color and Brown: Portrait of Arthur Jerome Eddy*, 1894. The Art Institute of Chicago, Arthur Jerome Eddy Memorial Collection, 1931.501.

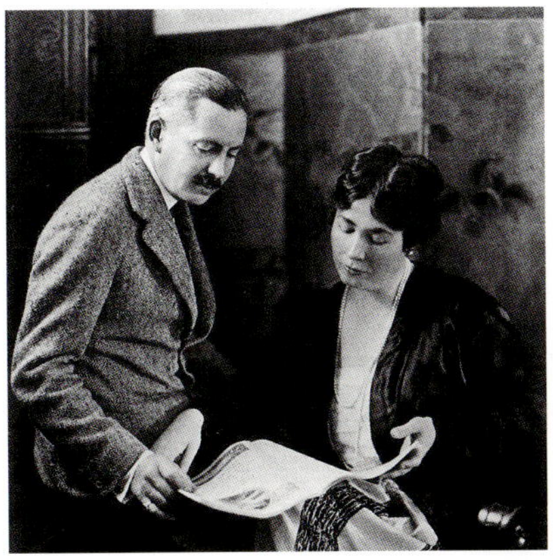

Frederic Clay (1873–1953) and Helen Birch Bartlett (1883–1925), c. 1923.

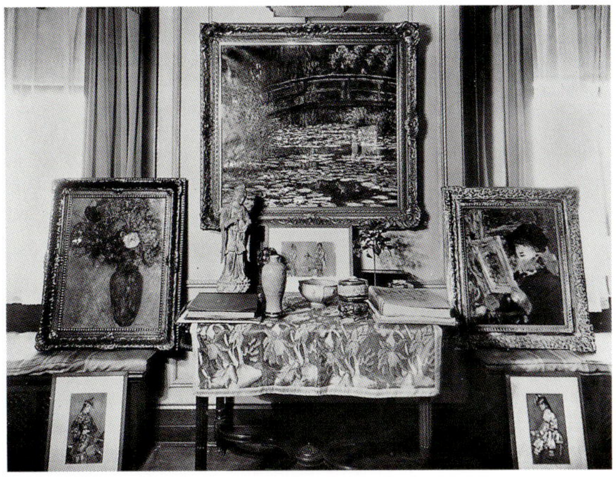

A view of Mrs. Lewis Larned Coburn's Blackstone Hotel apartment showing her casual, eccentric display of artwork, including Manet's *Woman Reading* (cat. 21) and Monet's *Water Lily Pond* (cat. 90).

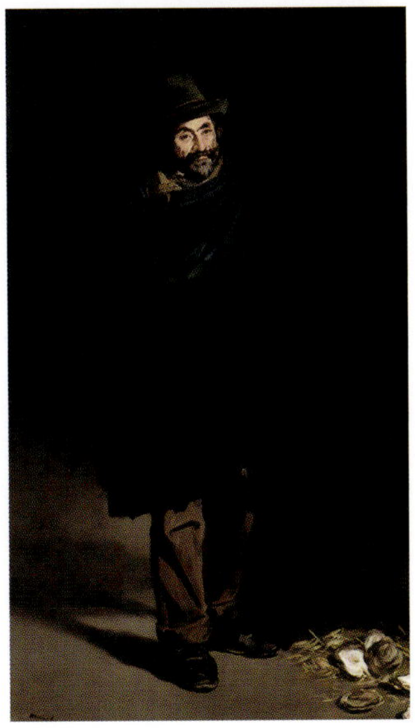

Édouard Manet. *Beggar with Oysters (Philosopher)*, 1865/67 (cat. 2). This canvas is acquired from the estate of Arthur Jerome Eddy (1859–1920) in 1931.

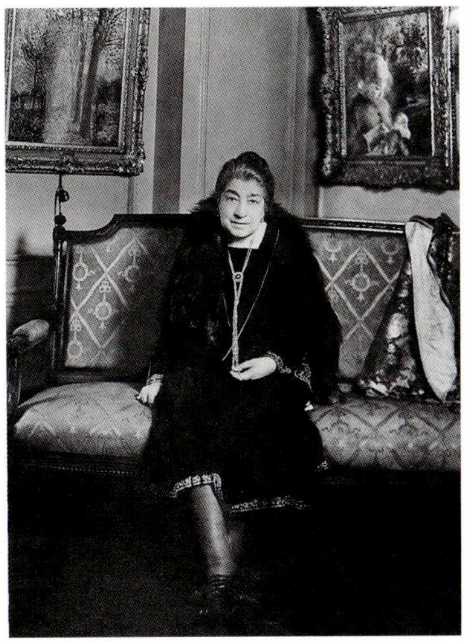

Mrs. Lewis Larned Coburn (1856–1932) with Renoir's *Young Woman Sewing* (cat. 29) at upper right.

1926

As a memorial to his second wife, Helen Birch (1883–1925), Frederic Clay Bartlett presents the Art Institute with *La Grande Jatte*, along with over twenty other significant Post-Impressionist paintings by artists such as Paul Cézanne (cat. 67), Gauguin (cat. 71), and Van Gogh (cats. 54 and 58). Proposed in December 1925, the Helen Birch Bartlett Memorial Collection officially enters the museum in 1926. Bartlett will make several additions and deletions to the content of the collection in the late 1920s, finally adding Lautrec's *Ballet Dancers* (1885–86) in 1931. Bartlett considers this collection of key Post-Impressionist pictures to be a way for the Art Institute to increase its representation of modern art, previously exemplified largely by the Impressionists.

1930

The Art Institute opens a loan exhibition of over 250 works—including paintings, drawings, prints, and posters—by Lautrec.

1931

The Art Institute receives twenty-three objects, including Manet's *Beggar with Oysters (Philosopher)* (cat. 2), from the estate of Arthur Jerome Eddy (1859–1920), a prominent Chicago lawyer. In addition to being a pioneering champion of modern art, Eddy wrote several books, including *Cubists and Post-Impressionism* (1914), which was the first comprehensive text published in English on the subject. He was also instrumental in bringing the 1913 Armory Show to Chicago and acquired many paintings and sculptures from it.

1932

The exhibition *Mrs. L. L. Coburn Collection of Modern Paintings and Watercolors* is displayed at the Art Institute from April 6 to October 9. Annie Swan Coburn (1856–1932) had initially purchased American art, gradually expanding her collection to include French Impressionist paintings. Upon her death, nearly two months after the opening of this exhibition, her will reveals a gift to the museum of over one hundred paintings, pastels, and watercolors, many of which are important Impressionist and Post-Impressionist works; they will be officially accessioned in 1933.

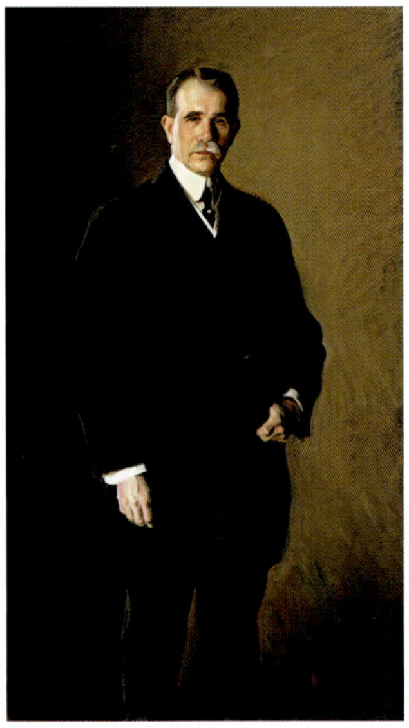

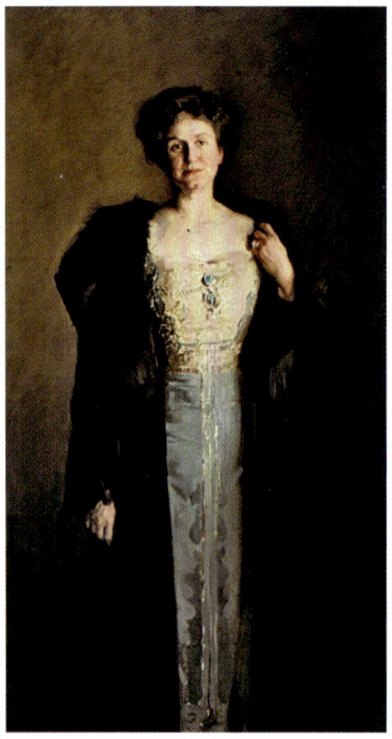

Louis Betts (American, 1873–1961). *Martin A. Ryerson*, 1913. The Art Institute of Chicago, Mr. and Mrs. Martin A. Ryerson Collection, 1933.1183.

Louis Betts. *Mrs. Martin A. Ryerson*, 1912. The Art Institute of Chicago, Mrs. Martin A. Ryerson Collection, 1935.433.

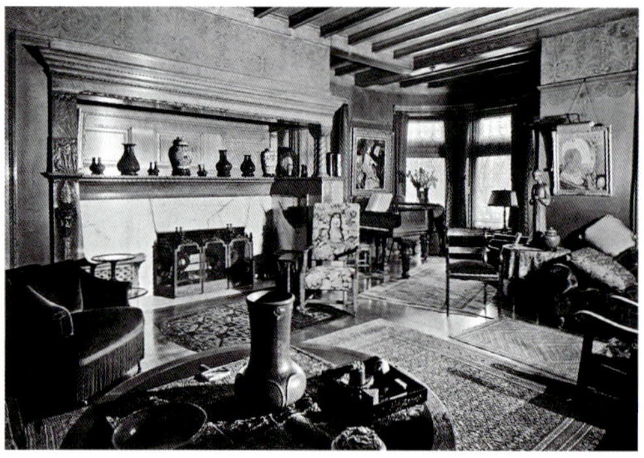

Interior of the Ryersons' Chicago home with Renoir's *Woman at the Piano* (cat. 24) hanging over the piano. This was Mrs. Ryerson's favorite painting.

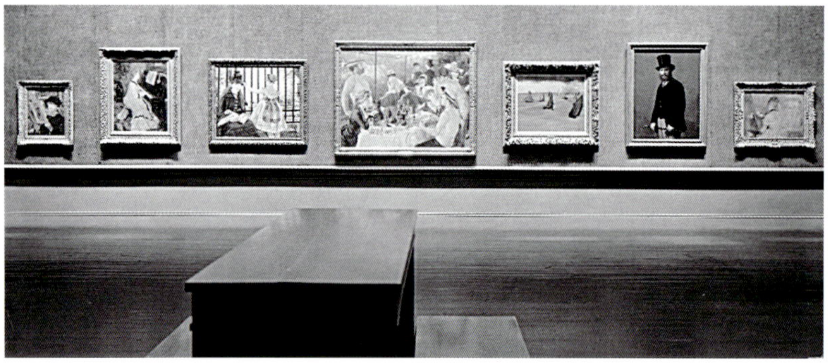

A gallery at the 1933 Century of Progress Exhibition of Paintings and Sculpture at the Art Institute. Among the works on view are, left to right, Manet's *Woman Reading* (cat. 21), Renoir's *Woman at the Piano* (cat. 24), Manet's *Steamboat Leaving Boulogne* (cat. 9), Henri Fantin-Latour's *Édouard Manet* (cat. 4), and Berthe Morisot's *Woman at Her Toilette* (cat. 19). In the center hangs Renoir's famous *Luncheon of the Boating Party* (1880–81; Phillips Collection, Washington, D.C.).

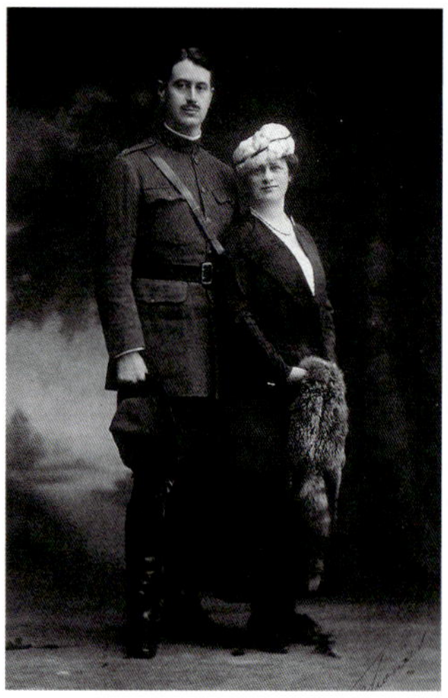

Colonel Robert R. (1880–1955) and Amy Irwin McCormick (1880–1939).

1933

Upon Martin A. Ryerson's death, the Art Institute receives the initial bequest of the Mr. and Mrs. Martin A. Ryerson Collection. This unprecedented gift—totaling over two hundred European and American paintings, in addition to textiles, European decorative arts, sculptures, prints, and drawings—remains the greatest single donation of art in the museum's history. A number of works will stay in the Ryerson home until Mrs. Ryerson's death in 1937.

In conjunction with the Century of Progress Exposition commemorating Chicago's centennial, the Art Institute organizes an exhibition of over one thousand works of art from the early Renaissance to the present. It runs from June 1 to November 1. Assembled primarily from North American collections, the show illuminates the progress of art collecting on this side of the Atlantic. The Century of Progress Exposition proves so popular that it will reopen the following year, to which the Art Institute will respond by staging a second loan exhibition, from June 1 to November 1, 1934.

Prior to the two Century of Progress exhibitions, the Art Institute's collections had been organized according to donor. These exhibitions prompt the museum to reinstall its permanent collection chronologically, an arrangement that has continued to the present day.

1940

The Art Institute stages an exhibition of paintings from the collection of Colonel and Mrs. Robert R. McCormick from April 17 to June 2. The show features nineteen primarily nineteenth- and twentieth-century French paintings, as well as four works painted by Mrs. McCormick (1880–1939). A great-nephew of the inventor and businessman Cyrus McCormick, the colonel (1880–1955) is the publisher of the *Chicago Tribune*. In addition to seven other works of art, he will give Cézanne's *The Bathers* (cat. 68) and Degas's *Two Dancers* (cat. 42) to the Art Institute in 1942 as part of the Amy McCormick Memorial Collection.

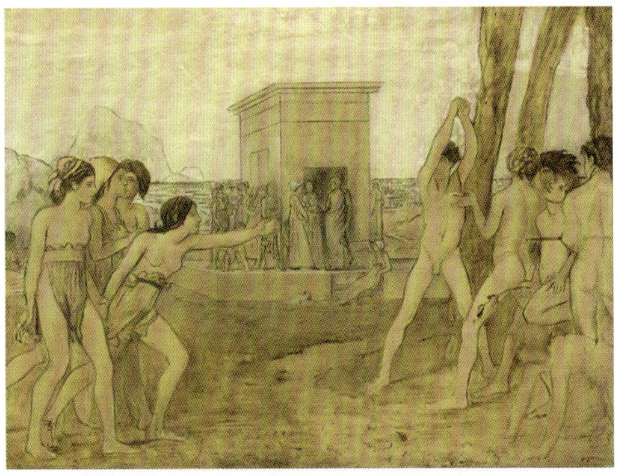

Edgar Degas. *Young Spartan Girls Challenging Boys*, c. 1860 (cat. 37). This painting will be purchased in 1961 through funds provided by the Worcesters.

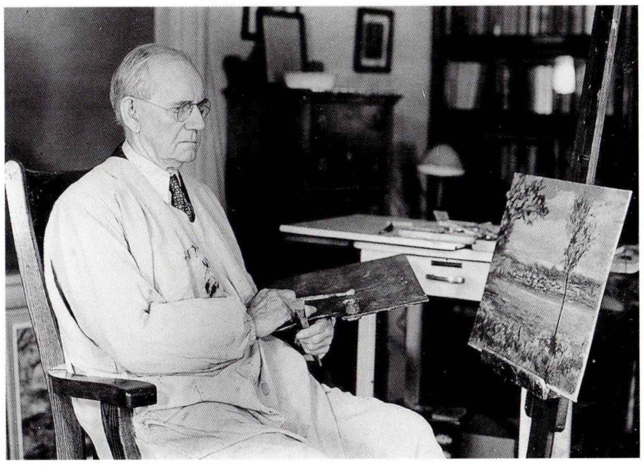

Charles H. Worcester (1864–1956) at his easel.

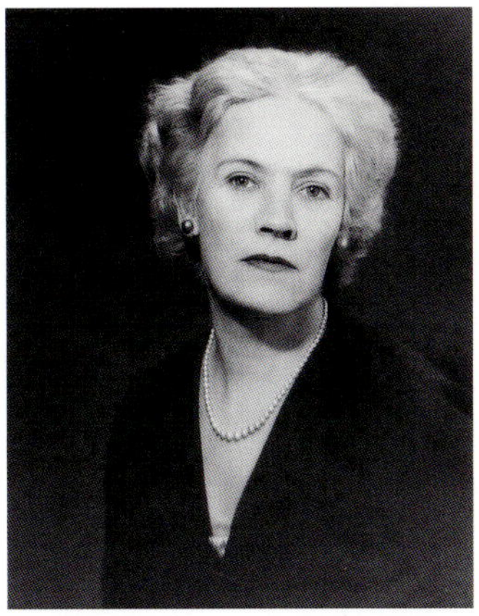

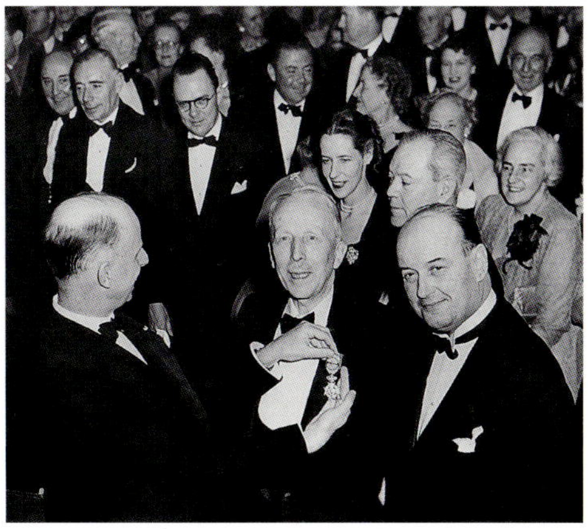

Vincent W. van Gogh (front row, center), the artist's nephew, at the 1950 Van Gogh exhibition opening. Behind him to the left is the Art Institute's director, Daniel Catton Rich.

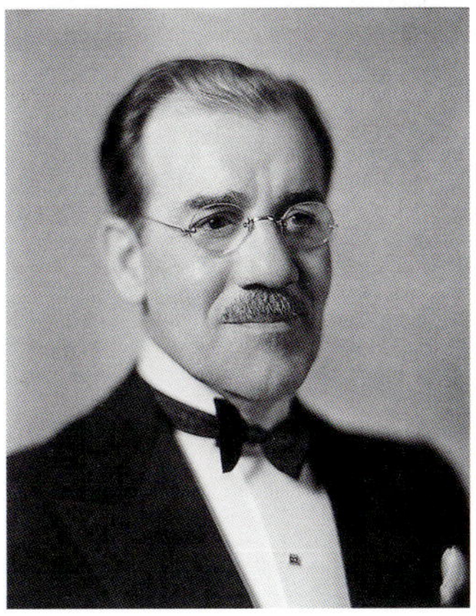

Kate Lancaster Brewster (1879–1947) as photographed by Man Ray (American, 1890–1976) in 1930 (Art Institute of Chicago, 1964.409).

Walter S. Brewster (1872–1954).

1941

A monumental loan exhibition of 272 primarily nineteenth-century French paintings, watercolors, and drawings from over twenty European institutions and many private collections opens at the Art Institute in April. Organized by the French government, it had traveled to South America in May 1939. When World War II broke out in Europe, the De Young Museum, San Francisco, arranged for the exhibition to tour the United States. Portions of the show are seen at the De Young and the Metropolitan Museum of Art, New York. The Art Institute is the first American venue to display the entire exhibition.

1944

For financial reasons, the Art Institute's Board of Trustees directs the administration to sell many works—including Old Master, Barbizon, and Impressionist paintings—at two auctions at Parke-Bernet Galleries, New York.

1947

Charles H. (1864–1956) and Mary F. S. (1861–1954) Worcester present seventy paintings, drawings, and sculptures from their wide-ranging collection to the Art Institute; the donation includes Monet's *Boats on the Beach at Étretat* (cat. 48) and Renoir's *The Laundress* (cat. 25). They also leave funds that will allow the museum to purchase Gustave Caillebotte's *Paris Street; Rainy Day* (cat. 18) and Degas's *Young Spartan Girls Challenging Boys* (cat. 37).

1950

A comprehensive exhibition of Van Gogh's work opens at the Art Institute on February 1. Co-organized with the Metropolitan Museum of Art, the Chicago show features over 150 works. Nearly fifty paintings and many drawings are lent by Vincent W. van Gogh, the artist's nephew, who attends the Chicago opening.

An exhibition of sixty-three paintings, sculptures, prints, and drawings recently donated to the Art Institute as part of the bequest of Kate Lancaster Brewster (1879–1947) goes on view. Kate Brewster was the president of the Chicago Public School Art Society, and her husband, Walter S. Brewster (1872–1954), a stockbroker, was a museum trustee. He contributes greatly to the Art Institute, including donations of funds, his collection of Whistleriana, and other gifts and bequests to the Department of Prints and Drawings.

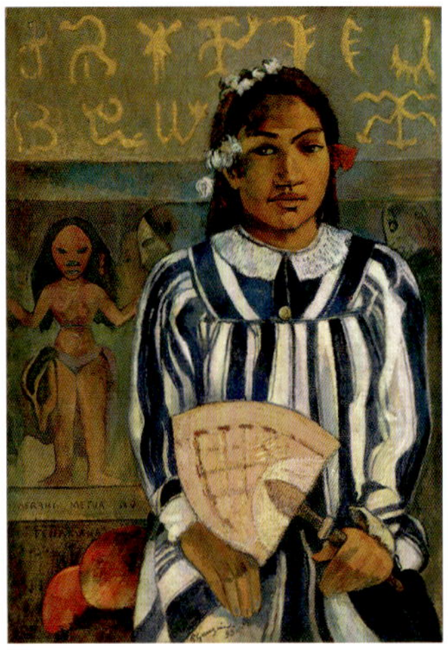

Paul Gauguin. *The Ancestors of Tehamana*, 1893 (cat. 70). This work is in a 1955 exhibition organized by the Art Institute in memory of Chauncey McCormick.

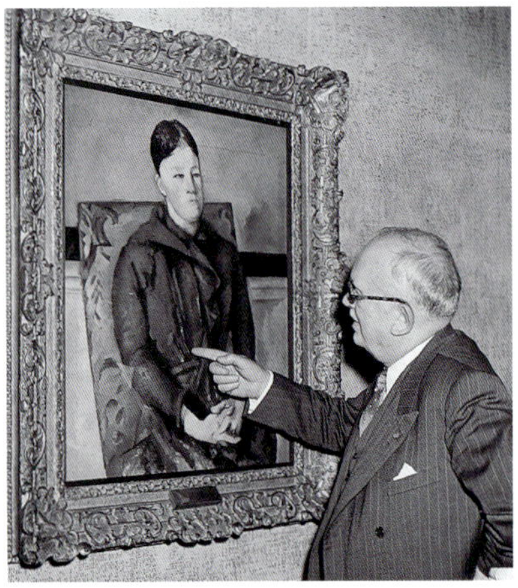

Vincent Auriol, president of France, in front of *Madame Cézanne in a Yellow Chair* (cat. 64), which appears in a 1952 Cézanne exhibition at the Art Institute.

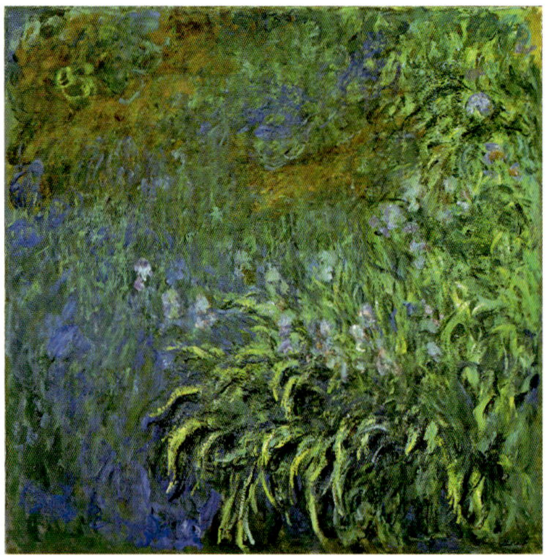

Monet's *Iris* (1922/26) is purchased by the Art Institute in 1956.

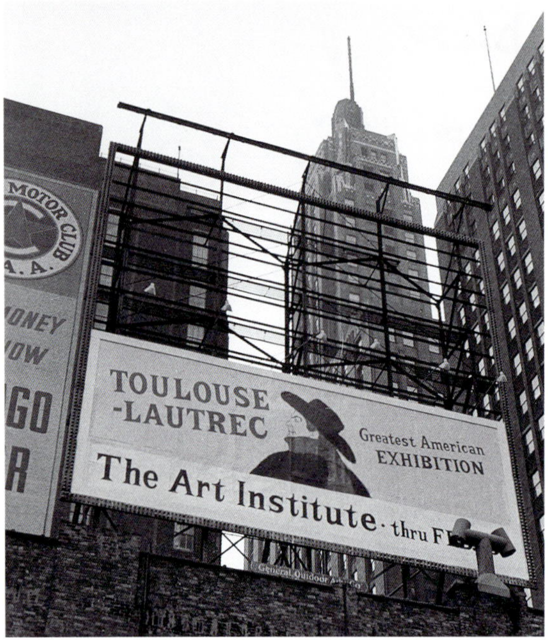

Billboard in the Chicago Loop advertising the Art Institute's 1956 Lautrec exhibition.

1952

In collaboration with the Metropolitan Museum of Art, the Art Institute holds an exhibition of over one hundred of Cézanne's paintings, watercolors, and drawings from February 7 to March 16. This retrospective includes loans from museums and collectors across four continents.

1955

From January 20 to February 20, the Art Institute exhibits *Great French Paintings: An Exhibition in Memory of Chauncey McCormick*. Chauncey McCormick (1884–1954), president of the Art Institute from 1944 to 1954, made a number of gifts to the museum, together with his wife, Marion Deering McCormick (1886–1965). Mrs. McCormick and her sister, Barbara Deering Danielson (1888–1987), also donated numerous masterpieces of Spanish painting that had belonged to their father, Charles Deering (1852–1927). The nearly forty works on view in this loan exhibition include Gauguin's *The Ancestors of Tehamana* (cat. 70). The McCormicks' son Charles Deering McCormick will present this painting to the museum in 1980. He, along with his brothers, Brooks and Roger McCormick, will make many other gifts to the Art Institute, including Van Gogh's *Fishing in Spring* (cat. 55).

1956

Nearly 250 paintings, drawings, prints, and posters by Lautrec are exhibited at the Art Institute from January 10 to February 15. This comprehensive show is organized in collaboration with the Philadelphia Museum of Art and the Albi Museum, France (now known as the Musée Toulouse-Lautrec).

Katharine Kuh, Art Institute publicist, educator, and curator from 1943 to 1959, facilitates the purchase of Monet's *Iris* from Katia Granoff's gallery in Paris. The painting, one of the canvases left in the artist's Giverny studio after his death, had recently been put on the market by his son Michel. This purchase, along with other late Monet works that will enter public and private collections around the same time, initiates a reevaluation of Monet's art, especially his *Water Lilies* series, now seen as the culmination of his career. Alfred H. Barr, Jr., director of the Museum of Modern Art, New York, is equally interested in buying *Iris*, but he fails to persuade Kuh to give up acquiring the painting for the Art Institute.

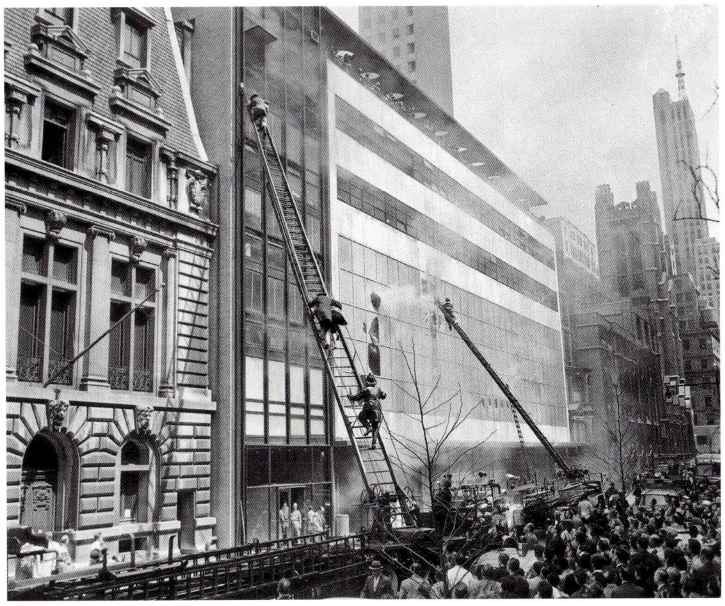

Fire at the Museum of Modern Art, New York, on April 15, 1958, during a Seurat exhibition, to which the Art Institute had loaned *La Grande Jatte*.

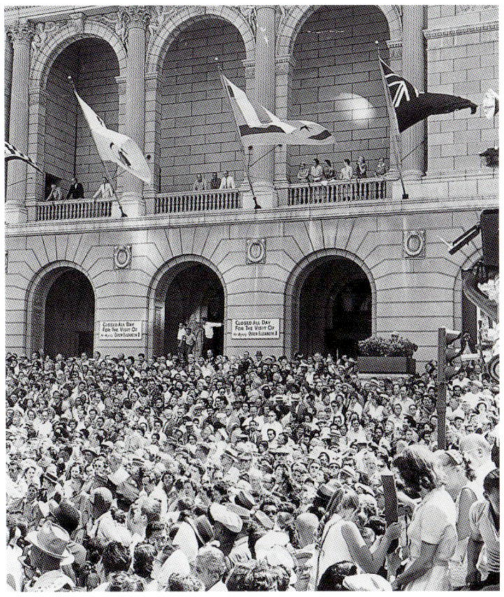

Crowd in front of the Art Institute during Queen Elizabeth's 1959 visit to Chicago.

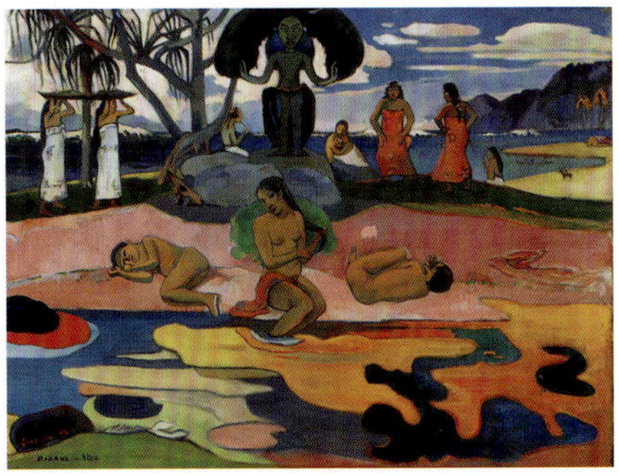

Paul Gauguin. *Day of the God (Mahana no Atua)*, 1894 (cat. 71). This painting is included in a 1959 Gauguin exhibition at the Art Institute.

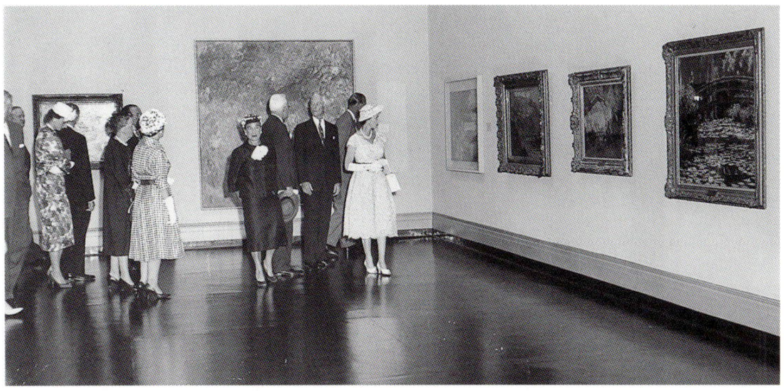

At the Art Institute, the queen tours a gallery of paintings by Monet. On the far wall is *Iris*; on the right wall are such canvases as *Arrival of the Normandy Train, Gare Saint-Lazare* (cat. 17) and *Water Lily Pond* (cat. 90). To the queen's right are board president William McCormick Blair and curator Katharine Kuh.

1957

Inspired by the acquisistion of Monet's *Iris* the previous year, in April the Art Institute holds the month-long exhibition *The Paintings of Monet*, which includes all thirty works by the artist in the museum's collection.

1958

A major retrospective of the art of Seurat is organized by Daniel Catton Rich, the Art Institute's director from 1938 to 1958. Featuring some 150 drawings and paintings, including *A Sunday on La Grande Jatte—1884*, the show also travels to the Museum of Modern Art. During the exhibition at MoMA, a fire breaks out in the galleries. Although the painting is unharmed, the Art Institute's trustees decide never to let it leave the museum again.

1959

An exhibition of work by Gauguin opens on February 12. Organized with the Metropolitan Museum of Art, it features paintings, drawings, watercolors, prints, and sculptures. The Art Institute is the single largest lender.

During a trip to Canada for the official opening of the St. Lawrence Seaway on June 26, Queen Elizabeth II comes to Chicago, the only United States stop on her itinerary. Arriving on July 6 aboard their royal yacht, accompanied by American, British, and Canadian destroyers, Queen Elizabeth and Prince Philip tour the city. Over two million Chicago spectators gather to catch a glimpse of the couple, who visit the Art Institute, among other Chicago sites.

1963–64

During a renovation of its galleries, the Museum of Modern Art loans its *Reflections of Clouds on the Water-Lily Pond* (c. 1920) by Monet to the Art Institute for several months. The monumental triptych, nearly forty-two feet long and over six feet high, is installed in a second-floor gallery of the Morton Wing.

1964

John Maxon, the Art Institute's director from 1958 to 1965, purchases Caillebotte's masterpiece *Paris Street; Rainy Day* (cat. 18), which quickly becomes an Art Institute favorite. Maxon will also serve as the museum's Associate Director (1965–72) and Vice President of Collections and Exhibitions (1972–77).

Pierre-Auguste Renoir. *Lunch at the Restaurant Fournaise (The Rowers' Lunch)*, 1875 (cat. 23). This painting is shown in the Art Institute's 1973 Renoir exhibition.

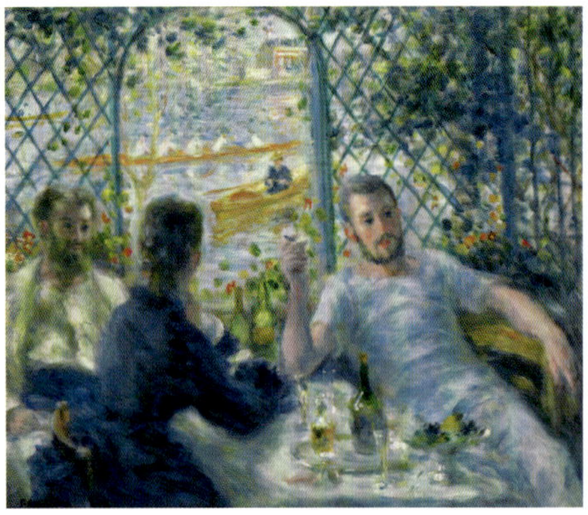

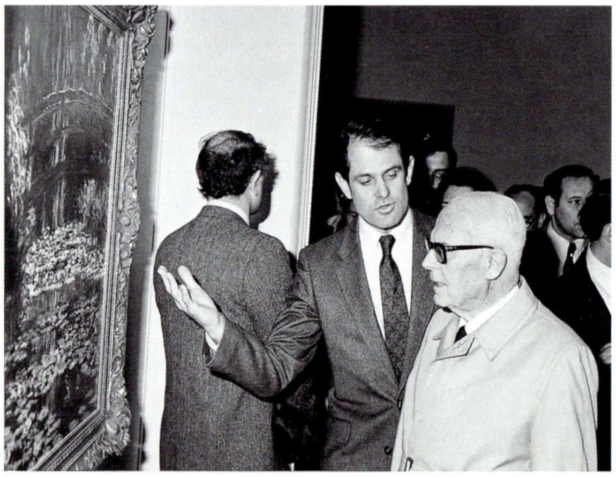

James N. Wood (center) discusses Monet's *Water Lily Pond* (cat. 90) with a museum visitor.

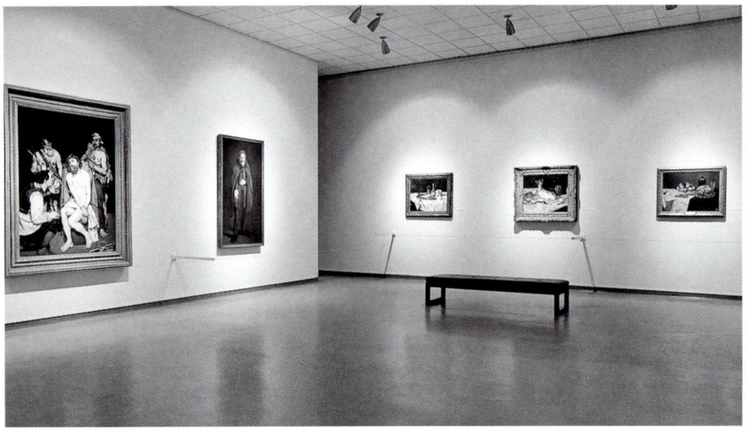

Installation view of a 1967 Manet exhibition at the Art Institute, including (from left) *The Mocking of Christ* (1865; Art Institute of Chicago), *Beggar with a Duffle Coat (Philosopher)* (cat. 3), and *Fish (Still Life)* (cat. 1).

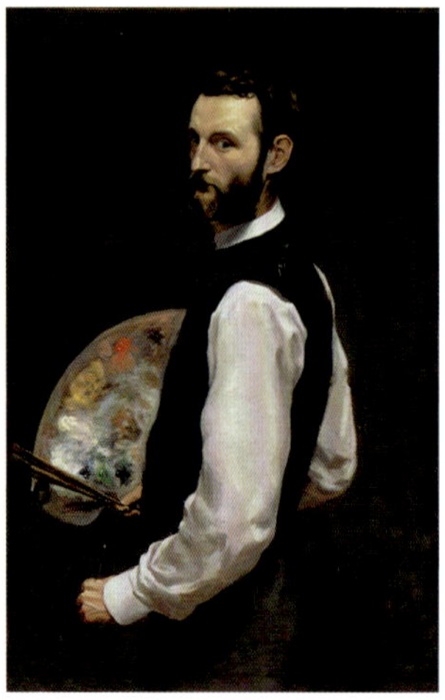

Frédéric Bazille. *Self-Portrait*, 1865/66 (cat. 5). This canvas is exhibited in the Art Institute's 1978 Bazille show.

1967

In collaboration with the Philadelphia Museum of Art, from January 13 to February 19 the Art Institute stages the most extensive exhibition of Manet's work in the United States to date. The show features approximately two hundred paintings, drawings, and works on paper from some eighty private and museum collections.

1973

The Art Institute holds a Renoir exhibition from February 3 to April 1. Shown only in Chicago, it is put together with the help of the artist's son Jean, the art historian François Daulte, and Charles Durand-Ruel, grandson of the dealer Paul Durand-Ruel. By the end of its two-month run, 354,169 visitors have seen it. This sets an attendance record for paid loan exhibitions at the Art Institute.

1975

An exhibition of over one hundred paintings from all phases of Monet's career is held at the Art Institute from March 15 to May 11.

1978

J. Patrice Marandel, Curator of Classical Art and European Painting at the Art Institute from 1974 to 1979, organizes *Frédéric Bazille and Early Impressionism*, on view from March 4 to April 30. Comprising nearly fifty paintings, as well as drawings, it introduces the work of this relatively unknown artist to the American public. Also included in the show are paintings by Bazille's close colleagues Manet, Monet, Renoir, and Sisley, among others.

1979

An exhibition of 109 paintings by Lautrec is organized by the Art Institute and is on view from October 4 to December 2. Forty works come from the Musée Toulouse-Lautrec, Albi. In exchange for this generous loan, in 1980 the Art Institute will lend the Albi museum fifty-nine French and American nineteenth-century paintings for the exhibition *Trésors impressionnistes du Musée de Chicago*.

1980

James N. Wood becomes Director and President of the Art Institute of Chicago, a position he will hold until 2004. During his long tenure, the museum will organize and host a number of major international loan exhibitions of Impressionist and Post-Impressionist art. He will also initiate the renovation of the Art Institute's Allerton Building, the construction of the Rice Building, and the planning of the Modern Wing.

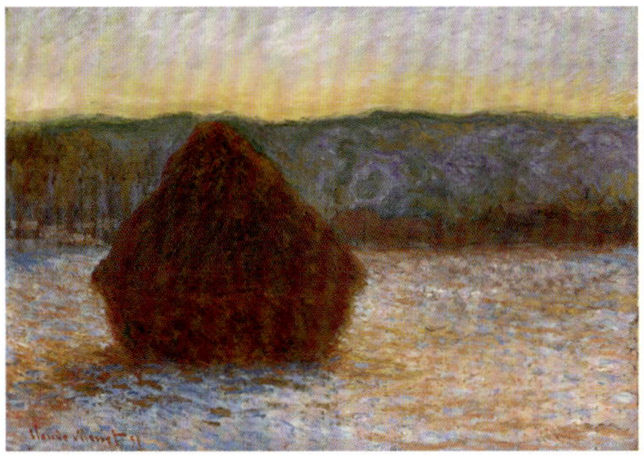
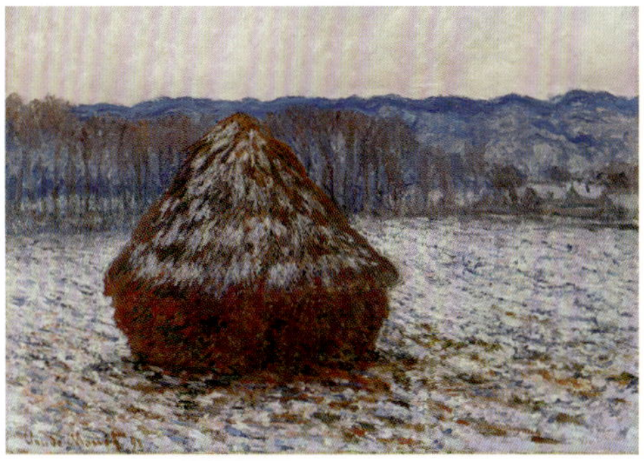
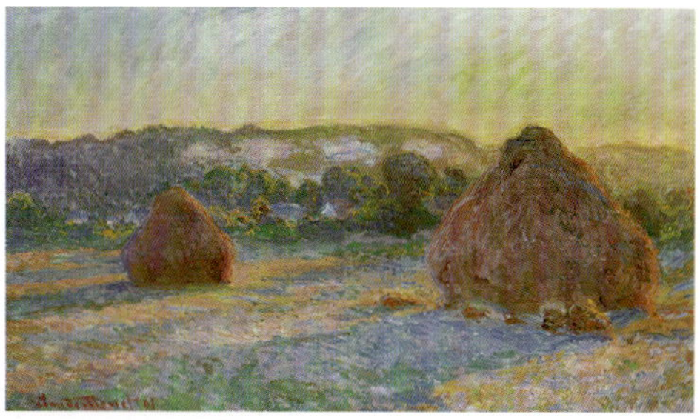

Claude Monet. *Stack of Wheat (Thaw, Sunset)*, 1890/91 (cat. 80); *Stack of Wheat*, 1890/91 (cat. 79); *Stacks of Wheat (End of Summer)*, 1890/91 (cat. 75). These canvases enter the Art Institute's collection in 1983 and 1985.

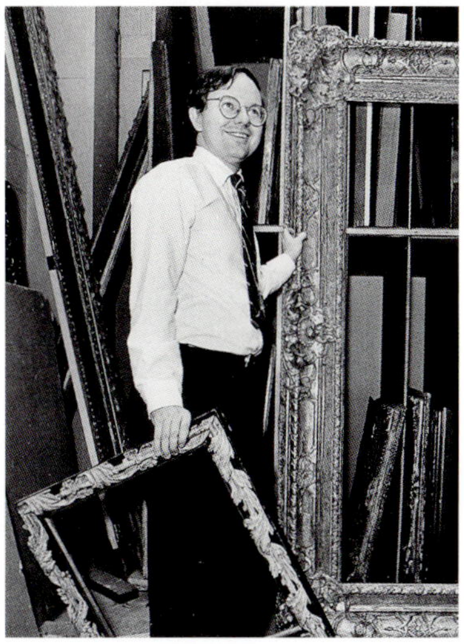

Richard Brettell in the Art Institute's frame storage area.

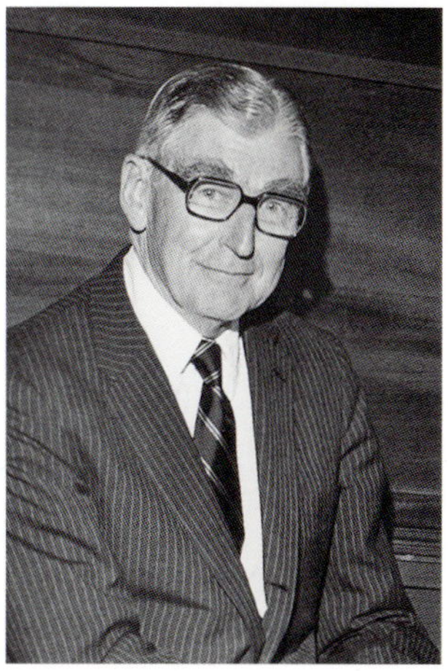

Arthur M. Wood, Sr. (1913–2006).

1983

The Art Institute acquires two paintings from Monet's *Stacks of Wheat* series. Mr. and Mrs. Daniel Searle are instrumental in both acquisitions, donating *Stack of Wheat (Thaw, Sunset)* (cat. 80) and providing additional funds for the purchase of *Stack of Wheat* (cat. 79).

1984

To celebrate Degas's 150th birthday, Richard Brettell, Searle Curator of European Painting from 1980 to 1988, and Suzanne Folds McCullagh, in the Department of Prints and Drawings since 1975 and Anne Vogt Fuller and Marion Titus Searle Curator of Earlier Prints and Drawings since 2001, mount an exhibition of ninety-one paintings, sculptures, prints, drawings, pastels, and monotypes by Degas owned by the Art Institute, supplemented by rarely seen works from Chicago-area collections. This show inaugurates a series of publications and loan exhibitions featuring the museum's holdings of a single artist's work in various media.

An unprecedented international loan exhibition of over 130 French Impressionist landscape paintings organized by Richard Brettell opens at the Art Institute on October 23. Including works by seventeen Impressionist and Post-Impressionist artists, *A Day in the Country: Impressionism and the French Landscape* is groundbreaking in its focus on landscapes as reflections of contemporary social, economic, and technical developments, such as expanding railroad lines, suburbanization, and industrialization. The exhibition is organized by the Los Angeles County Museum of Art in collaboration with the Art Institute and the Réunion des Musées Nationaux, Paris.

1985

Arthur M. Wood, Sr. (1913–2006), trustee of the Art Institute for several decades and chairman of the board from 1978 to 1981, donates Monet's *Stacks of Wheat (End of Summer)* (cat. 75) to the Art Institute in honor of his late wife, Pauline Palmer Wood (1917–1984). Mrs. Wood was the daughter of Potter Palmer II and Pauline Kohlsaat Palmer and a granddaughter of Potter and Bertha Honoré Palmer. This gift adds a sixth *Stacks of Wheat* canvas to the Art Institute's collection, making it the largest group from a single series to be owned by any museum in the world.

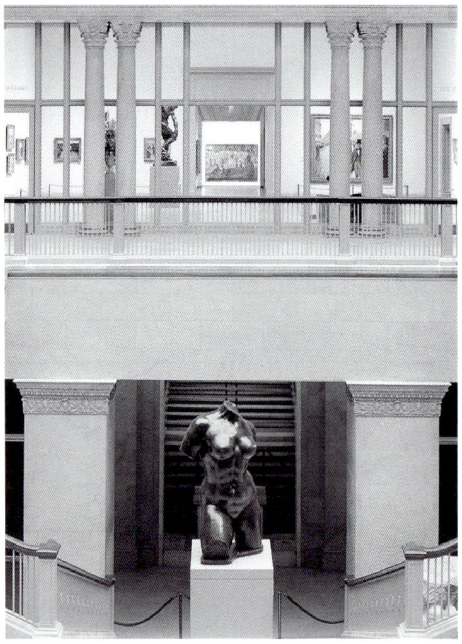

Installation view of the Art Institute's renovated galleries looking through Gallery 201 onto Seurat's *A Sunday on La Grande Jatte—1884* in Gallery 240, 1987.

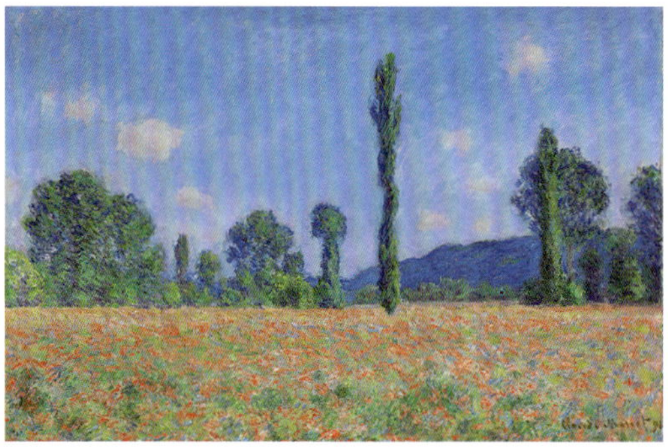

Claude Monet. *Poppy Field*, 1890–91 (cat. 74). This painting is included in the 1990 exhibition *Monet in the '90s: The Series Paintings.*

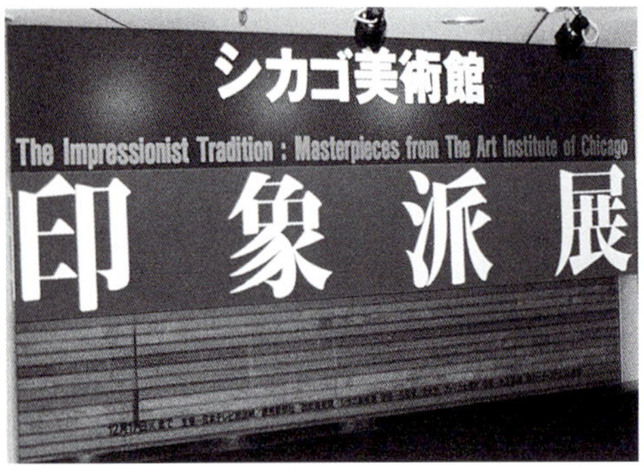

A sign in the Seibu Museum of Art, Tokyo, promoting the 1985–86 exhibition *The Impressionist Tradition: Masterpieces from The Art Institute of Chicago.*

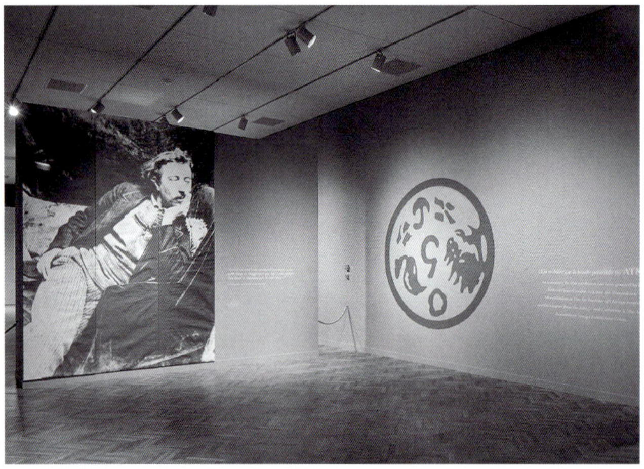

View of the installation of the Art Institute's 1988 Gauguin exhibition.

1985–86

During a renovation of its galleries, the Art Institute loans sixty-five important Impressionist and Post-Impressionist paintings to Japan. *The Impressionist Tradition: Masterpieces from The Art Institute of Chicago* travels to three museums in Japan, attracting large crowds.

1987

The Art Institute's galleries of European Art reopen to the public after a two-year renovation overseen by Chicago architectural firm Skidmore, Owings and Merrill. With the reinstallation, works on paper can be exhibited in the corridor galleries adjacent to the daylit spaces where paintings and sculptures are displayed. This allows the viewer to appreciate the work of an artist in a variety of media. The project also includes a renovation of the Art Institute's lobby and Grand Staircase by Chicago architect John Vinci.

1988

The Art of Paul Gauguin opens at the Art Institute in September, organized by Richard Brettell and Charles Stuckey, Frances and Thomas Dittmer Curator of Twentieth-Century Painting and Sculpture from 1987 to 1995. They are assisted by Gloria Groom, in the Department of European Painting since 1984 and David and Mary Winton Green Curator of Nineteenth-Century European Painting since 1999; and Peter Zegers, in the Department of Prints and Drawings since 1986 and Rothman Family Research Curator since 1996. Five years in the making, this comprehensive exhibition features over 250 paintings, sculptures, ceramics, prints, and drawings from the artist's early Impressionist phase to his time in Brittany, Tahiti, and the Marquesas. Co-organized by the Art Institute, the National Gallery of Art, Washington, D.C., and the Réunion des Musées Nationaux, this show inaugurates Regenstein Hall, the exhibition space in the Art Institute's new Daniel F. and Ada L. Rice Building.

1990

Organized by the Museum of Fine Arts, Boston, *Monet in the '90s: The Series Paintings* opens in Chicago on May 19. This exhibition brings together approximately ninety works related to the series Monet executed between 1889 and 1900, including *Poppy Field*, *Stacks of Wheat*, and *Water Lily Pond* (cats. 74, 75–80, and 90). The Chicago presentation is facilitated by Douglas Druick, Prince Trust Curator of Prints and Drawings since 1985 and recently appointed Searle Curator and head of the Department of European Painting.

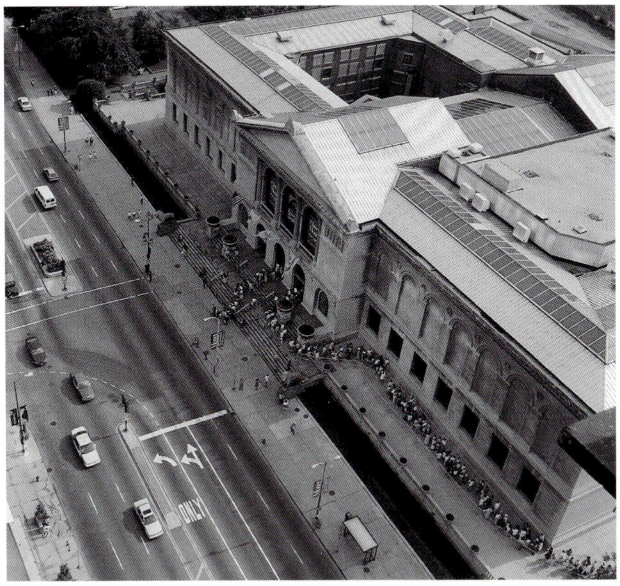

A long line of visitors waiting to enter the Art Institute to see a 1995 Monet exhibition.

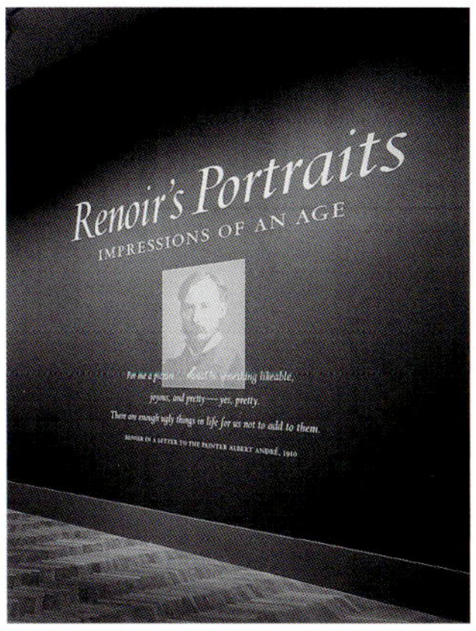

Title wall for the 1997 exhibition *Renoir's Portraits* at the Art Institute.

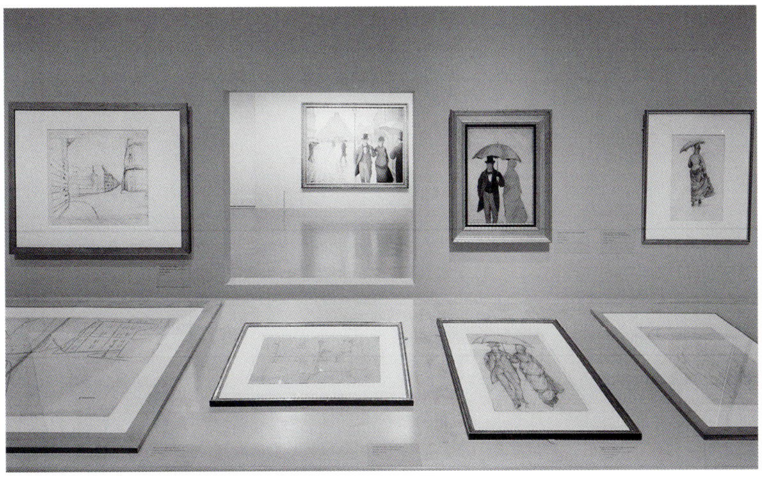

View of the installation of the Art Institute's 1995 exhibition *Gustave Caillebotte: Urban Impressionist.* A cutout in the wall of the exhibition space allows viewers to catch a glimpse of the artist's *Paris Street; Rainy Day* (cat. 18) while in an adjacent gallery of related drawings.

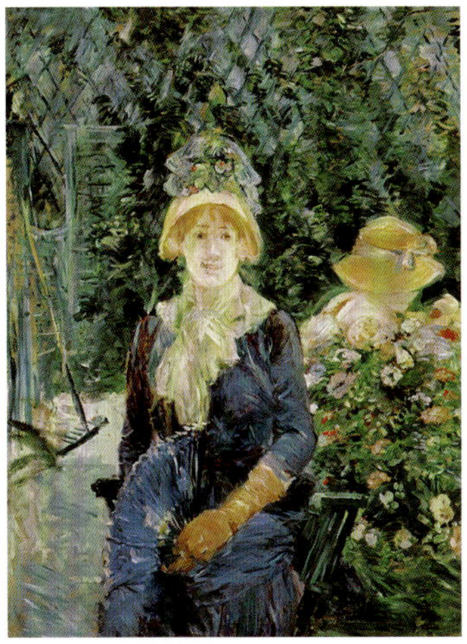

Berthe Morisot. *Young Woman in a Garden*, 1882/83 (cat. 20). This work is part of the Millennium Gift of Sara Lee Corporation.

1995

In recognition of the one hundredth anniversary of Caillebotte's 1894 death, the Art Institute collaborates with the Réunion des Musées Nationaux and the Musée d'Orsay, Paris, to present a major international retrospective of the artist, patron, and collector. *Gustave Caillebotte: Urban Impressionist* features over one hundred works. Following the exhibition, the Art Institute acquires Caillebotte's *Calf's Head and Ox Tongue* (cat. 36) directly from the artist's family.

The largest and most comprehensive exhibition ever devoted to the art of Monet is held exclusively at the Art Institute. *Claude Monet: 1840–1926* brings together over 150 works from international public and private collections. Nearly one million people visit the exhibition between July 22 and November 26.

1996

Co-organized with the National Gallery, London, *Degas: Beyond Impressionism* opens at the Art Institute. It is the first in-depth exhibition devoted to the artist's late years, focusing on the period between 1886, the date of the last Impressionist exhibition, and 1917, the year of his death.

1997

The Art Institute presents the first major survey of Renoir's portraits. Organized by the National Gallery of Canada, Ottawa, in conjunction with the Art Institute and the Kimbell Art Museum, Fort Worth, *Renoir's Portraits: Impressions of an Age* reflects all phases of the artist's career and attests to the rich relationships he had with family, friends, patrons, and fellow artists.

1998

Sara Lee Corporation announces that it will donate fifty-two works from its art collection (assembled by its founder, Nathan Cummings) to forty museums around the world. The Art Institute receives twelve (they will officially enter the collection in 1999), including Berthe Morisot's *Young Woman in a Garden* (cat. 20) and Pissarro's *Woman Bathing Her Feet in a Brook* (cat. 46). Before the collection is dispersed, it will tour the world in the exhibition *Monet to Moore: The Millennium Gift of Sara Lee Corporation*. The show will visit the Art Institute in 2000.

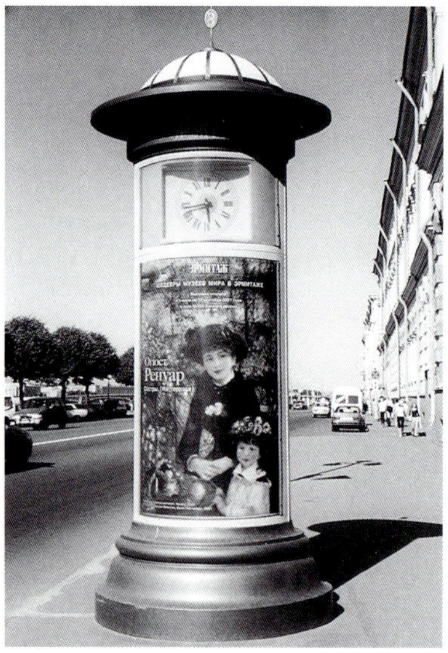

Kiosk outside the State Hermitage Museum, St. Petersburg, promoting the Art Institute's 2001 loan of Renoir's *Two Sisters* (cat. 28).

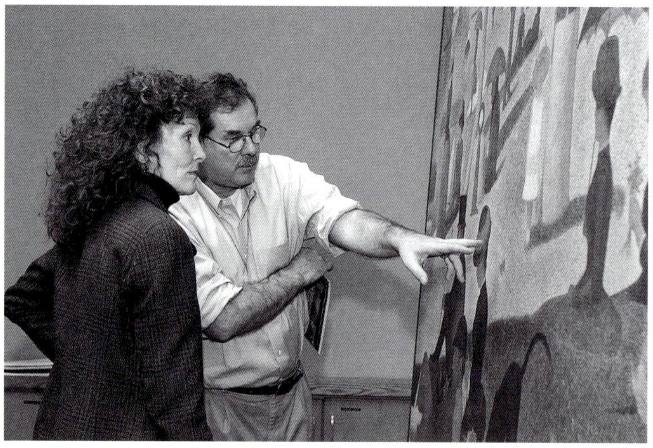

Gloria Groom and Frank Zuccari, Executive Director of Conservation at the Art Institute, examine *La Grande Jatte* in the conservation laboratory.

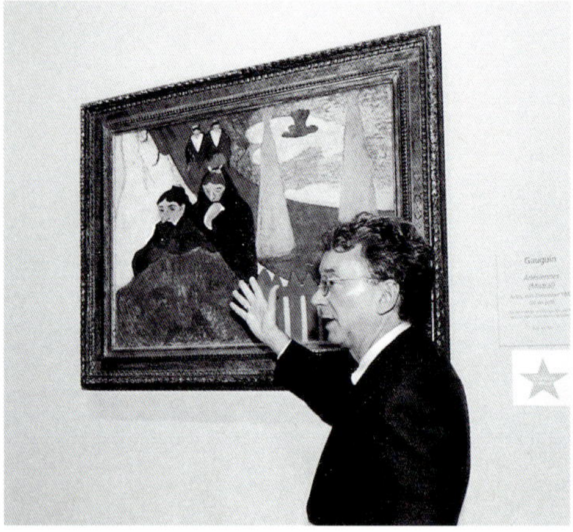

Douglas Druick speaking about Gauguin's *Arlésiennes (Mistral)* (cat. 59) at the 2001 opening gala for the exhibition *Van Gogh and Gauguin: The Studio of the South.*

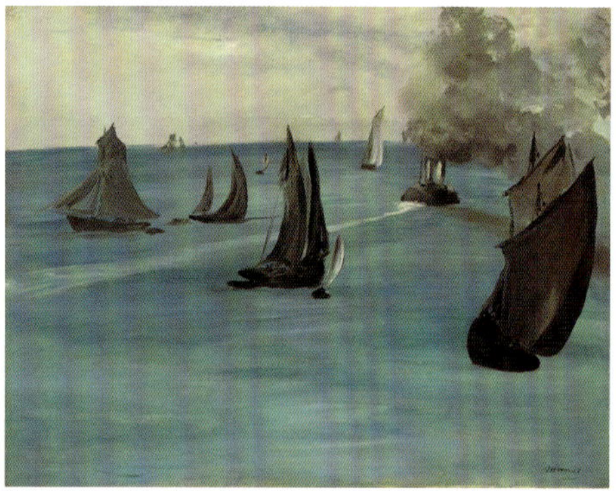

Édouard Manet. *Steamboat Leaving Boulogne*, 1864 (cat. 9). This painting appears in the 2003 *Manet and the Sea* exhibition.

2001

Organized by Art Institute curator Gloria Groom, in collaboration with the Metropolitan Museum of Art, *Beyond the Easel: Decorative Painting by Bonnard, Vuillard, Denis, and Roussel, 1890–1930* opens in February. It is the first exhibition to explore the mural-size paintings of these Post-Impressionist artists.

The Art Institute loans Renoir's *Two Sisters (On the Terrace)* (cat. 28) to the State Hermitage Museum, St. Petersburg, as the star work in an exhibition in their series *Masterpieces from the World's Museums in the Hermitage*.

In September Art Institute curators Douglas Druick and Peter Zegers present the groundbreaking exhibition *Van Gogh and Gauguin: The Studio of the South*. Many years in the making, this show explores the complicated personal and professional relationship between this pair of artists. Co-organized with the Van Gogh Museum, Amsterdam, it brings together paintings, works on paper, ceramics, and sculptures from public and private collections worldwide. It also incorporates new evidence for dating works and understanding their development that has come to light from technical investigations into the artists' working practices.

2003

Opening in October, *Manet and the Sea*, the first major exhibition exploring the marine paintings of Manet, is organized with the Philadelphia Museum of Art and the Van Gogh Museum. This show traces Manet's innovative interpretations of the sea and demonstrates how he approached the theme and, in turn, influenced other artists painting this subject. The organizing curator for Philadelphia, Joseph Rishel, was a curator in the Art Institute's paintings department from 1968 to 1971.

2004

James Cuno becomes President and Eloise W. Martin Director of the Art Institute of Chicago. Previously he had served as Professor and Director of the Courtauld Institute of Art, University of London, and as Professor and Director of the Harvard University Art Museums, Cambridge, Massachusetts, both of which are known for their Impressionist collections.

One of the Art Institute's most famous paintings, Seurat's masterwork *A Sunday on La Grande Jatte—1884*, is the focus of the exhibition *Seurat and the Making of "La Grande Jatte,"* which opens in June. The show brings together many of the numerous studies (see cat. 51), in various media, that the artist produced in conjunction with his magnum opus, helping to trace the painting's conception and evolution. Research by the Art Institute's conservation, curatorial, and imaging staff plays a critical role in elucidating the stages of the

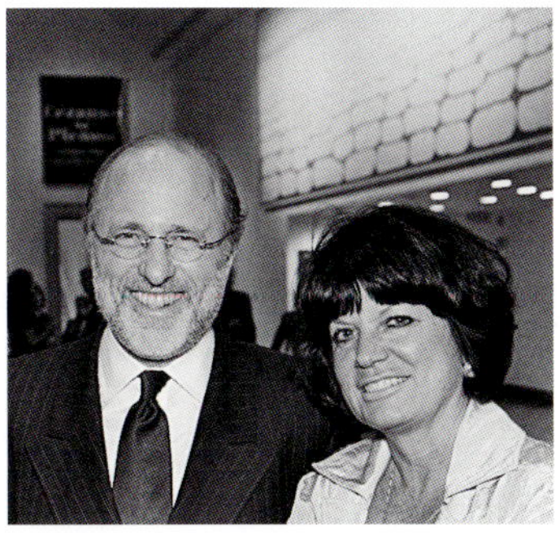

James Cuno with Dorothy Schroeder, Vice President for Exhibitions and Museum Administration at the Art Institute, at the opening gala for ***Cézanne to Picasso: Ambroise Vollard, Patron of the Avant-Garde***, 2007.

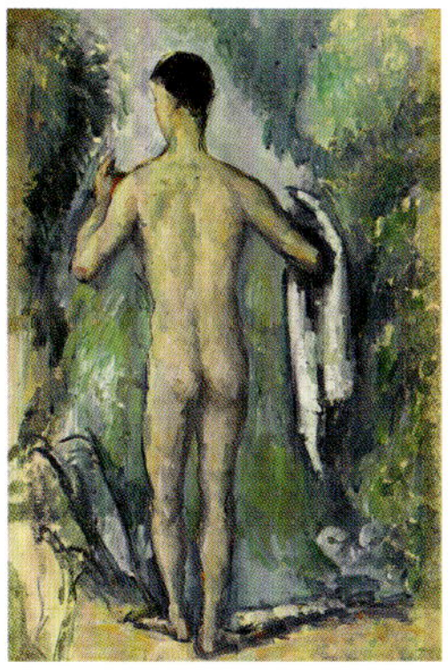

Paul Cézanne. ***Standing Bather, Seen from the Back***, 1879/82. The Art Institute of Chicago, bequest of Brooks McCormick, 2007.289.

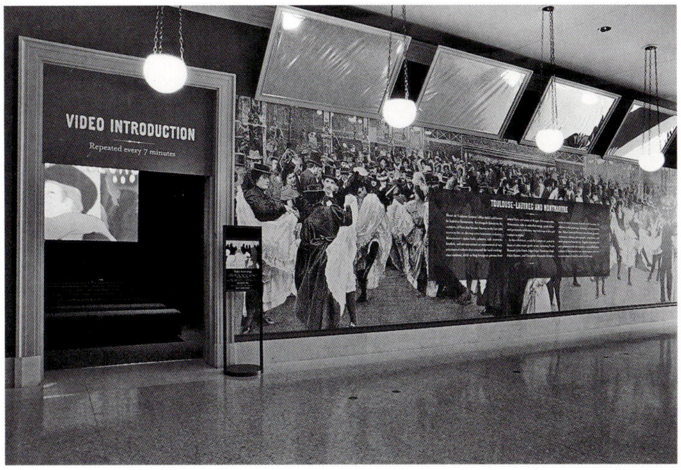

Entryway of the 2005 exhibition ***Toulouse-Lautrec and Montmartre*** at the Art Institute.

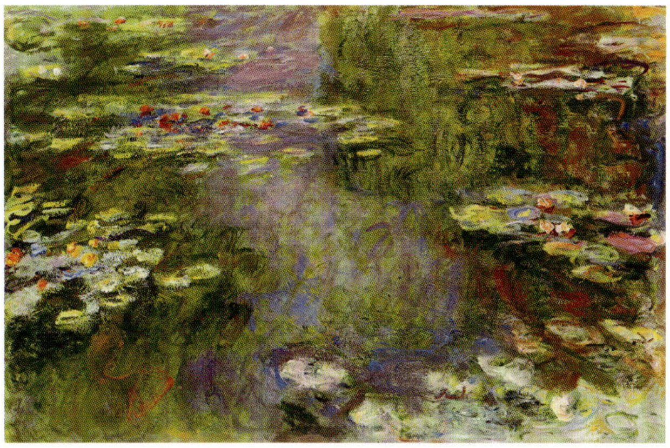

Claude Monet. ***Water Lily Pond***, 1917–22 (cat. 92). This painting is given to the Art Institute by Mrs. Harvey (Ruth) Kaplan.

painting's development, as well as in analyzing the exact nature of its discoloration. The show also includes other relevant works by Seurat and a number of his contemporaries.

2005

Organized with the National Gallery of Art, Washington, D.C., the Art Institute presents *Toulouse-Lautrec and Montmartre*. Featuring over 250 works in various media by Lautrec and nearly fifty other artists, the exhibition explores the bohemian Parisian district, a hub of avant-garde entertainment at the end of the nineteenth century.

The Art Institute acquires the late Monet painting *Water Lily Pond* (cat. 92) upon the death of Mrs. Harvey (Ruth) Kaplan (1910–2005). A Life Member and distinguished benefactor of the museum, she had announced the gift in 1982 but kept the painting until her death. This donation allows the Art Institute to fully represent the evolution of Monet's motif of the water-lily pond.

2007

Cézanne to Picasso: Ambroise Vollard, Patron of the Avant-Garde is shown at the Art Institute. This exhibition, co-organized with the Metropolitan Museum of Art, the Musée d'Orsay, and the Réunion des Musées Nationaux, explores the career of the legendary art dealer and publisher Ambroise Vollard. The Chicago exhibition features nearly 250 paintings, sculptures, prints, ceramics, and books—by artists like Cézanne, Degas, Gauguin, Van Gogh, and Renoir—that Vollard handled, commissioned, exhibited, or owned.

The Art Institute receives a generous bequest from Brooks McCormick (1917–2006), a trustee of the museum from 1954 to 1987 and vice chairman of the board for many years. Included in this gift is Cézanne's *Standing Bather, Seen from the Back*, which joins another painting on this theme, *The Bathers* (cat. 68), bequeathed to the museum by a relative of McCormick's in 1942.

2008

During the renovation of the European Painting and Sculpture galleries, ninety-two Impressionist and Post-Impressionist masterpieces from the Art Institute travel to the Kimbell Art Museum for the exhibition *The Impressionists: Master Paintings from the Art Institute of Chicago*, which is on view from June to November.

In December the Art Institute's Impressionist and Post-Impressionist paintings, along with European paintings and sculptures from the Middle Ages through 1900, reopen in a resplendent suite of galleries refurbished by Vinci/Hamp Architects, Inc., Chicago, on the Allerton Building's second floor.

Landscape and Figure Painting: New Approaches

TRADITION AND INNOVATION

MANET: RACES AND BULLFIGHTING

SEA AND SKY

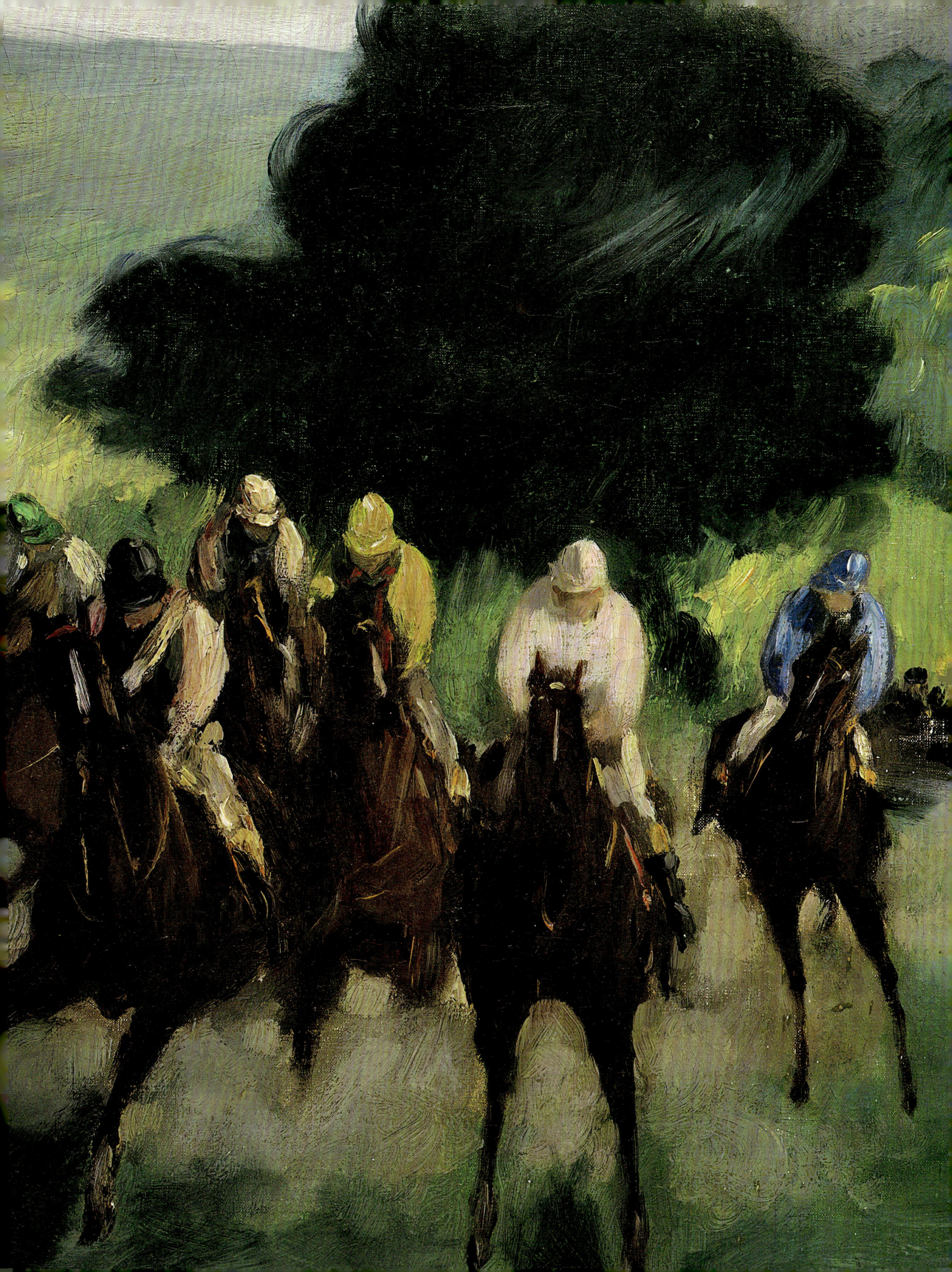

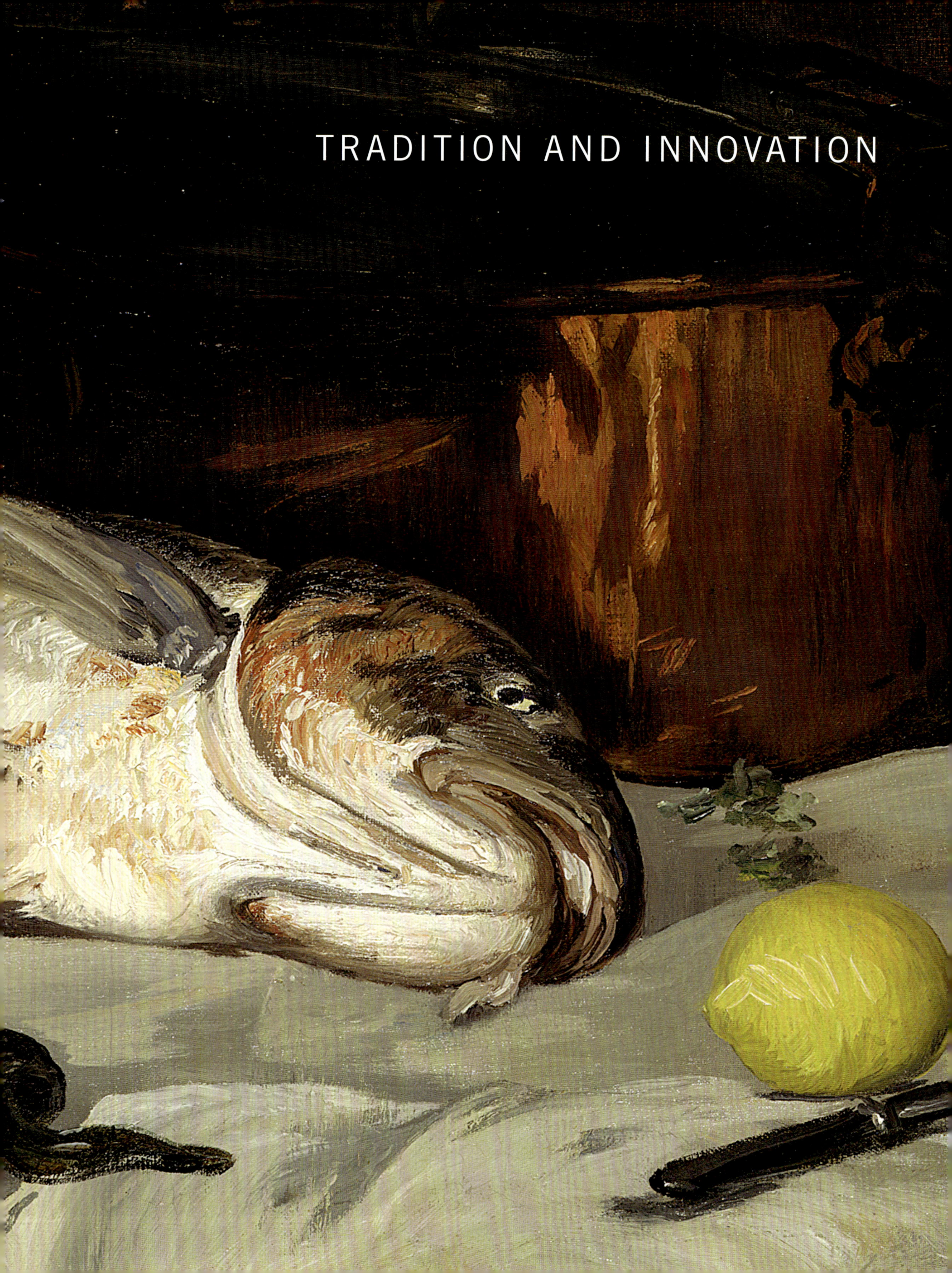
TRADITION AND INNOVATION

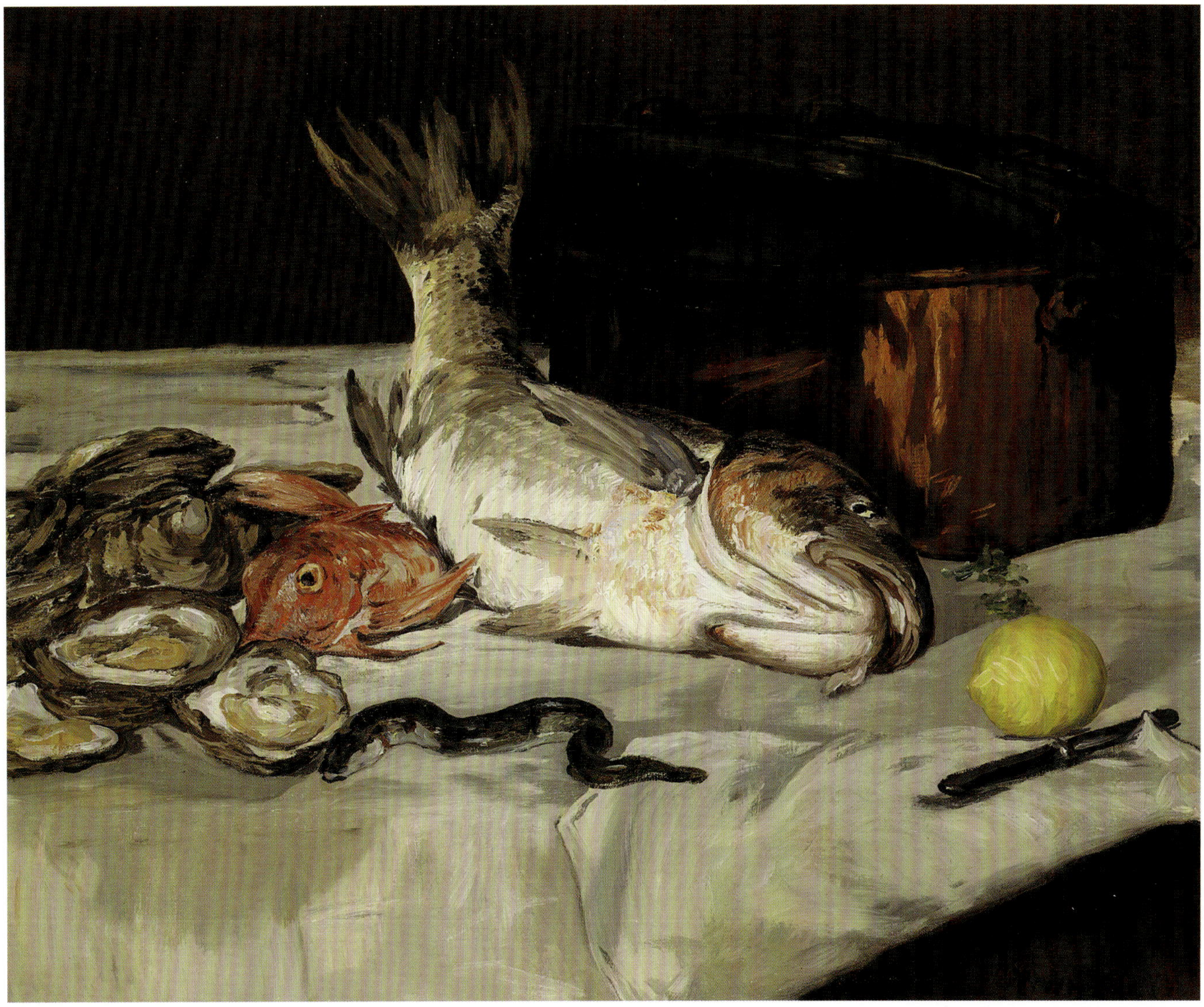

1

Fish (Still Life), 1864

Oil on canvas; 73.4 x 92.1 cm (28⅞ x 36¼ in.)
Mr. and Mrs. Lewis Larned Coburn Memorial Collection, 1942.311
Signed lower right: *Manet*

By age thirty, Édouard Manet had garnered recognition at the state-sponsored Salon exhibition in Paris and established himself as the artist to watch, producing works that translated Old Master painting into a modern idiom. In its subject, light, and handling, *Fish (Still Life)* recalls the work of seventeenth-century Dutch still-life painters, the *bodegones* of the Spanish Baroque masters, and especially the humble kitchen arrangements of the eighteenth-century French painter Jean-Baptiste Chardin, all of which had gained new currency by the mid-nineteenth century among artists of the Realist school.

This imposing arrangement of carp, red mullet, eel, oysters, lemon, stockpot, and knife is one of numerous still lifes that Manet painted in 1864, the year of his most intense engagement with the genre. Having been vilified for his Salon submissions that year, Manet may have found *nature morte* (literally "dead nature") an easily accessible and therapeutic alternative to working with live models on history paintings, which were subjected to stricter academic standards for technique and finish. The resulting composition, however, is anything but mild. In this and smaller still-life variants, Manet created a pulse-quickening sense of immediacy and instability by raising the tail of the central fish and strategically positioning elements along the diagonal of the tablecloth so that they seem to slide forward into the viewer's space. This feeling of slipperiness is further suggested by the precariously balanced knife, the still-slithering eel, and, above all, the painterly rendering of the oiliness of the fish and oysters, whose watery trail has soaked through the crisp white tablecloth.

Manet never submitted any of his still lifes to the official Salon, preferring instead to exhibit them through the burgeoning network of Parisian art galleries, such as Galerie Cadart, where *Fish (Still Life)* was probably first shown in 1865.

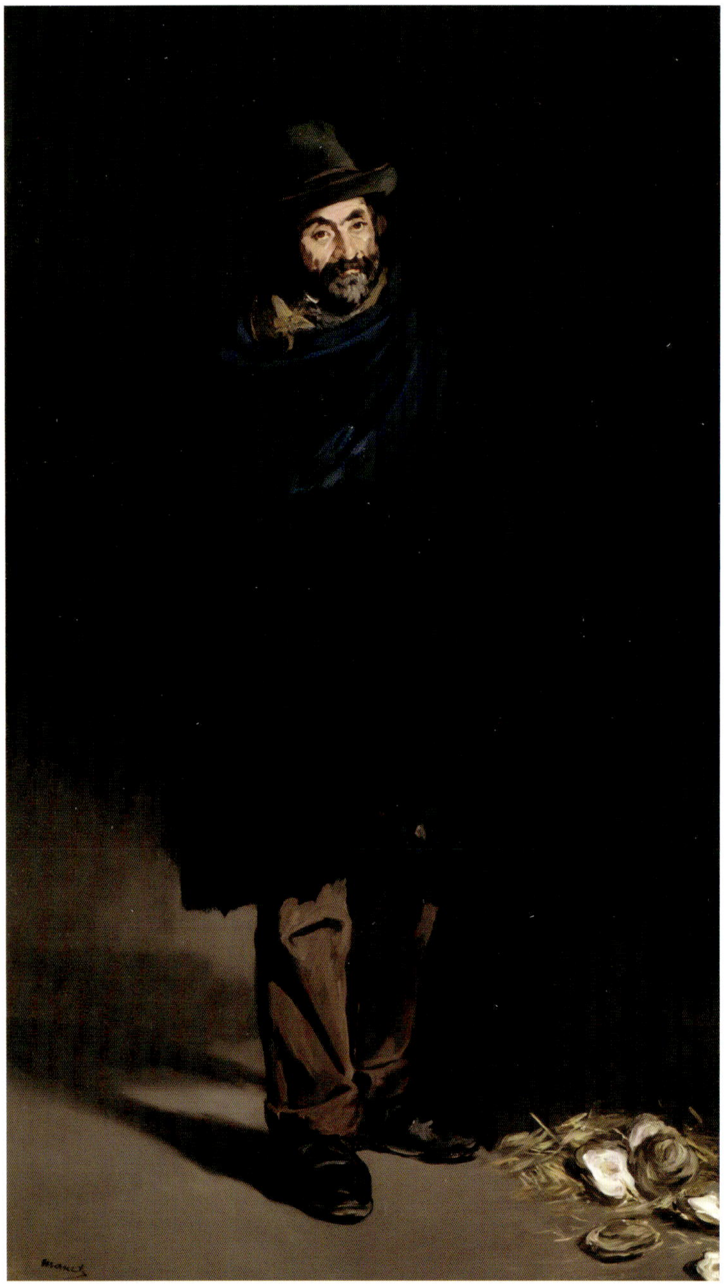

2

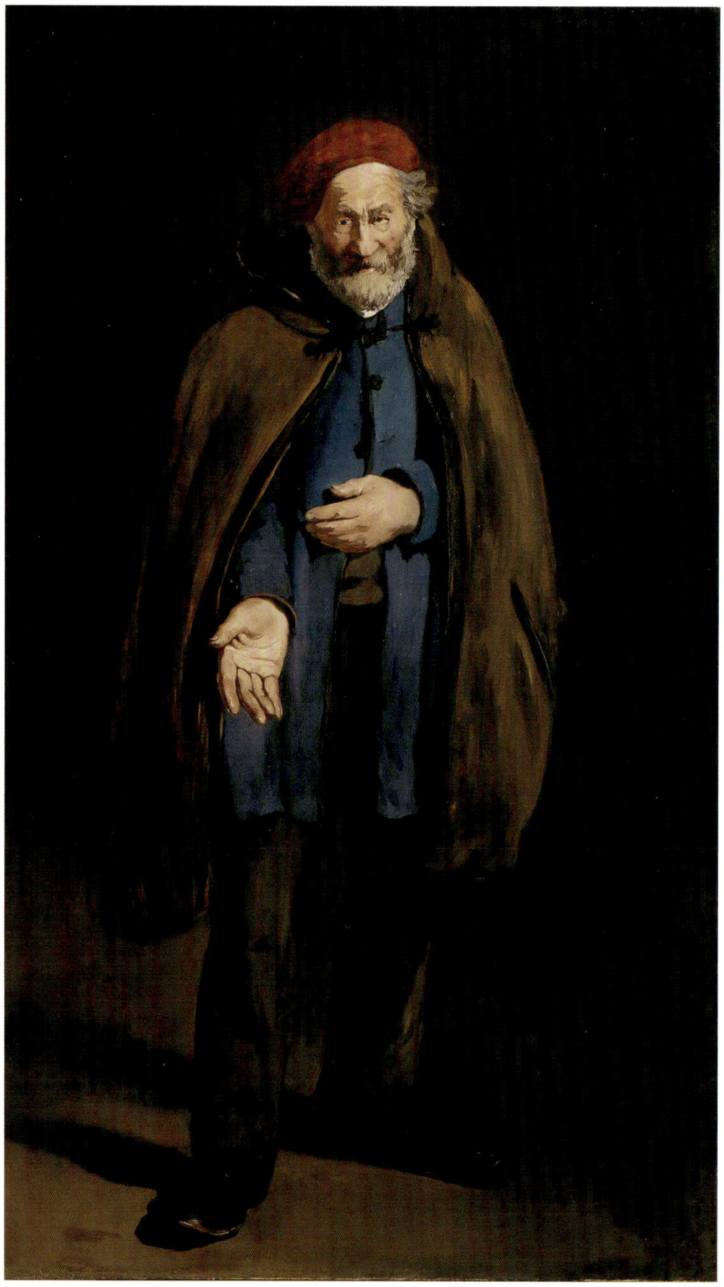

3

2

Beggar with Oysters (Philosopher), 1865/67

Oil on canvas; 187.3 x 108 cm (73¾ x 42½ in.)
Arthur Jerome Eddy Memorial Collection, 1931.504
Signed lower left: *Manet.*

3

Beggar with a Duffle Coat (Philosopher), 1865/67

Oil on canvas; 187.7 x 109.9 cm (73⅞ x 43¼ in.)
A. A. Munger Collection, 1910.304
Signed lower right: *Manet*

Édouard Manet's fascination with Spanish art reflected a passion among the French for all things Spanish (*espagñolisme*), which was stimulated by the court of Empress Eugénie, Napoleon III's Spanish wife. Nonetheless, the artist's depictions of Spanish singers, bullfighters, and bullfights were highly criticized. Because his unorthodox compositions and rough, vigorous brushwork ran so counter to the detailed and polished paintings of the French academicians, his works found little favor when they were exhibited. Indeed, Manet may have embarked on a long-contemplated trip to Spain in 1865 to recover from the devastating reviews of the two paintings he submitted to the Salon that year (one of which was the infamous *Olympia*, 1863; Musée d'Orsay, Paris). At the Museo del Prado, Madrid, he was overwhelmed by the works of the Baroque artist Diego Velázquez, commenting in particular on his life-size portrayals of Aesop and Menippus (both c. 1638). Undoubtedly as a result of that encounter, upon his return to Paris, Manet began work on these two similarly scaled canvases depicting beggar-philosophers.

Probably conceived as pendants, the paintings were shown together for the first time in 1867, along with *Absinthe Drinker* (1858/59; Ny Carlsberg Glyptotek, Copenhagen). By 1872 Manet had grouped these and an additional canvas, *Ragpicker* (1865/70; Norton Simon Museum, Pasadena), under the collective title *Philosophers*. In the Art Institute's canvases, Manet paid special homage to the subjects, stark compositions, earth-toned palette, and vigorous brushwork of Velázquez, whose ancient Greek philosophers Manet updated with these equally impoverished, world-weary, and dignified members of what the French called the *classe dangereuse*. Like the ancient stoics, whose poverty is associated with wisdom, Manet's beggar-philosophers fit into the popular notion of the social outcast as a seer possessing rare insight. Beggars and ragpickers (nocturnal scavengers of garbage unsuitable for resale) held a particular fascination for Realist artists and writers, who saw these figures as resourceful, proud, and appealingly nonconformist types threatened by government "regularization" projects intended to drive them out of the city.

In *Beggar with Oysters*, the pose of the dark-bearded man, a ragged mantle (or blanket) thrown over his shoulders, suggests an element of rugged independence. The oysters at his feet—some opened, some not—remain mysterious, since it is not clear why or how he obtained them. When the painting was shown in 1867, its hint of unpleasant confrontation inspired one cartoonist to draw the beggar holding a knife behind his cloak. This disturbing ambiguity is more explicitly felt in *Beggar with a Duffle Coat*, which features a man with narrowed eyes sporting a beret and *caban* (a duffle coat often worn by mariners) and soliciting alms with his crudely rendered hand extended provocatively to the viewer. As is the case with many of his early figure paintings, Manet's beggar-philosophers reflect historical precedents that the artist made modern, thus creating a new imagery for contemporary types and events that confronts and confounds easy categorization.

By a remarkable coincidence, at the turn of the twentieth century, these two closely related works found their way by very different means to the Art Institute's collection, where they can again be viewed as they were originally in 1867.

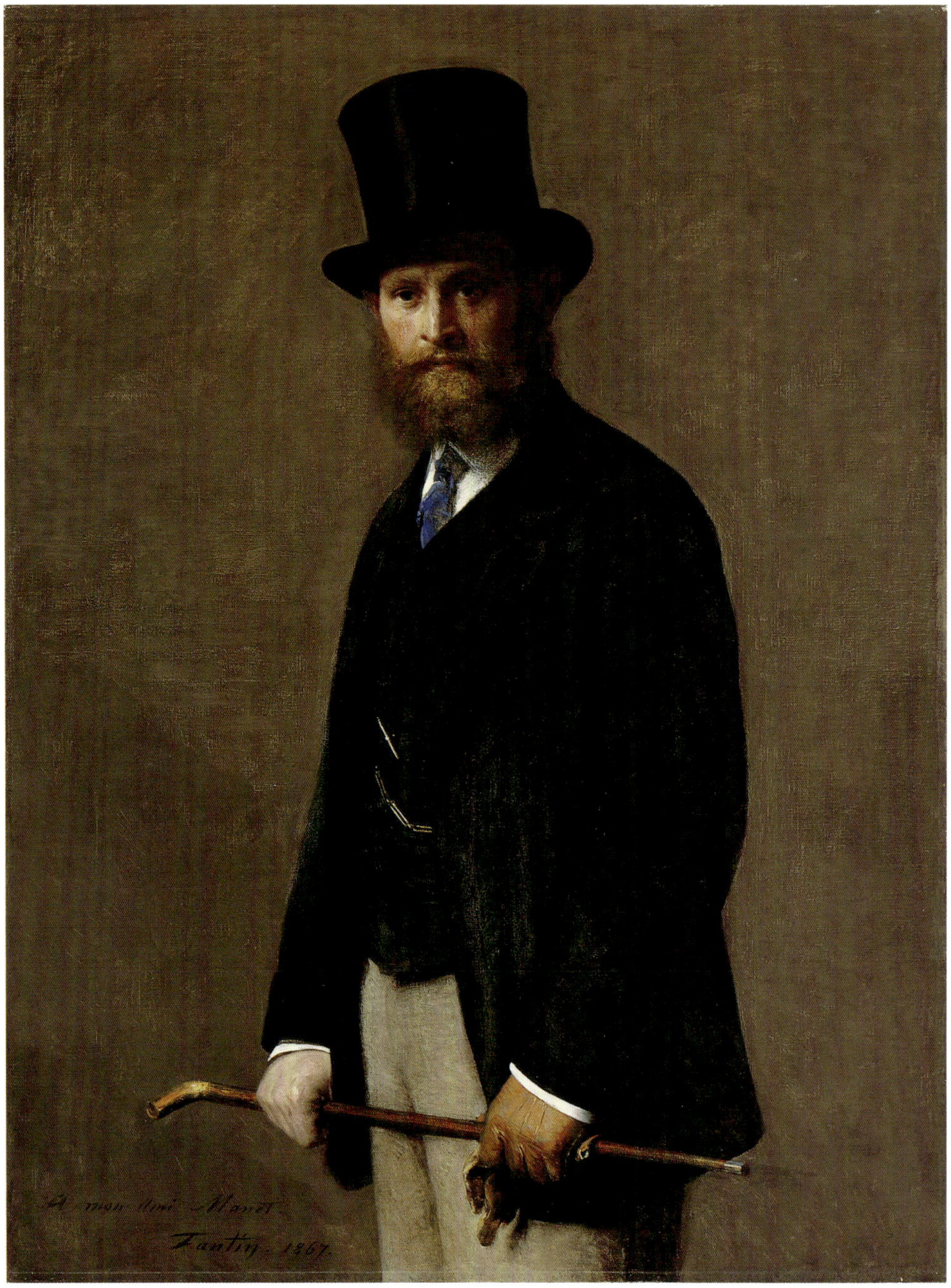

4

Édouard Manet, 1867

Oil on canvas; 117.5 x 90 cm (46 1/4 x 35 7/16 in.)
Stickney Fund, 1905.207
Signed lower left: *A mon ami Manet. / Fantin. 1867.*

Henri Fantin-Latour and Édouard Manet's friendship began sometime in 1857, while they were copying Old Master paintings at the Musée du Louvre, Paris, as part of their artistic training. Despite their increasing involvement in the early 1860s with the young artists who would come to be known as the Impressionists, both continued to look to the Salon for recognition and official approval. In 1867, after having been regularly rejected by that institution since his first submission in 1859, Manet decided not to exhibit there, instead paying for a private show of fifty-six of his works in an independent pavilion very near the Exposition Universelle. Fantin's decision to submit a portrait of his friend to the Salon that year may have been calculated to play off Manet's increasing notoriety. Inscribed in relatively large script in the lower-left corner, "To my friend Manet / Fantin 1867," the picture not only underscored his support for the embattled artist but also won Fantin a new level of critical respect.

Manet chose his own pose, which conveys decorous determination and alludes to the bourgeois social sphere in which both he and Fantin moved. The silver-tipped cane that he holds horizontally across his legs may hint at his readiness to fend off artistic attacks; however, it also suggests his preparedness for an urban outing in his role as artist-flaneur, a detached spectator of modern city life. The frank and easy confidence of this dignified gentleman both impressed and startled critics. As one of them admitted, he found it difficult to reconcile his preconceived image of Manet as a "long-haired art student"—as he had anticipated the author of the infamous *Olympia* to be—with the "well-gloved, well-dressed young man" who confronts the viewer in this canvas.

5

Self-Portrait, 1865/66

Oil on canvas; 108.9 x 71.1 cm (42⅞ x 28⅜ in.)
Restricted gift of Mr. and Mrs. Frank H. Woods in memory of Mrs. Edward Harris Brewer, 1962.336

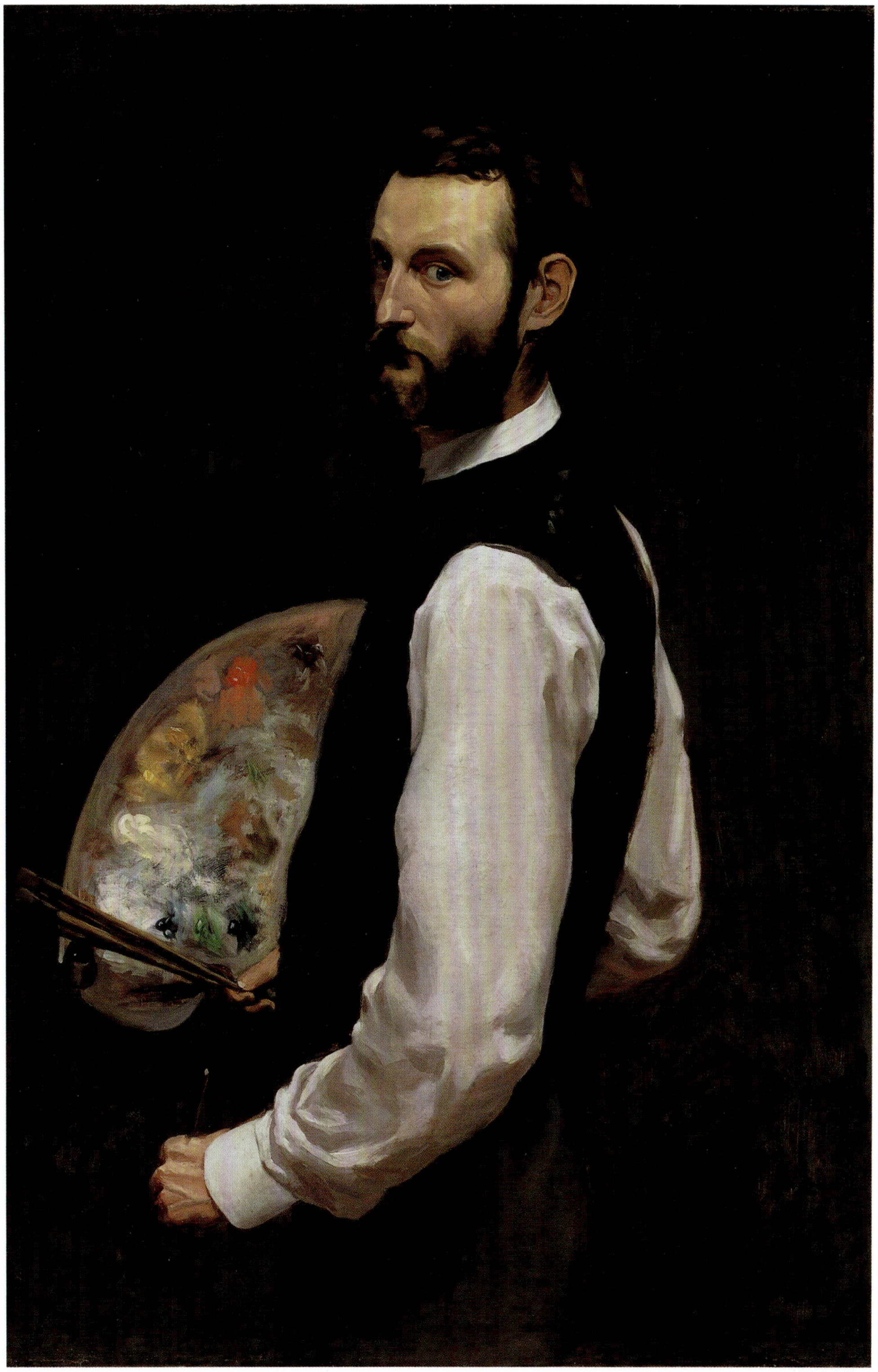

During his brief career, which ended in 1870 when he was killed in the line of duty during the Franco-Prussian War, Frédéric Bazille produced about seventy paintings, four of which are self-portraits. Among these, the Art Institute's work is unique in the pose and scale of the figure. In fact, it could be the painting that Bazille began in 1865 and described as "a big portrait, life size," undertaken "especially to train myself." For the twenty-four-year-old artist, the portrait may have been both a practice piece (in which he observed and painted his reversed image as seen in a mirror) and a professional manifesto. Only a year earlier, he had failed his examinations for a medical career and received parental consent to rent an atelier. By December he was sharing an apartment-studio with Claude Monet and experimenting with new painting techniques that would be central to the Impressionist movement. Perhaps Bazille's exaggeration of the palette in this image, held vertically so that all eight pigments are visible, was intended to announce his commitment to a full-time artistic career.

In direct contrast to Henri Fantin-Latour's depiction of Édouard Manet as a poised and elegant boulevardier (cat. 4), Bazille presented himself as highly focused, an artist hard at work. His torso is angled away, but his head turns toward the viewer with a startled look, as if he wanted to capture his own image by surprise, or as if his portrait session had been unexpectedly interrupted. His strained neck muscles, the protruding veins of his left hand, and his short brush—snapped off at the handle so as to better render details—further convey the physical nature of the artist's craft. Recent conservation revealed that the background of the painting, formerly thought to be flatly monochromatic, is made up of sweeping brushstrokes of a dark brownish gray that complement the intense mood of the subject.

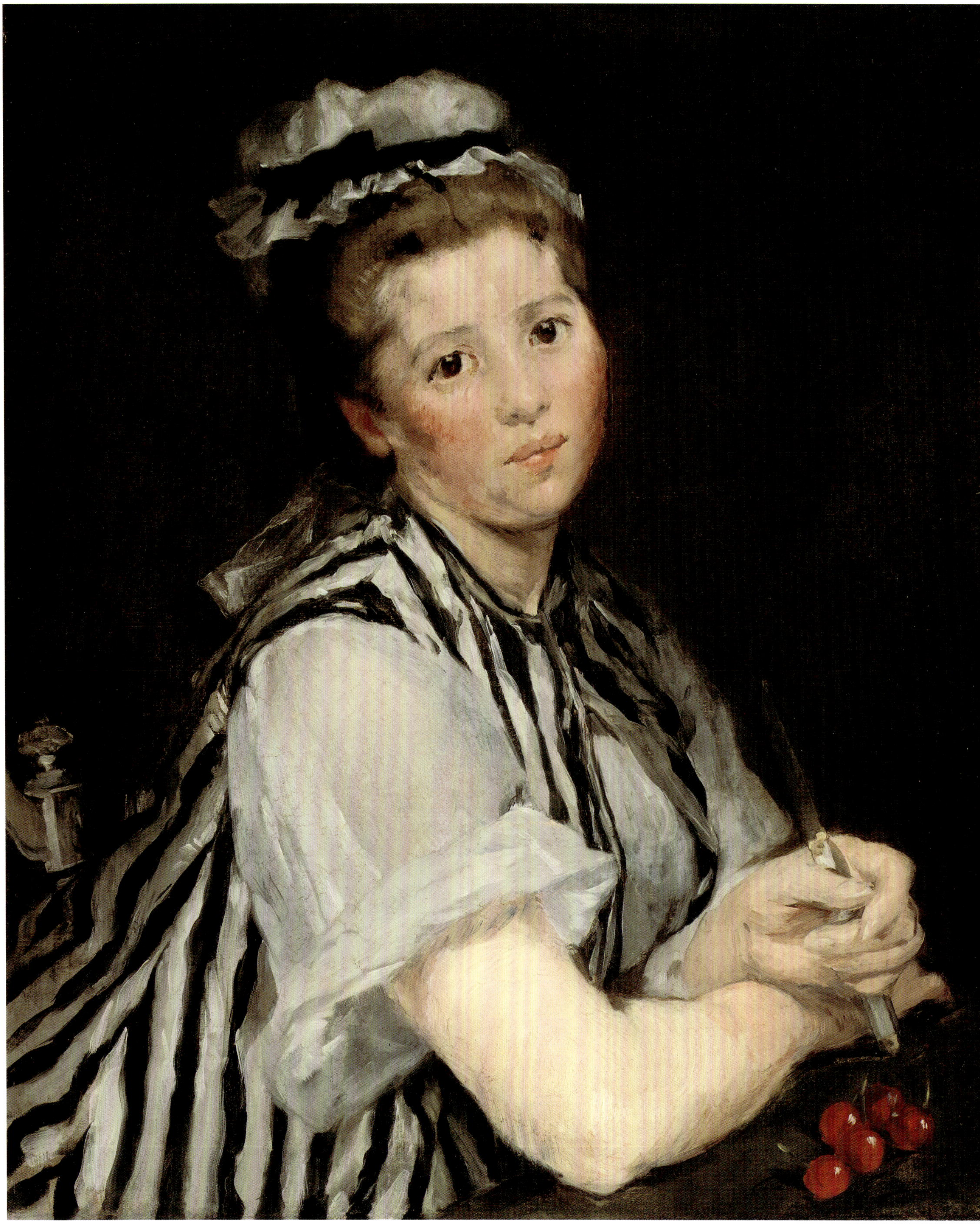

EVA GONZALÈS French, 1849–1883

6

Girl with Cherries, c. 1870

Oil on canvas; 56.2 x 47.4 cm (22 1/16 x 18 5/8 in.)
Mr. and Mrs. Lewis Larned Coburn Memorial Collection, 1940.32
Signed lower right: *Eva Gonzalès*

When Eva Gonzalès, the cultivated, beautiful, and affluent daughter of a celebrated novelist and an accomplished musician, began taking painting lessons in 1865, her choice of the fashionable society portraitist Charles Chaplin as a teacher was completely appropriate for a woman of her standing. Less acceptable was her decision four years later to leave Chaplin to study with Édouard Manet, becoming his first and only official pupil. For the painter Berthe Morisot, Manet's friend and sometime model, Gonzalès was a serious rival. Indeed, Morisot complained, "Manet lectures me, and holds up that eternal Mlle Gonzalès as an example: she has poise, perseverance, she is able to carry an undertaking to a successful issue, whereas I am not capable of anything." *Girl with Cherries*, painted shortly after Gonzalès signed on with Manet, is indebted to her teacher's Spanish-style works, such as *Beggar with Oysters* and *Beggar with a Duffle Coat* (cats. 2–3), which are characterized by dramatically lit figures set against dark backgrounds.

The model for this intimate portrait wears the frilled linen cap and loose striped gown (*robe à la française*) of an eighteenth-century servant—an occupation further hinted at by her rolled-up sleeve. Having adopted Manet's Realist subjects and painterly techniques (which are particularly visible in the long, loose peachy white strokes that describe the woman's foreshortened arm), Gonzalès softened the sense of confrontation between model and viewer that appears in many of her teacher's works. Although *Girl with Cherries* adheres to Manet's use of artifice and observation, the subject is far removed from his images of his favorite model, Victorine Meurent, whose immodest gaze so affronted the art establishment in *Déjeuner sur l'herbe* (1863; Musée d'Orsay, Paris) and *Olympia*. Instead, Gonzalès's demure young servant girl returns the viewer's gaze with gentle candor, holding a fruit knife in mid-air as if caught unawares. In her choice of costume and pose, Gonzalès paid homage to the eighteenth-century artist Jean-Baptiste Chardin, who specialized in painting quiet domestic scenes of servants and children.

As model, muse, and pupil, Gonzalès is forever linked to Manet, who died in April 1883, just five days before her own premature death.

MANET: RACES AND BULLFIGHTING

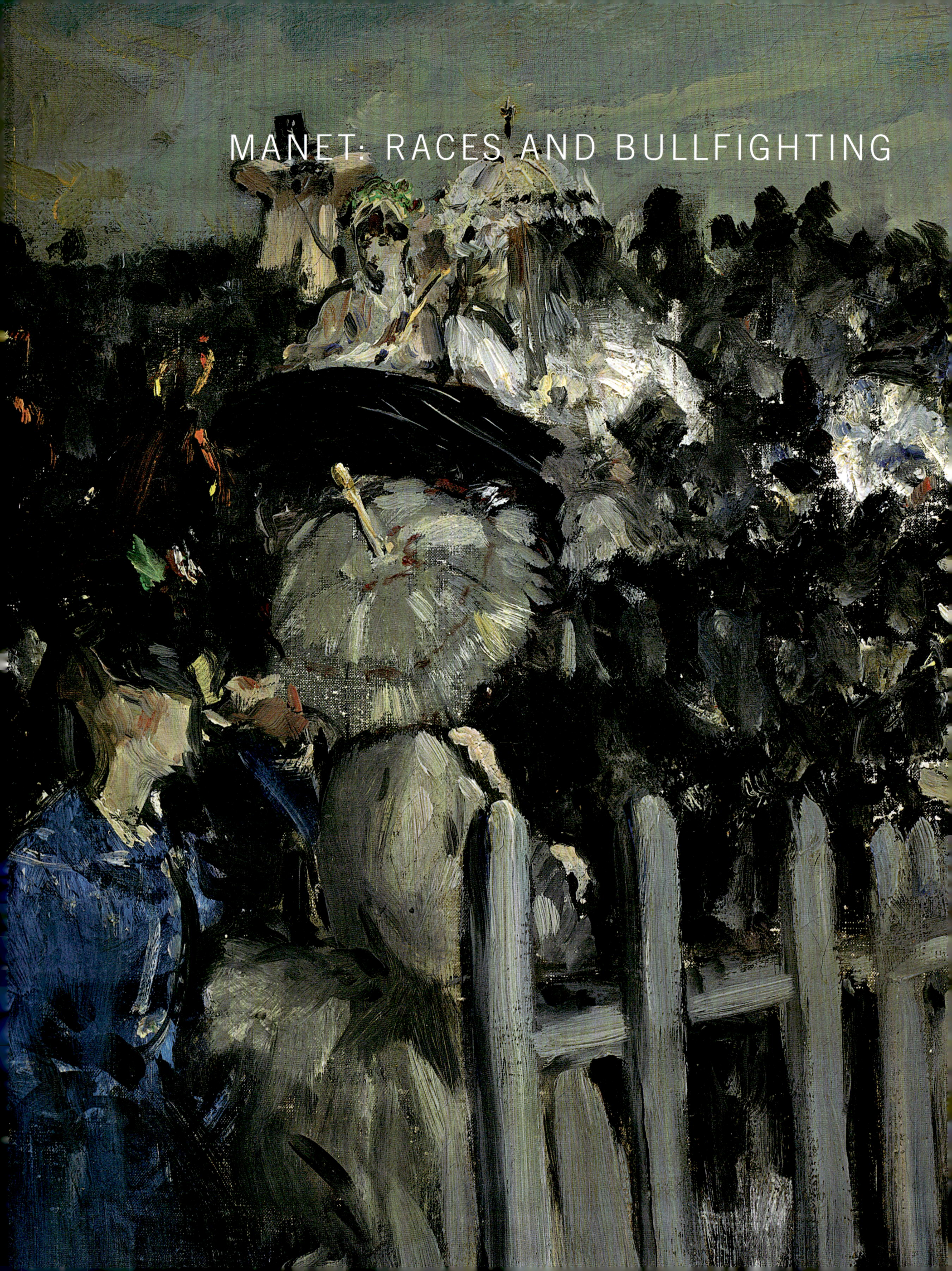

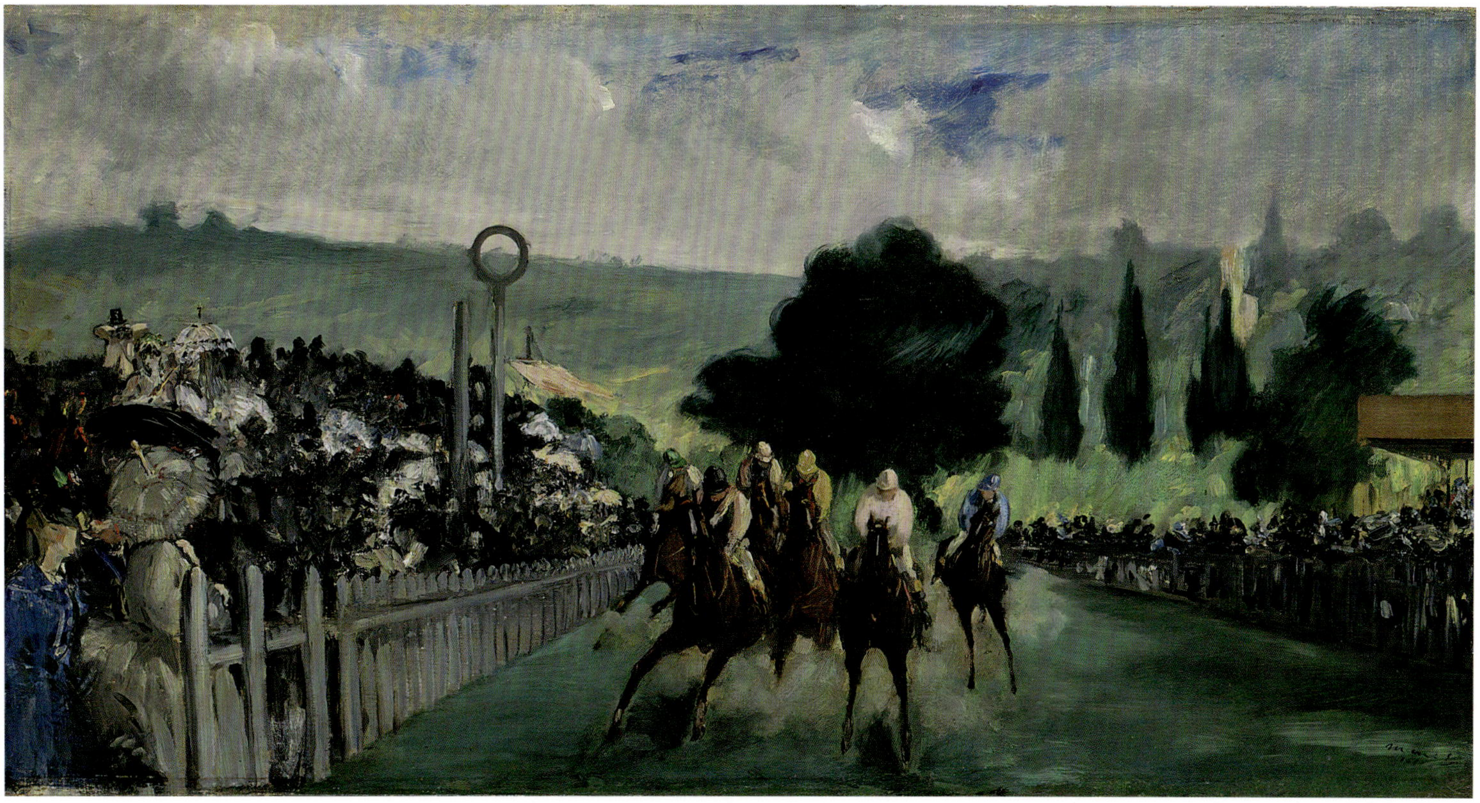

7

The Races at Longchamp, 1866

Oil on canvas; 43.9 x 84.5 cm (17 ¼ x 33 ¼ in.)
Potter Palmer Collection, 1922.424
Signed lower right: *Manet. / 1866*

The 1860s saw a growing trend among artists to paint ambitious canvases of the pleasures of modern life. Few are as savory as those by Édouard Manet, who introduced into the contemporary Realist project a deadpan irony, offhand elegance, and historical self-consciousness that utterly transformed it. In *The Races at Longchamp*, however, there is no sense of the classical or Old Master sources that inspired many of his early works. Instead, Manet suggested the explosive speed of the horses, the teeming crowds, and the masses of trees and hills in an exciting new pictorial language.

Manet's subject reflects the revival of horse racing during the Second Empire (1852–70), signaled by the opening in 1857 of the Longchamp track in the Bois de Boulogne, a park on the western outskirts of Paris. Although the artist took liberties with the surrounding landscape, he was specific when it came to the details of the track, from the viewing stands at left to the tribunal building at right. His faithful and innovative rendering of modern life was further exemplified by his depiction of the race itself. Manet chose to capture the last moments of the event, when the horses rush past the finish line, indicated by the pole with an open, circular disk on the left sideline. Revolutionizing the long tradition of pictures showing races from the side (clearly indicating which horse is in the lead), the artist dared to compose the scene so that the deafening and frantic throng of horses and satin-clad jockeys appears to thunder straight toward us. Rising above the flurry of horses and spectators is a man in a top hat looking at the finish through binoculars; he may be a stand-in for the artist himself.

When this painting was first shown at the artist's posthumous exhibition, one reviewer judged it "a pretty sketch that might have been a painting," but there is little doubt that this signed and dated composition represents the artist's full-fledged response to the attempts of other vanguardists to visually express motion and temporality.

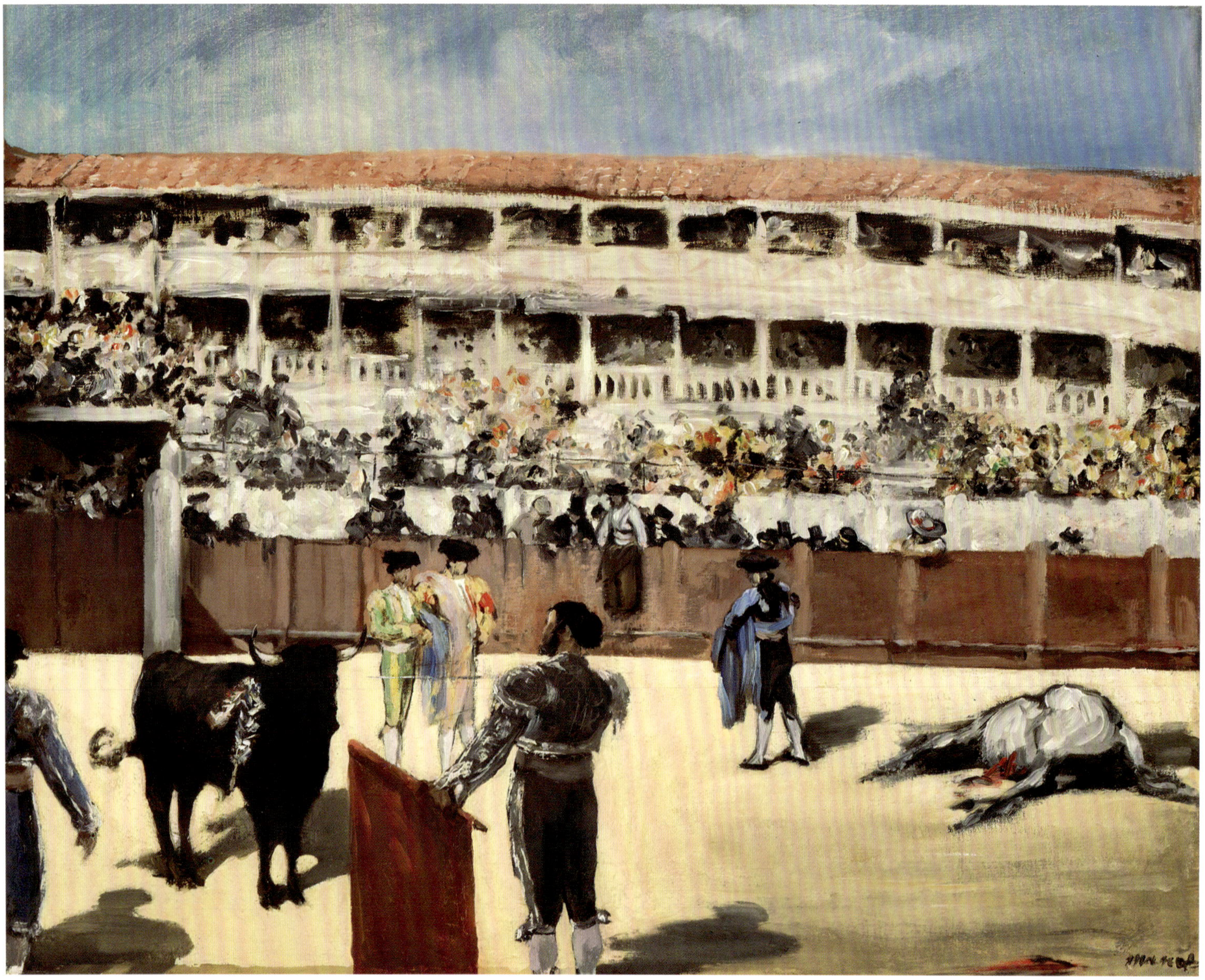

ÉDOUARD MANET French, 1832–1883

8

Bullfight, 1865/66

Oil on canvas; 48 x 60.4 cm (18⅞ x 23¾ in.)
Mr. and Mrs. Martin A. Ryerson Collection, 1937.1019
Signed lower right: *Manet*

Édouard Manet's trip to Spain in the fall of 1865 lasted only about ten days, but it had a profound impact on the artist. In addition to visits to the Museo del Prado, he attended a bullfight in Madrid, which he called "one of the finest, most curious and most terrifying sights to be seen" in a letter of September 14 to his friend the poet and critic Charles Baudelaire. To capture the excitement of the bullfight, he made quick sketches that informed several canvases. Of these, the Art Institute's *Bullfight* is both the smallest and the most carefully composed.

Although the fallen and bleeding horse on the right signals the aftermath of violence, the painting is devoid of the deadly combat (bull goring horse) or cruel actions (*banderillos* aggravating the bull to wear him out) of the two larger works (*Bullfight*, 1865; Musée d'Orsay, Paris; and *Bullfight*, 1865–66; formerly Matsukata Collection, present location unknown). Instead of showing the *espada* (bullfighter) in action, Manet presented the moment of truth, the confrontation between man and bull, as indicated by the bullfighter's muleta (a piece of red wool cloth hanging on a wood stick) and sword, which dramatically connect the two.

In this stop-action scene, Manet's primary actors and their shadows create decorative surface patterns. The focus, however, is on the silhouetted shape of the black bull, which joins with the flattened forms of the humans and their shadows in a triangular zone of danger and threat. As a backdrop for this mortal face-off, Manet painted the spectators with short, airy strokes, creating a blurred image of a crowd that mirrors his treatment of onlookers in a contemporaneous scene of modern entertainment, *The Races at Longchamp* (cat. 7).

The modernity of *Bullfight* was underscored by the fact that in 1913 its owner, Chicago collector Martin A. Ryerson, lent it to the controversial Armory Show, which introduced American audiences in Chicago, as well as New York and Boston, to many trends in avant-garde European and American art.

SEA AND SKY

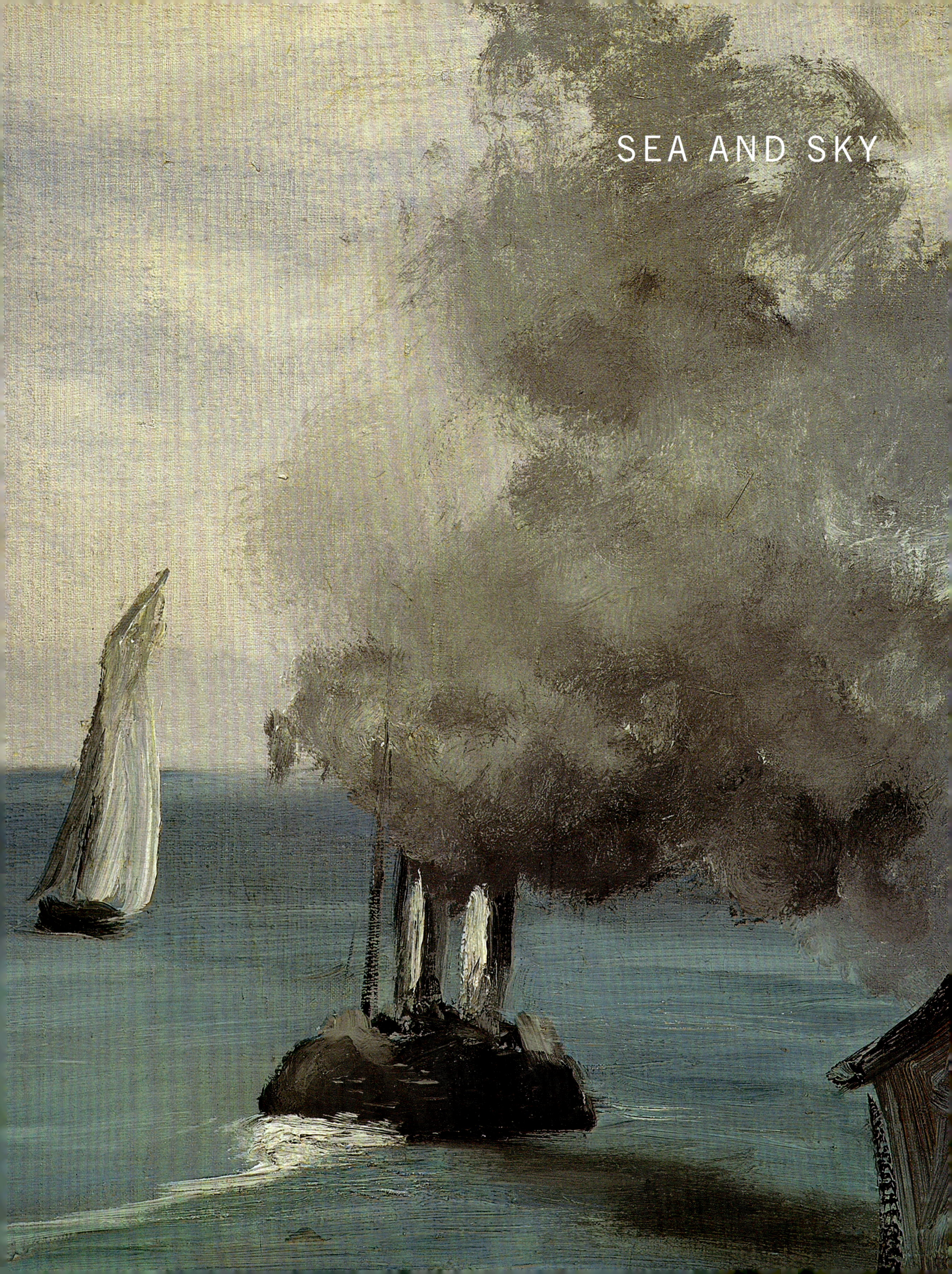

ÉDOUARD MANET French, 1832–1883

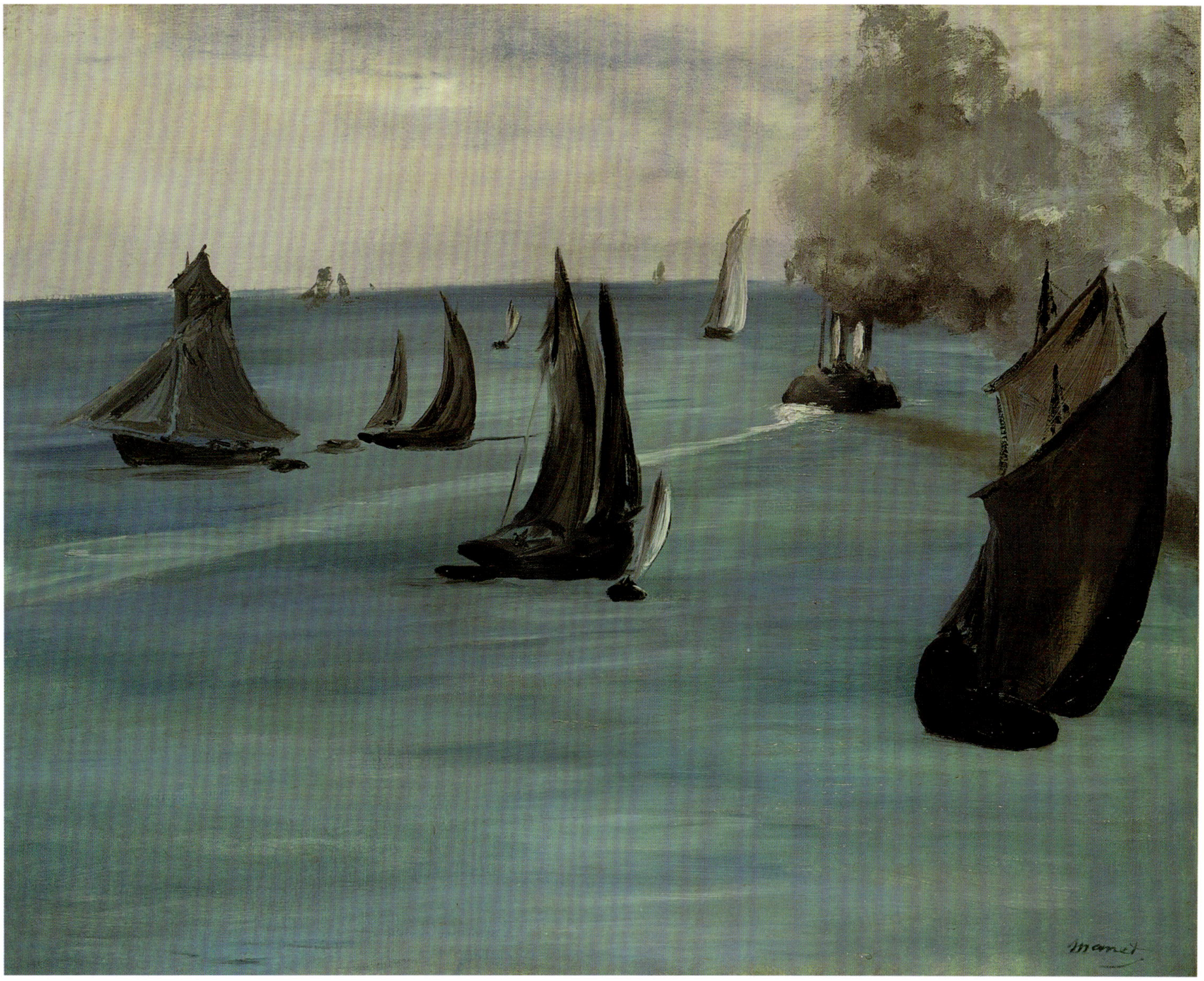

9

Steamboat Leaving Boulogne, 1864

Oil on canvas; 73.6 x 92.6 cm (29 x 36½ in.)
Potter Palmer Collection, 1922.425
Signed lower right: *Manet.*

Édouard Manet was thirty-two years old when he began painting the sea. Although they represent the least known aspect of his oeuvre, his marine pictures chart an artistic journey that lasted from 1864 until shortly before his death in 1883. During this time, Manet experimented relentlessly, pushing the boundaries of his craft and building on his own and others' achievements while responding to the emerging generation of avant-garde artists who would become known as the Impressionists. *Steamboat Leaving Boulogne* is one of three or four marines that Manet painted in Paris on the basis of sketches made on vacation with his family in the northern port town of Boulogne-sur-Mer. In stark contrast to the dark, solidly constructed and crowded still lifes from his Boulogne sojourn (see cat. 1), these seascapes are remarkable for their sense of light, wind, and water. Of the marines known to have been painted in 1864, this is the smallest and most formally audacious. X-ray examinations revealed that Manet painted the sea first, liquefying his pigments in order to apply them smoothly over a finely woven linen canvas that shows through the paint in places. Over this glossy, blue-green expanse, which fills more than two-thirds of the canvas, creating a high horizon line, he added eleven boats, boldly brushed and almost calligraphic in form. Seemingly decorative and *japonisant* (influenced by the fashion for Japanese woodblock prints), these can be identified as specific boat types, including the side-wheel packet steamer heading up the Channel and leaving in its long wake the slower, sail-powered vessels. When Manet first showed this picture, in 1867, a caricaturist illustrated it in *Le Journal amusant* and titled it *Le Steam-Boat*, leaving no doubt as to its focus.

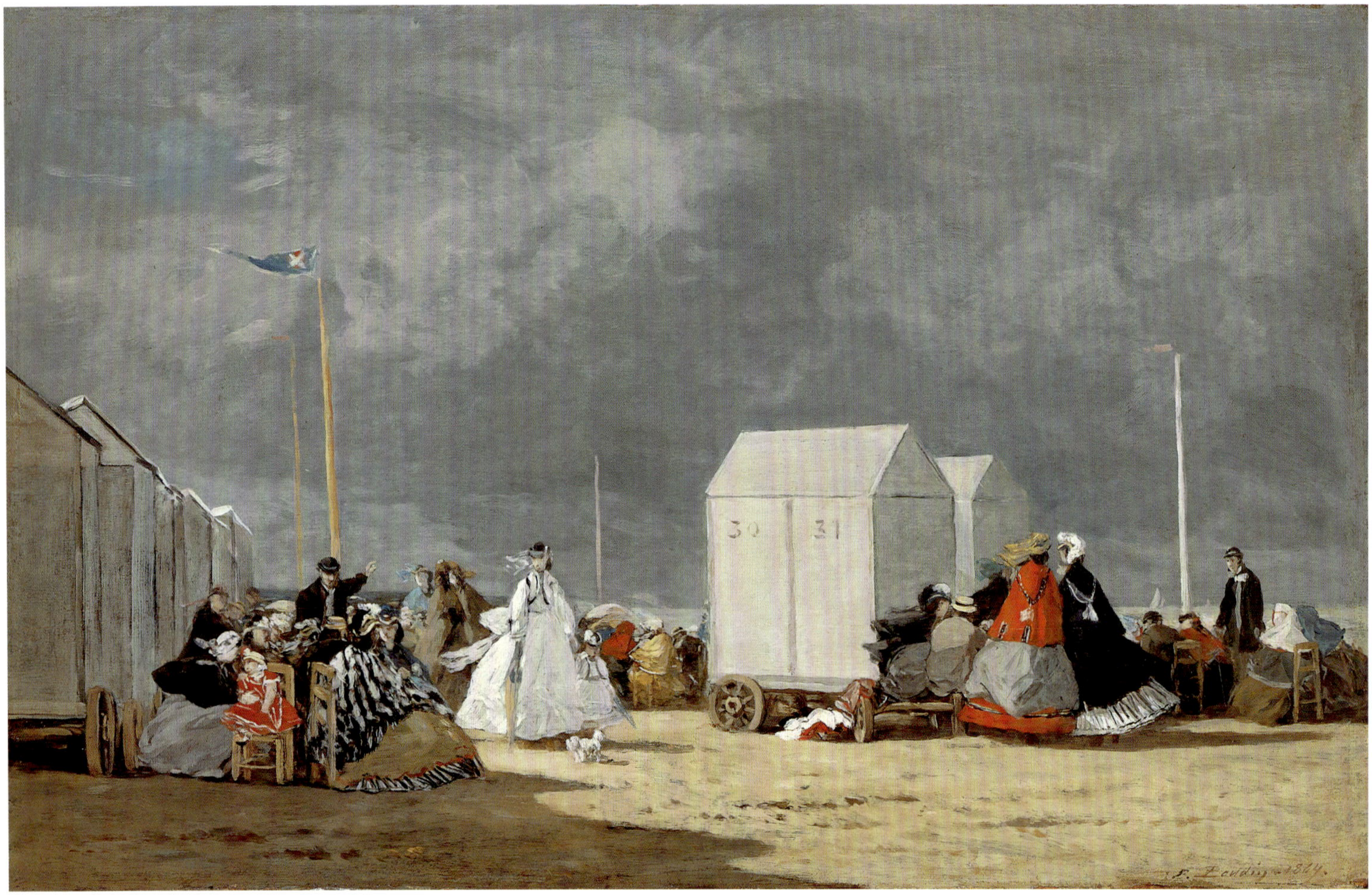

10

10

EUGÈNE-LOUIS BOUDIN

Approaching Storm, 1864

Oil on cradled panel; 36.3 x 57.9 cm (14 3/8 x 22 1/2 in.)
Mr. and Mrs. Lewis Larned Coburn Memorial Collection, 1938.1276
Signed lower right: *E. Boudin. 1864.*

11

JOHAN BARTHOLD JONGKIND

Entrance to the Port of Honfleur, 1863/64

Oil on canvas; 42.2 x 56.2 cm (16 5/8 x 22 1/4 in.)
Louise B. and Frank H. Woods Purchase Fund in honor of The Art Institute of Chicago Diamond Jubilee, 1968.614
Signed lower right: *Jongkind 1864*

Eugène-Louis Boudin and Johan Barthold Jongkind changed the face of marine and seascape painting with works in which content, palette, and technical agility helped to develop plein-air (outdoor) painting. Claude Monet met Boudin in 1858 and adopted the artist as his principal mentor, but he claimed that it was Jongkind who "educated his eye." As they began to gain recognition from younger artists, Boudin and Jongkind also found admirers and buyers for their works. The rising popularity of their paintings relatively late in their careers coincided with a growing interest in the beach as a vacation spot. The Normandy coast in particular had become easily accessible for tourists and artists alike, thanks to the extension of the French railway system from Paris to the Atlantic Ocean.

Entrance to the Port of Honfleur is one of two seascapes that Jongkind showed at the Salon of 1864. At the same Salon, Boudin exhibited a work entitled *Beach near Trouville*, previously identified as the Art Institute's *Approaching Storm* but now thought to be a larger work (possibly *Vacationers on the Beach at Trouville*, 1864; Minneapolis Institute of Art). The majority of the beach scenes that Boudin painted in the fashionable tourist spots of Trouville and nearby Deauville date from 1864, his most intense period of work on the subject. These paintings usually feature the constantly changing Normandy skies over a beach populated by what the artist called his "little dolls." As he wrote to a friend in 1863, "People really like my ladies on beaches. Some claim that there is a gold mine there to be exploited."

Boudin's beach scenes translated the life of the Paris boulevards to the seashore. At a time when bathing costumes were a rarity, women, men, and children wore the same

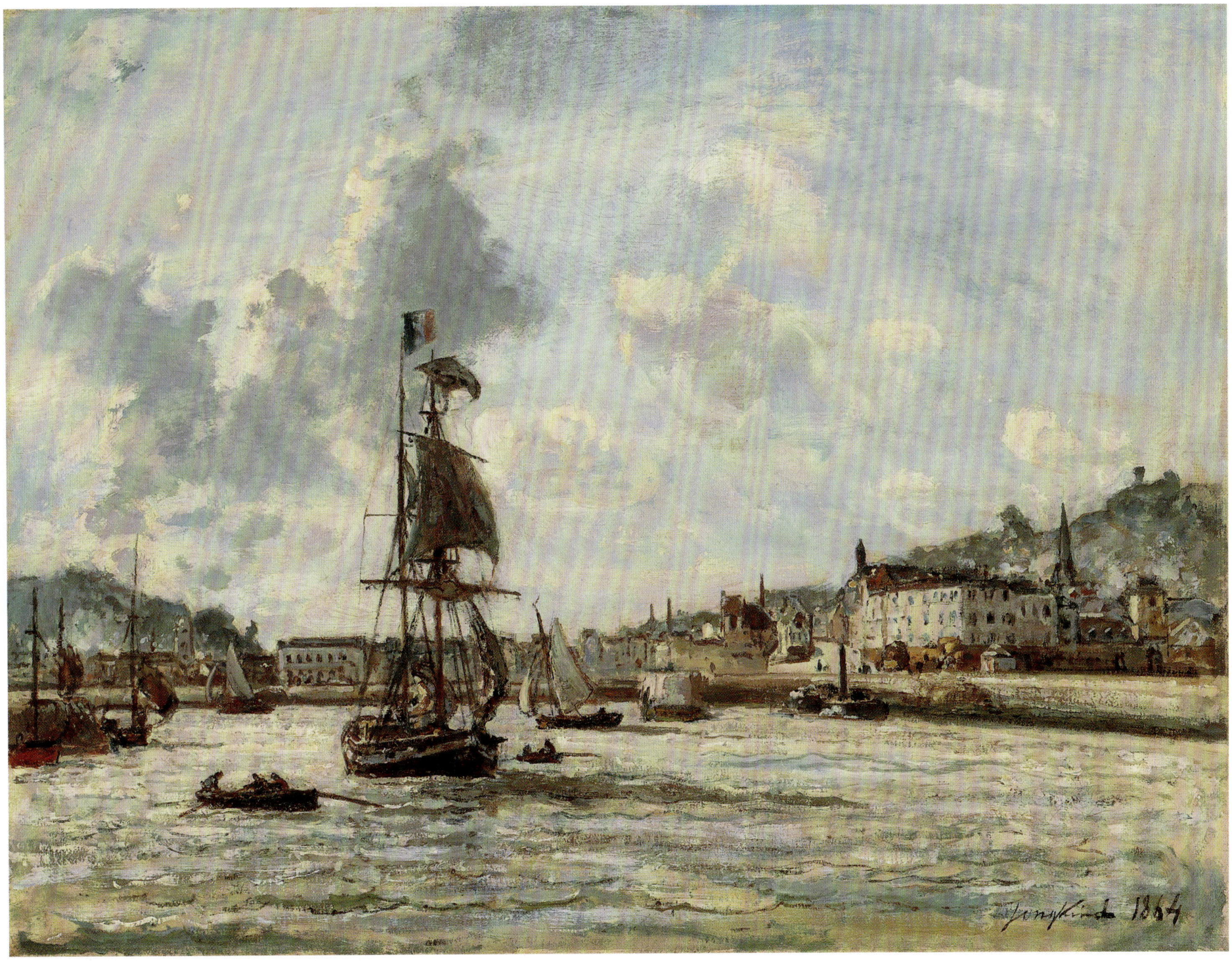

11

ponderous crinolines, frock coats, felted hats, and buckled shoes and participated in the same promenades, visits, and dinners at the beach as they did in their urban lives. Jongkind, on the other hand, focused on the sea rather than the crowds. During his early career in Paris, he was known as the "painter of the Seine," and on the Normandy coast, he continued to focus on waterways and ships entering and leaving the harbor, with only hints of the accompanying commercial activities.

Despite differences in the content of their paintings, both artists executed their final compositions in their studios, trying to retain the moist light and vivid spontaneity of the plein-air sketches from which they worked. They looked to the seventeenth-century Dutch marine tradition, and their compositions share a similar horizontal format and low horizon line. In each of the Art Institute's paintings, the eye travels from the lower-left corner to a central focal point—the woman and child in fluttering white crinolines in the Boudin, and the flapping sails of the wind-whipped ship in the Jongkind. Both artists included details that reveal an insider's knowledge of the scenes they depicted. At the right of *Port of Honfleur*, Jongkind showed the Hôtel Le Cheval Blanc in front of the hillside known as Côte de Grace. Equally precise (although not specifically identified) is the large sailing ship, with meticulously rendered masts punctuating the sky.

Boudin was no less exact in his representations of beach crowds. In *Approaching Storm*, he gave special emphasis to the portable changing machines (which were pulled into the water so that bathers could put on bathing suits without fear of being seen), whose silhouettes break up the frieze of figures and cast dramatic shadows. The darkening sky and high winds (indicated by snapping skirts and fluttering scarves) provide both entertainment for the seated figures at the shoreline and a sense of impending danger.

High Impressionism

CRADLE OF IMPRESSIONISM

CITIES AND SUBURBS

RENOIR'S TRANSFORMATIVE VISION

STILL LIFE

DEGAS: CLASSICAL TRADITION AND MODERN LIFE

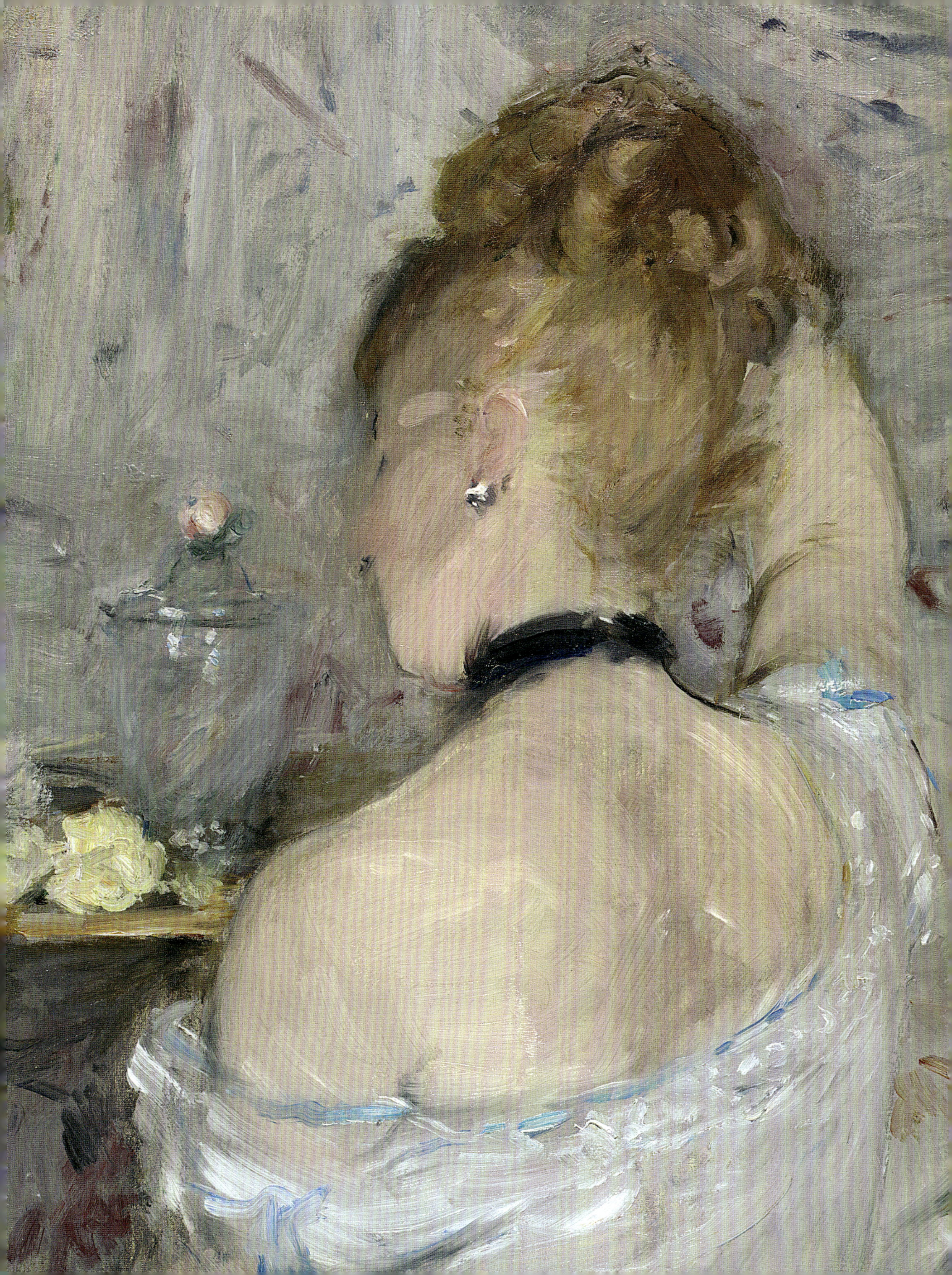

CRADLE OF IMPRESSIONISM

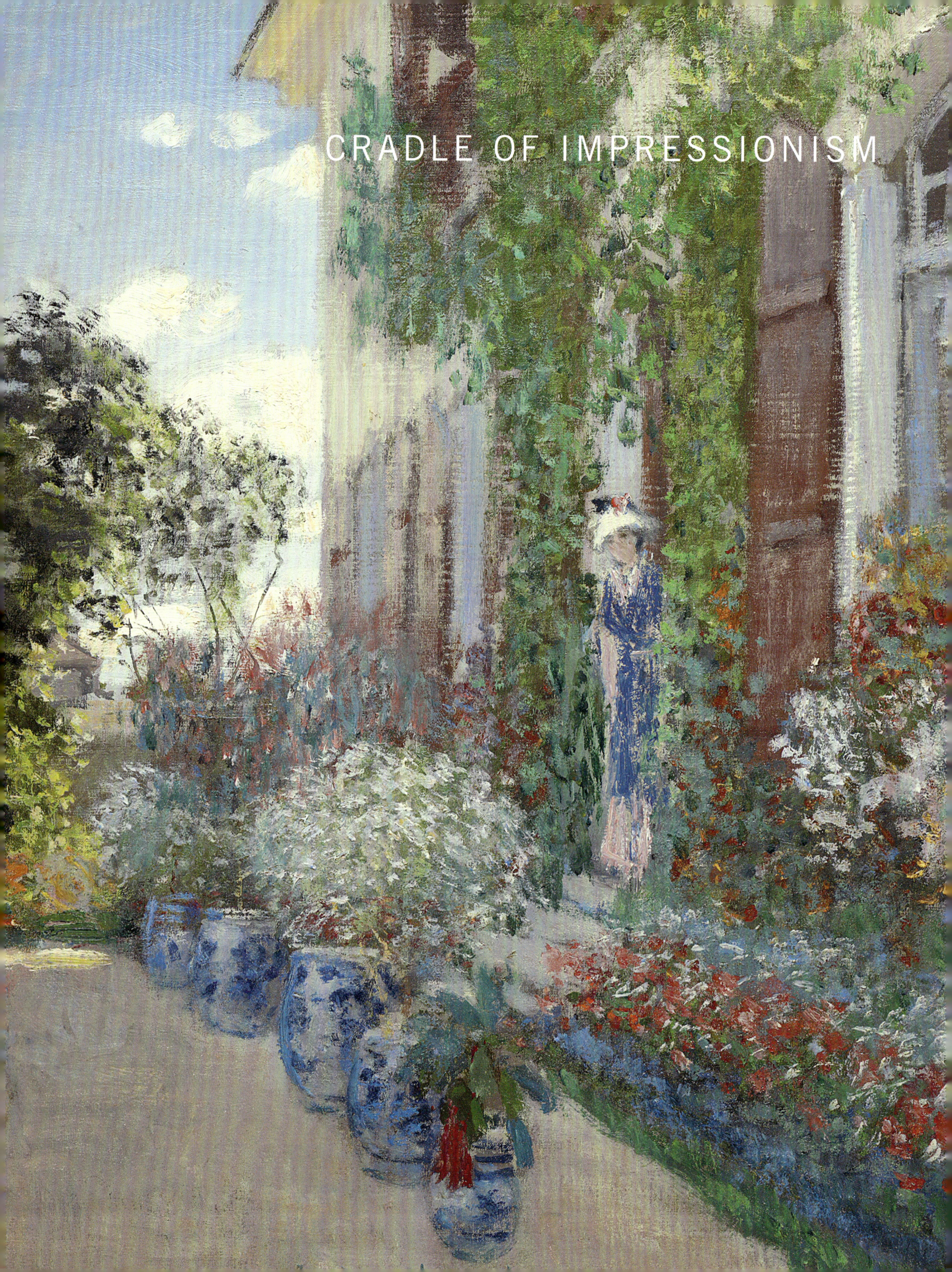

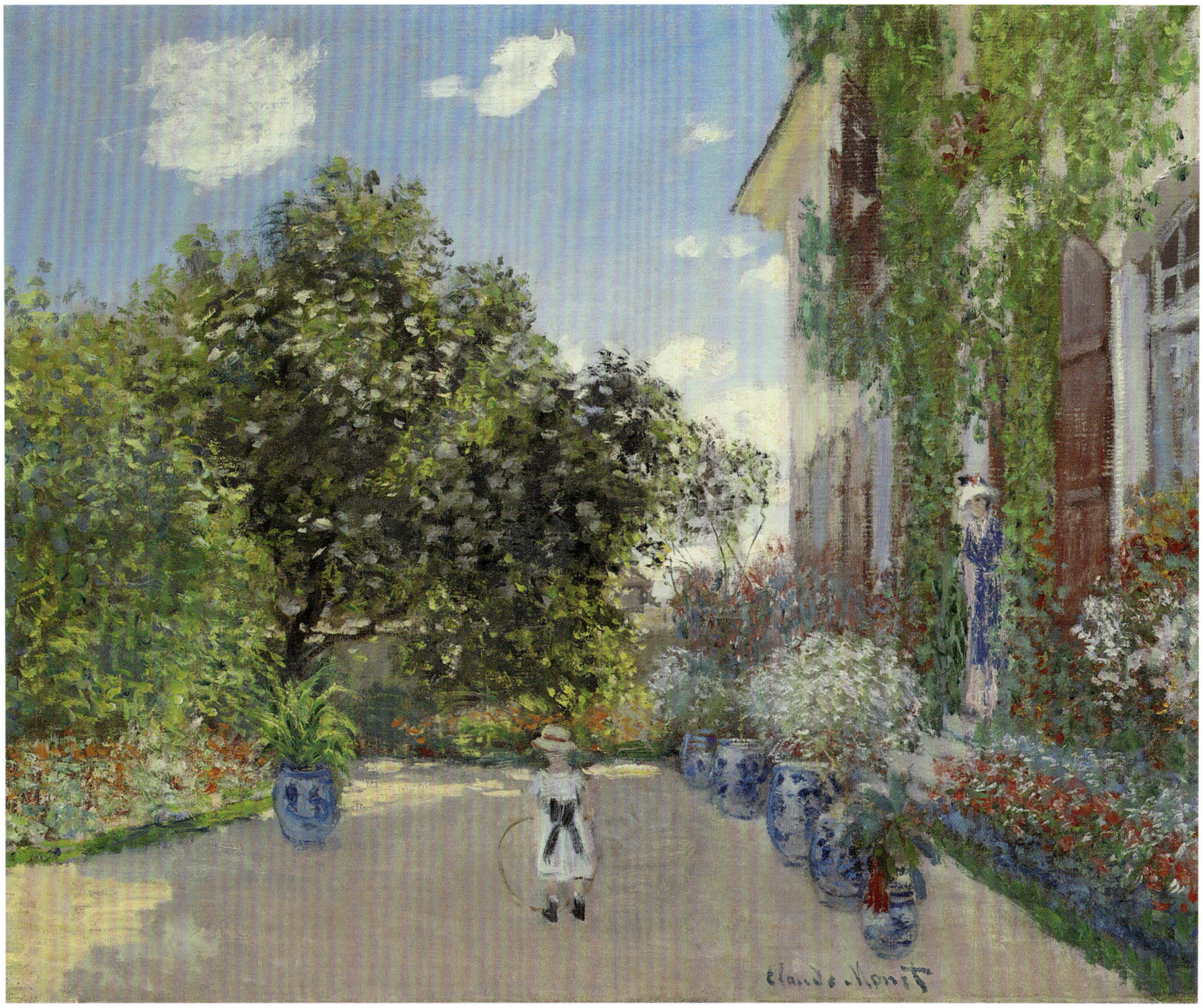

12

The Artist's House at Argenteuil, 1873

Oil on canvas; 60.2 x 73.3 cm (23 11/16 x 28 7/8 in.)
Mr. and Mrs. Martin A. Ryerson Collection, 1933.1153
Signed lower right: *Claude Monet*

This quintessentially Impressionist scene shows the garden of the house where Claude Monet and his family took up residence in late 1871. Its lush vegetation and sense of tranquility give visual testimony to the artist's material comfort at this time, thanks to recent sales of his work to the Paris dealer Paul Durand-Ruel.

The sun-dappled house, shaded gravel path, and circular flower beds form the stage on which Jean, the first of Monet's two sons (born in August 1867), plays with a wood hoop, while Camille Doncieux, whom Monet had married in 1870, watches from the open doorway. There are distinct similarities between Monet's famous final home in Giverny and this two-story, vine-covered house, whose back steps led to a profusion of multicolored flower beds and fruit trees. Over time Monet became exclusively a landscape painter; even in this candid familial scene, it is the garden setting and not the human activity that he chose to foreground. Unlike the many portraits that Monet made of his son, in this composition, Jean turns away from the viewer. Wearing a white linen frock over matching short pants tied with a blue sash (a popular outfit for boys because of its sailor connotations), he appears, like the blue-and-white glazed flowerpots, as a strategically placed decorative element.

Although Monet's financial security was short-lived and his relationship with Camille became increasingly fraught as a result of her deteriorating health (she would die in 1879), the seven years he spent at Argenteuil were significant. There he produced, in addition to numerous pictures of his home and its garden, some of his most celebrated landscapes and river views. Argenteuil was also close to Paris, where Monet and his colleagues planned a series of independent exhibitions, the first of which was held just one year after he executed this painting.

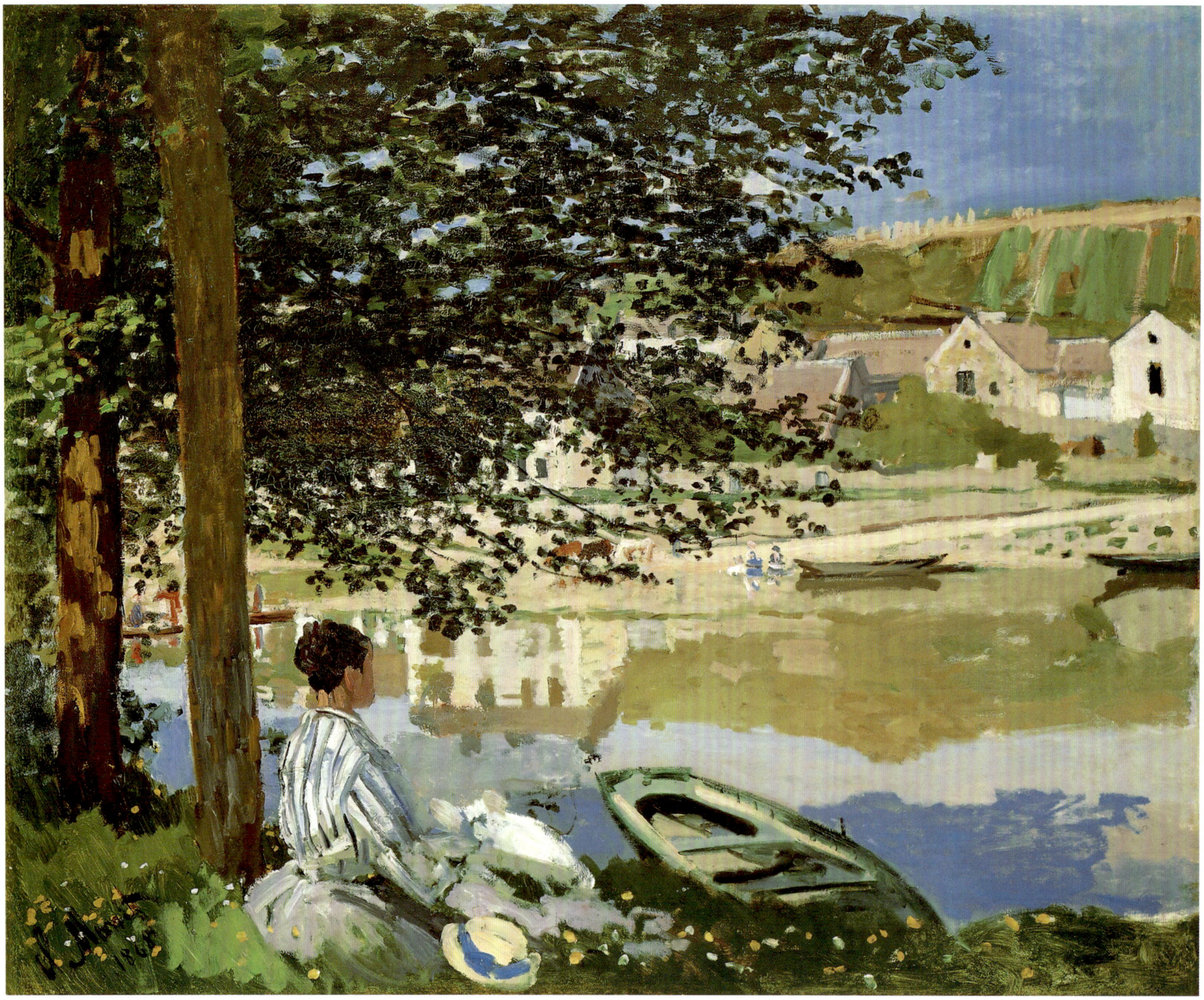

13

On the Bank of the Seine, Bennecourt, 1868

Oil on canvas; 81.5 x 100.7 cm (32 1/16 x 39 5/8 in.)
Potter Palmer Collection, 1922.427
Signed lower left: *Cl. Monet / 1868*

In this nearly square canvas, Claude Monet depicted his future wife, Camille Doncieux, with whom he had been only recently reunited after a separation of almost a year, seated on a riverbank on an island in the Seine River. Framed by trees on the left, she looks across the river to the hamlet of Gloton, next to the town of Bennecourt, from where she (and Monet) have just rowed. The writer Émile Zola recommended Gloton to Monet as a cheap rural retreat that was easily accessible from Paris. Perhaps acknowledging his friend's suggestion, Monet focused Camille's, and thus the viewer's, attention on the water's reflection of the hotel where Zola had stayed in 1866 and 1868.

Exhibited for the first time in 1889, with the title it now bears, this canvas—surprisingly experimental in both facture and coloration—is sometimes described as proto-Impressionist. Although the fluid blue and white stripes of Camille's dress appear to have been painted quickly over the still-wet green strokes that define the grass, X-radiographs reveal that Monet heavily reworked this area. In an early stage, Camille held a bonneted child (presumably the couple's nine- or ten-month-old son, Jean), whom Monet eventually painted out; he also added the white patch suggesting a fluffy dog to the right of Camille at a late stage in the process. The thick bands of color used in the river have a solidity that has little in common with the short, horizontal strokes Monet employed a few years later to suggest translucency and reflection. Indeed, with its decorative, near-abstract brushwork, Monet's *Bennecourt* has more in common with Paul Cézanne's structural facture (see cat. 14) or Paul Gauguin's zones of flat color (see cat. 71) than with the flickering brushstrokes that characterize the Impressionist touch.

Shortly after painting this image, Monet was forced to leave Bennecourt for non-payment of his rent. The fact that *On the Bank of the Seine, Bennecourt* is the only work to survive from the artist's short but tumultuous stay suggests how highly he valued it.

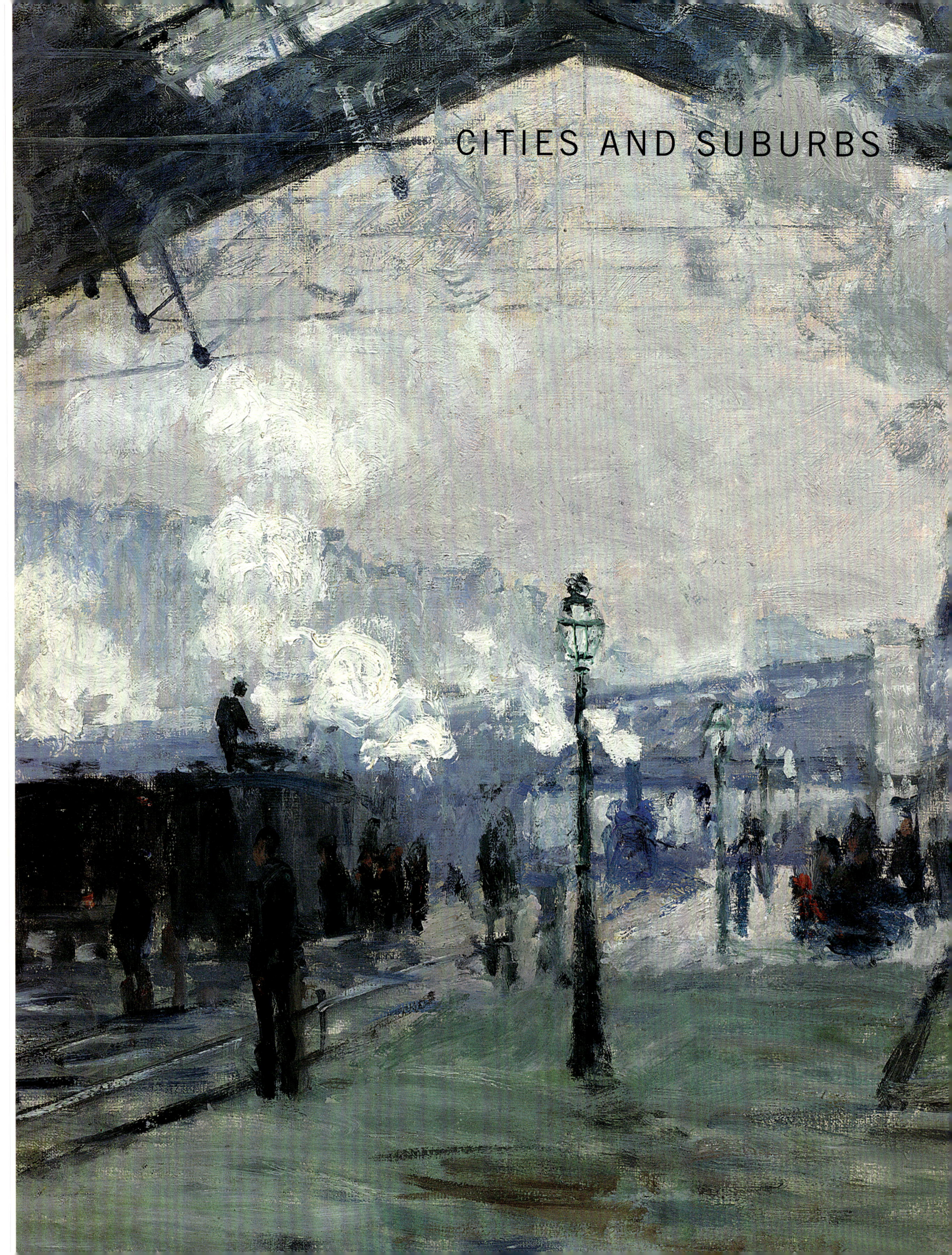

CITIES AND SUBURBS

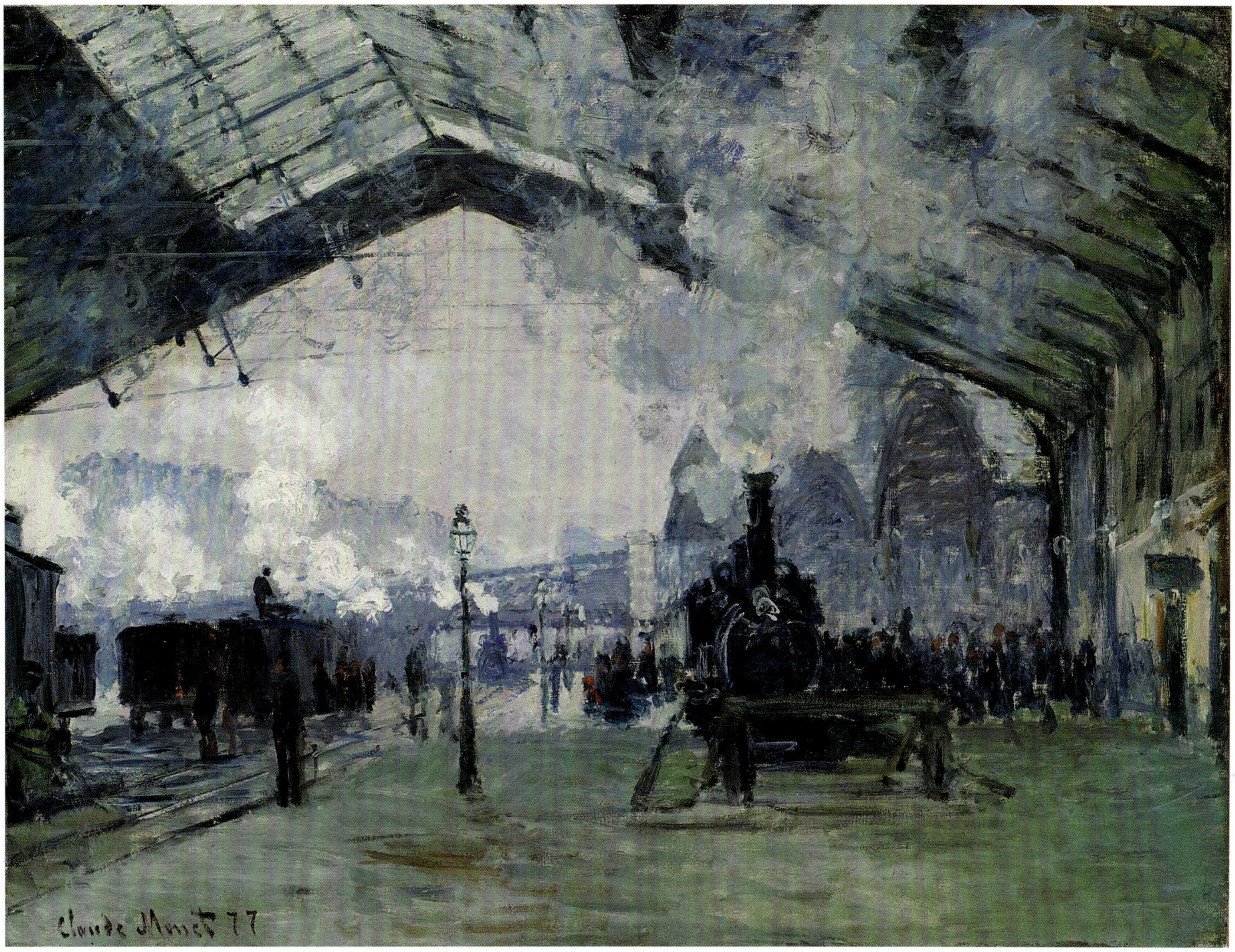

17

Arrival of the Normandy Train, Gare Saint-Lazare, 1877

Oil on canvas; 59.6 x 80.2 cm (23 ½ x 31 ½ in.)
Mr. and Mrs. Martin A. Ryerson Collection, 1933.1158
Signed lower left: *Claude Monet 77*

The Gare Saint-Lazare, which opened in 1837, quickly became the largest and busiest train station in Paris, attracting painters and printmakers who were interested in creating views of the modern city. But when, in early 1877, Claude Monet (financed by the artist Gustave Caillebotte) rented an apartment in the nearby rue Moncey and began the first of twelve canvases relating to the station, his aims, technique, and focus were quite different.

For Monet the train station represented the practical and critical link between his suburban home at Argenteuil and the business of art in Paris. In this particular canvas, one of four sold in March 1877 and included among seven shown at the third Impressionist exhibition the following month, the artist depicted the inside of the structure, whose lines serviced the villages along the route to Normandy that the Impressionists frequented. His use of the word *arrival* in the work's title signifies his desire to capture a specific moment—an intention reinforced by the use of dark strokes to show faceless workers and travelers, along with girders, signals, and engines. Legend has it that Monet even arranged for the stationmaster to add coal to the standing locomotives so that the painter could capture the effect of belching steam—dull gray when trapped inside the station, white and cloudlike when seen against the sky.

Despite its immediacy, the composition shows what a contemporary critic summarized as Monet's "skill in arrangement, that organization of the canvas"; at least one existing drawing (*Within the Gare Saint-Lazare: View of the Normandy Line*, 1877; Musée Marmottan, Paris) suggests a planned, rather than spontaneous, approach to the final composition. Its central lamppost aligns exactly with the apex of the glass canopy, bifurcating the work in much the same way as the lamppost in Caillebotte's *Paris Street; Rainy Day* (cat. 18), with which Monet would almost certainly have been familiar.

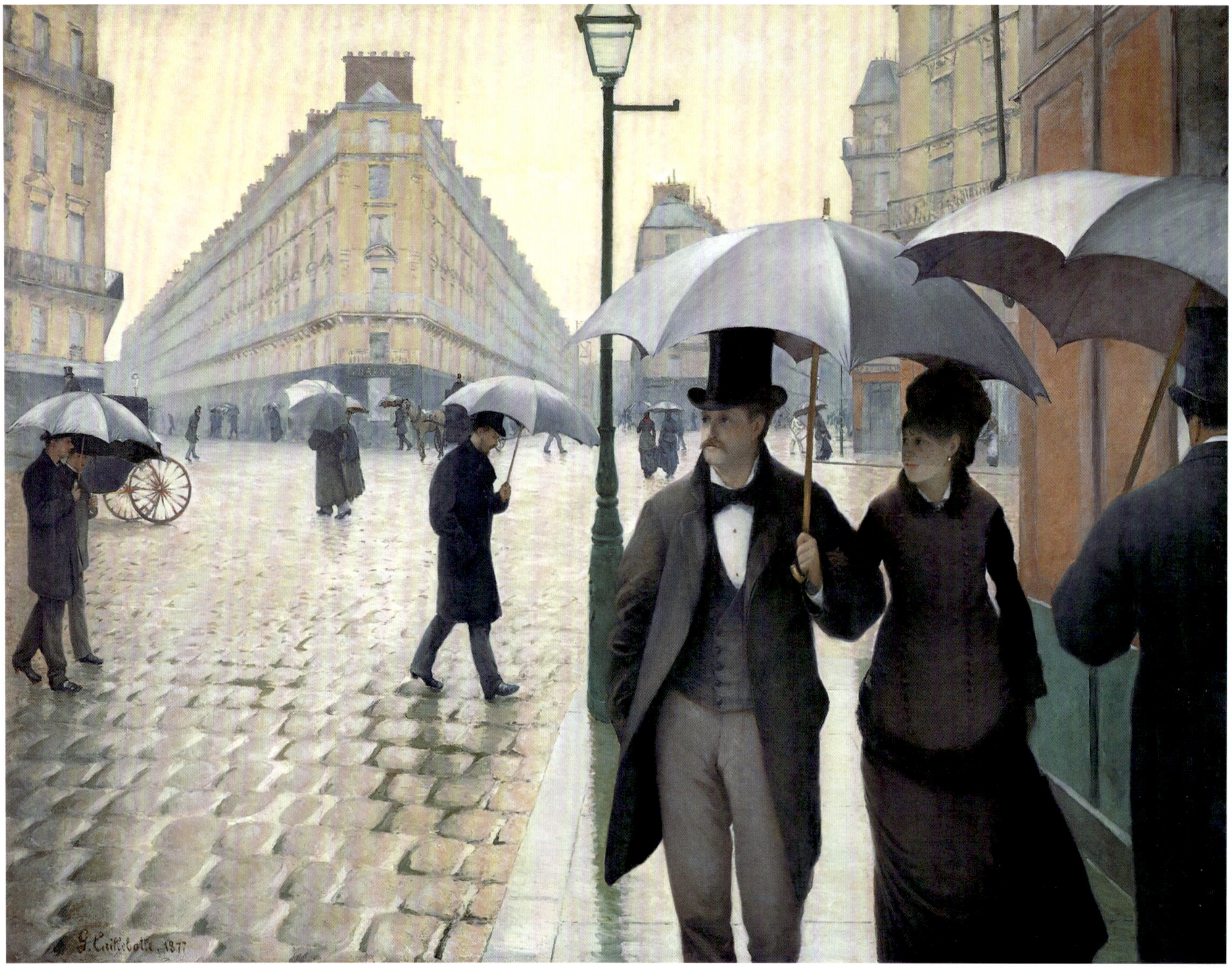

18

Paris Street; Rainy Day, 1877

Oil on canvas; 212.2 x 276.2 cm
(83½ x 108¾ in.)
Charles H. and Mary F. S. Worcester Collection, 1964.336
Signed lower left: *G. Caillebotte. 1877*

Paris Street; Rainy Day was, as one French anglophile reviewer said, "la masterpiece" of the third Impressionist exhibition, held in April 1877. Just four years earlier, the painting's creator, Gustave Caillebotte, had enrolled at the prestigious École des Beaux-Arts, Paris, where he received the technical grounding in painting and composition that would feature importantly in his future works. By 1877 the twenty-nine-year-old artist, a man of considerable wealth, was the youngest and most active member of the Impressionist group. He not only contributed six of his own canvases to the exhibition, but he also organized, financed, advertised, installed, and even lent works by Edgar Degas, Claude Monet, Camille Pissarro, and Pierre-Auguste Renoir from his personal collection. Upon his death at age forty-six, his collection was bequeathed to the state (only two-thirds of it was actually accepted), and it now forms the core of the Impressionist holdings of the Musée d'Orsay, Paris.

In this nearly ten-foot-wide canvas, Caillebotte took on a quintessentially Impressionist urban subject in a completely anti-Impressionist manner. Unlike Monet, who blurred architectural elements and abbreviated figures in his canvases of the Gare Saint-Lazare in order to express motion and immediacy (see cat. 17), Caillebotte here presented a frozen moment—one made permanent by his crisp technique and rigorously structured spatial composition. What makes the canvas so compelling is that it is both an irresistibly realistic depiction of life and a highly choreographed fiction. To achieve this balance, Caillebotte contrasted the minutely detailed cobblestones and two strolling city dwellers in the foreground with the smaller, less distinct figures in the background, who occupy the expansive spaces of the star-shaped intersection of the streets Saint-Pétersbourg, Turin, and Moscou. With their umbrellas providing visual links, these figures form rhythmic patterns while remaining firmly locked in the giant plus-sign structure of the composition, which is created by the vertical lamppost and its reflection, and by the imaginary horizontal axis connecting the bases of the buildings.

The pewter tones of the painting reinforce a sense of wetness that is both palpable and permanent, yet differs considerably from the Impressionists' depictions of atmospheric conditions. Indeed, the scene is not a captured impression, but a preconceived scenario based on a calculated perspective, into which Caillebotte added figures as both aesthetic and psychological elements. The sideways gaze of the nearly life-size woman at the right draws attention to the gleam of her pearl earring—a subtle reference to her bourgeois elegance. Behind her, framed by the umbrella handle and top hat of her male companion, the glint of a housepainter's ladder alerts the viewer to the presence of men and women of other social classes cohabiting the same urban space.

Although Caillebotte's title suggests a single street on a generically wet day, *Paris Street; Rainy Day* encapsulates both the monotony and the poetry of the boulevards designed by Baron Georges-Eugène Haussmann as part of his new Parisian city plan. The detached, noncommunicative character of the figures occupying the intersection may indicate Caillebotte's disdain for the anonymous and anti-picturesque nature of Haussmann's boulevards, which the novelist Edmond de Goncourt described as "without turnings, without chance perspectives, implacable in their straight lines." Although certainly different from Monet's and Renoir's lively views of the boulevards, which celebrate the spectacle of the capital, this work nonetheless pays homage to the quiet magic of the city, and more specifically to this intersection—topographically unremarkable from the many similar crossings of modern Paris, yet personally significant for the artist. Caillebotte's family residence was just a few blocks away, and in 1874 it had been expanded to include a studio space with a separate entrance, thus allowing him ready access to the streets he would immortalize.

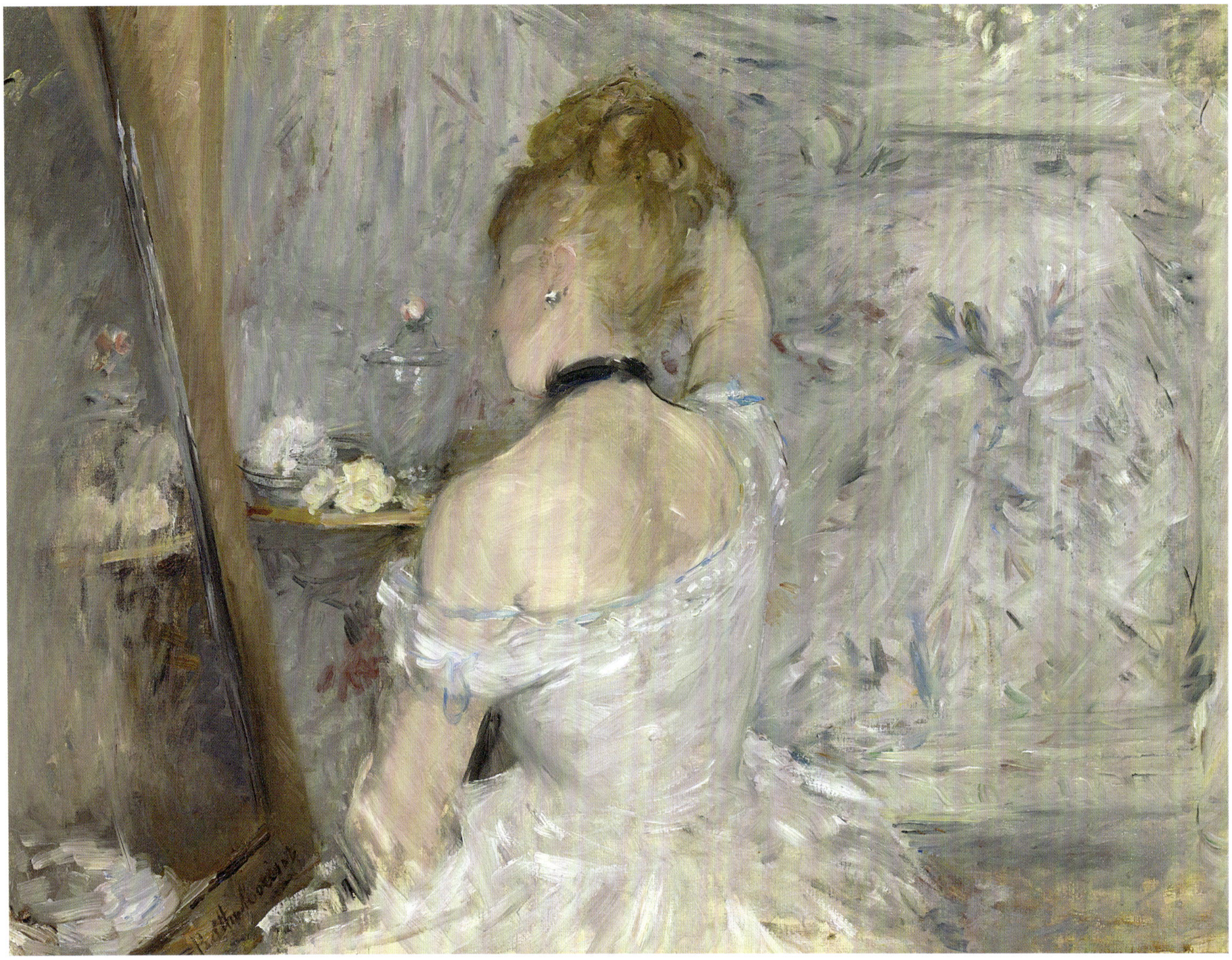

19

Woman at Her Toilette, 1875/80

Oil on canvas; 60.3 x 80.4 cm (23¾ x 31⅝ in.)
Stickney Fund, 1924.127
Signed lower left: *Berthe Morisot*

Berthe Morisot was, with Mary Cassatt, part of the small female contingent of the group of artists that came to be known as the Impressionists. In 1868, after studying with Camille Corot and showing her works at the official Salon, Morisot met Édouard Manet, who gave her entrée into the Impressionist circle. Although Manet (whose brother she later married) never felt entirely comfortable with the Impressionist style, Morisot became an enthusiastic and faithful adherent, exhibiting in all but one of the group's eight shows.

Woman at Her Toilette, presented at the fifth Impressionist exhibition, in 1880, is one of numerous canvases Morisot painted in the mid-1870s and early 1880s that depict the successive phases of well-to-do women dressing and readying themselves to appear in public. Although her brother-in-law often took on similar subjects, he eroticized his women—sometimes through the addition of a male admirer, other times by the attention given to undergarments or the model's state of undress. The sensuality of Morisot's boudoir scenes, on the contrary, results as much from her feathery soft, yet boldly free brushwork as from the pictures' narratives. Gustave Geffroy, a critic sympathetic to the Impressionists, admired the evanescent quality of Morisot's paintings and her ability to "fix the play of colors, the quivering between things, and the air that envelops them." In his view, "No one represents Impressionism with more refined talent or with more authority than Morisot." Geffroy applauded the balance that the artist established between her audacious painting style and her discretion in approaching her subjects, which allowed her to express a modernist vision of a private sphere without overstepping the limitations of what a respectable woman might paint.

In the rarified and perfumed realm of *Woman at Her Toilette*, Morisot's model adds the finishing touches to her apparel and makeup in preparation for a society ball. Turned so that only her neck and the back of her head are visible, she has also inclined the cheval glass toward her, effectively denying the viewer the pleasure of observing her or her reflection. Only the objects used in the process of creating her public persona—the powder puff, crystal jar, and flowers—can be seen, indirectly, in the mirror. Morisot's virtuoso brushwork and pale color harmonies merge her model's pinkish white flesh and the silvery satin of her dress with the floral background, from which emerges, as if floating, the headboard of an Empire bed. Probably Morisot's own bed (based on its appearance in other interior scenes by the artist), it is barely distinguishable, dissolved through her handling of paint, which one critic described as akin to spreading ground-up flower petals onto her surfaces "with airy, witty touches, thrown down almost haphazardly."

In fact, Morisot's technique was highly calculated to suggest the contours of the model, whose nuanced delicacy contrasts with the relative legibility of her toilette. Having donned her sparkling white earrings and navy blue velvet neckband, Morisot's young model need only pin to her chignon the two yellow and white roses sitting on the shelf in order to complete her sophisticated and refined evening ensemble. The silvery palette, delicate brushwork, and carefully composed, discreet view of a private moment result in an image celebrating femininity and artifice. The presence of Morisot's signature on the lower edge of the mirror suggests that both the artist and her subject are engaged in creating a fictive image of beauty: the former with paint and color and the latter with clothing and makeup.

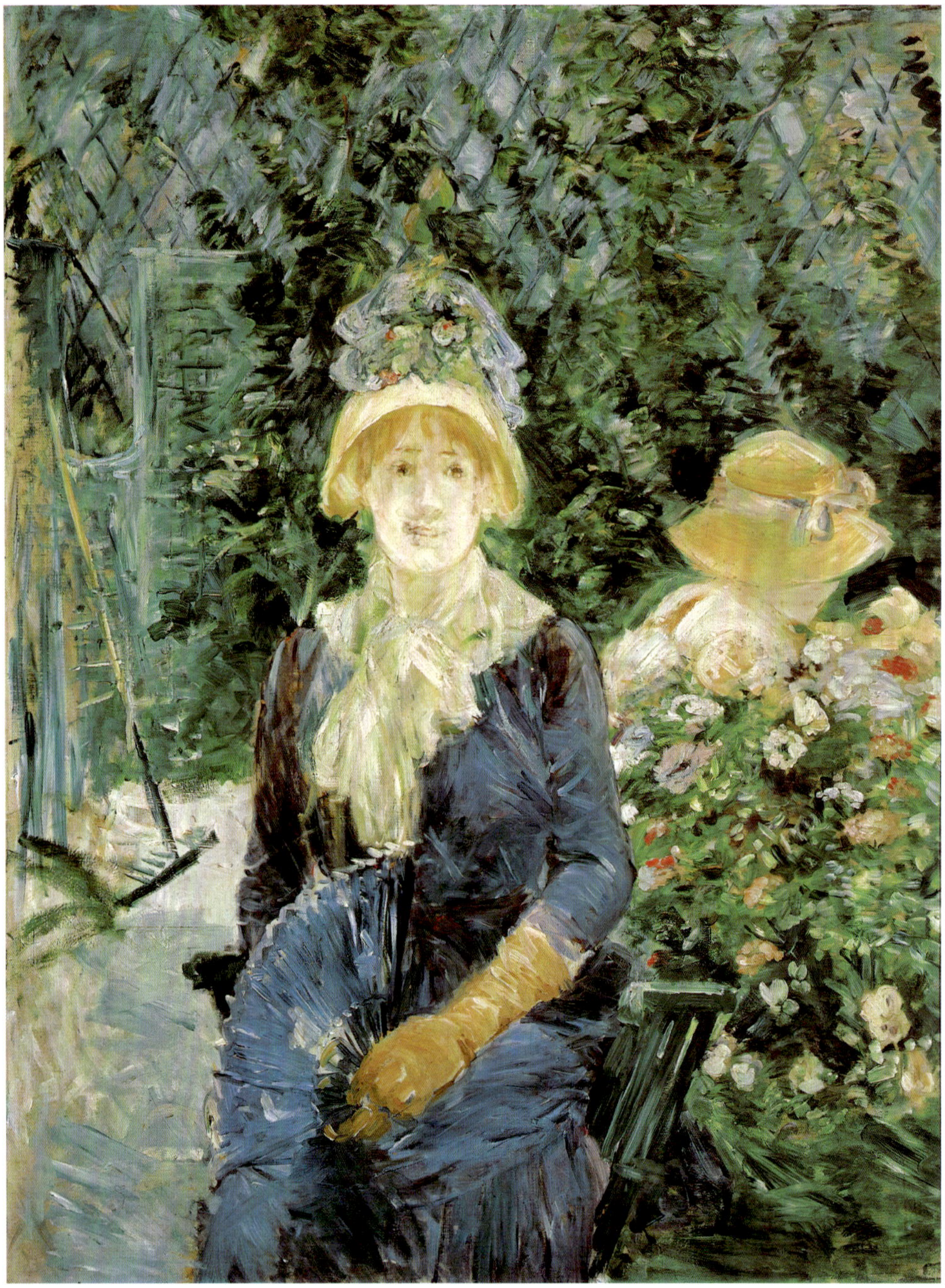

20

Young Woman in a Garden, 1882/83

Oil on canvas; 123 x 94 cm (48½ x 37 in.)
A Millennium Gift of Sara Lee Corporation, 1999.363

This ambitious canvas challenges the conventions of portraiture both compositionally and technically. Instead of flattering the sitter and making her the object of visual interest, Berthe Morisot deliberately treated the young woman as one of several focal points that serve to move the viewer's eye around the freely painted, yet highly structured composition.

Although undated, the work was probably begun in the summer of 1882, when Morisot, her husband, Eugène Manet, and their daughter, Julie, rented a house in Bougival, a picturesque village along the Seine River. The child wearing a straw hat and pinafore, who plays alone just behind the sitter, is undoubtedly the nearly four-year-old Julie. Both figures are surrounded by a profusion of flowers (some of which seem to have taken root atop the young model's hat) in a densely vegetated garden punctuated by the geometries of the trellis, the chair in the lower right, and the rake placed casually against the fence at the left. Far from creating a portrait likeness, Morisot applied paint as if she was making an Impressionist landscape, slashing acid green pigments and bluish ochers across the canvas to transcribe the effects of dappled sunlight without differentiating between the strokes used for the figure and setting. The resulting composition is both jarring—because it thwarts the anticipated treatment of the female as a beautiful complement to the natural setting—and captivating. Its rigorous and seemingly spontaneous brushwork unifies and electrifies the surface.

Although it was not exhibited at any of the Impressionist exhibitions, Morisot allowed the Paris dealer Paul Durand-Ruel to send the painting to London for an exhibition at a commercial gallery in April 1883. The fact that it remained in the artist's family for sixty years following her death may indicate that it was not marketable or, conversely, that it had been particularly important to her.

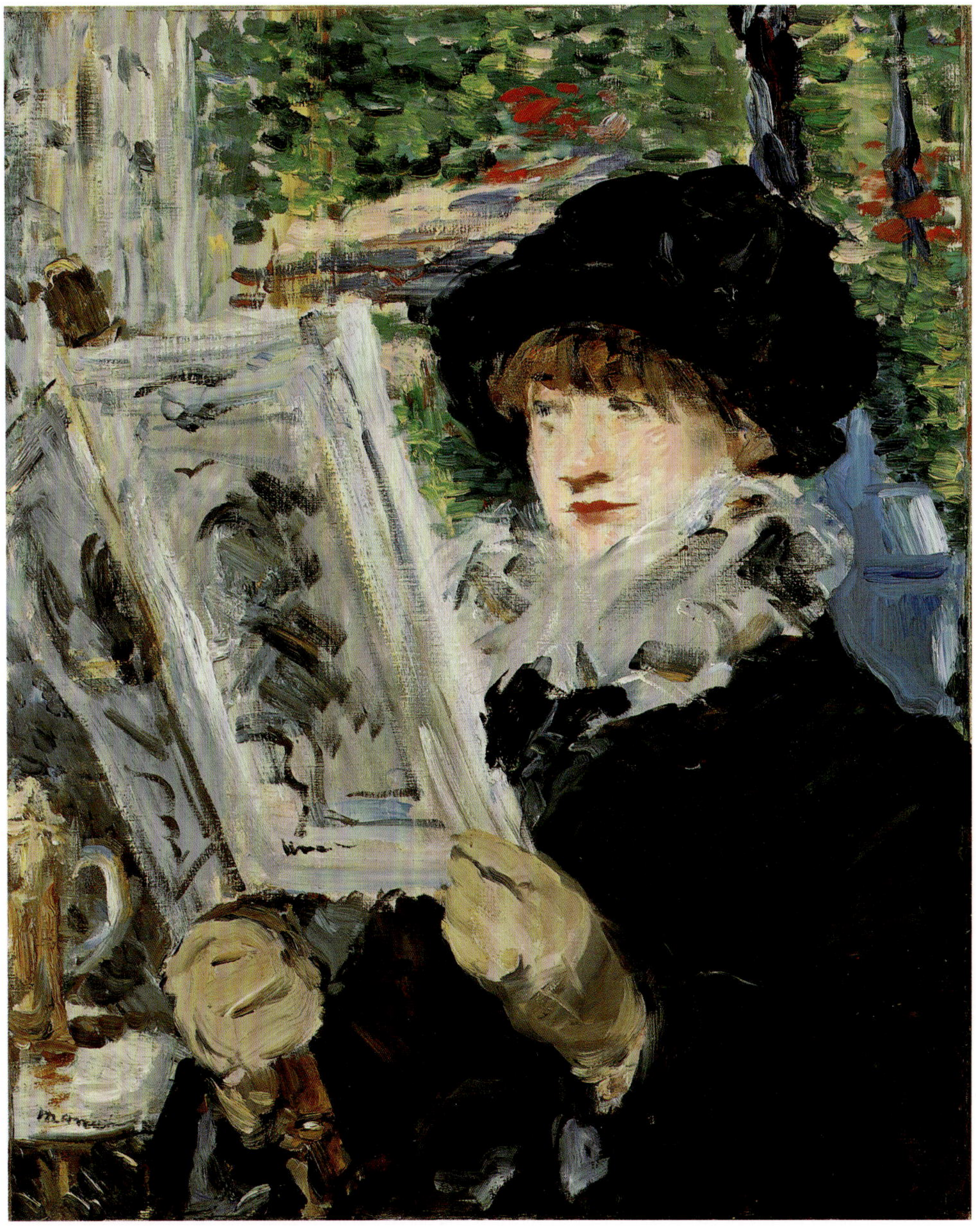

21

Woman Reading, 1879/80

Oil on canvas; 61.2 x 50.7 cm (24 1/16 x 19 7/8 in.)
Mr. and Mrs. Lewis Larned Coburn Memorial Collection, 1933.435
Signed lower left: *Manet*

Woman Reading may be Édouard Manet's most "impressionist" canvas. Although traces of a drawing visible beneath certain areas of the paint speak to a more deliberate execution in the studio, the canvas conveys just the sort of quick impression that a passerby might have had of a young and unaccompanied Parisienne in a café (or brasserie, since beer is being served).

The staccato reds, greens, and blues in the background—which has been variously described as a garden, a mirror, or a painting—intensify the sense of flux, as does the beer, whose frothy head indicates it has just been served. Even the woman's features consist of a few quick strokes, thinly painted on a white-primed canvas, as if Manet were applying makeup (kohl, lipstick, and rouge) to his model, rather than painting a flesh-and-blood woman.

The paper in her hands has a wooden rod holder, suggesting that she took it from the café's magazine rack. Its small format implies that it is an illustrated magazine, possibly *La Vie moderne*, a recently inaugurated journal with advertisements and short articles on literature, art, and society that appealed to men and women alike. Not only did Manet contribute drawings to this publication, but he also exhibited works in the magazine's offices, including this painting in April 1880. In *Woman Reading*, the journal's text is articulated with vigorous black and gray strokes that are teasingly illegible. These appear to fuse with the tulle collar of the stylish young woman, further connecting her to notions of modernity and consumerism in café life, advertising, and fashion. Perhaps the journal itself, with its schematic short texts and sketches, can be seen as a metaphor for the spirited painterly shorthand with which Manet treated his subject, just as the artist's flickering brushwork hints at her vivacious character.

RENOIR'S TRANSFORMATIVE VISION

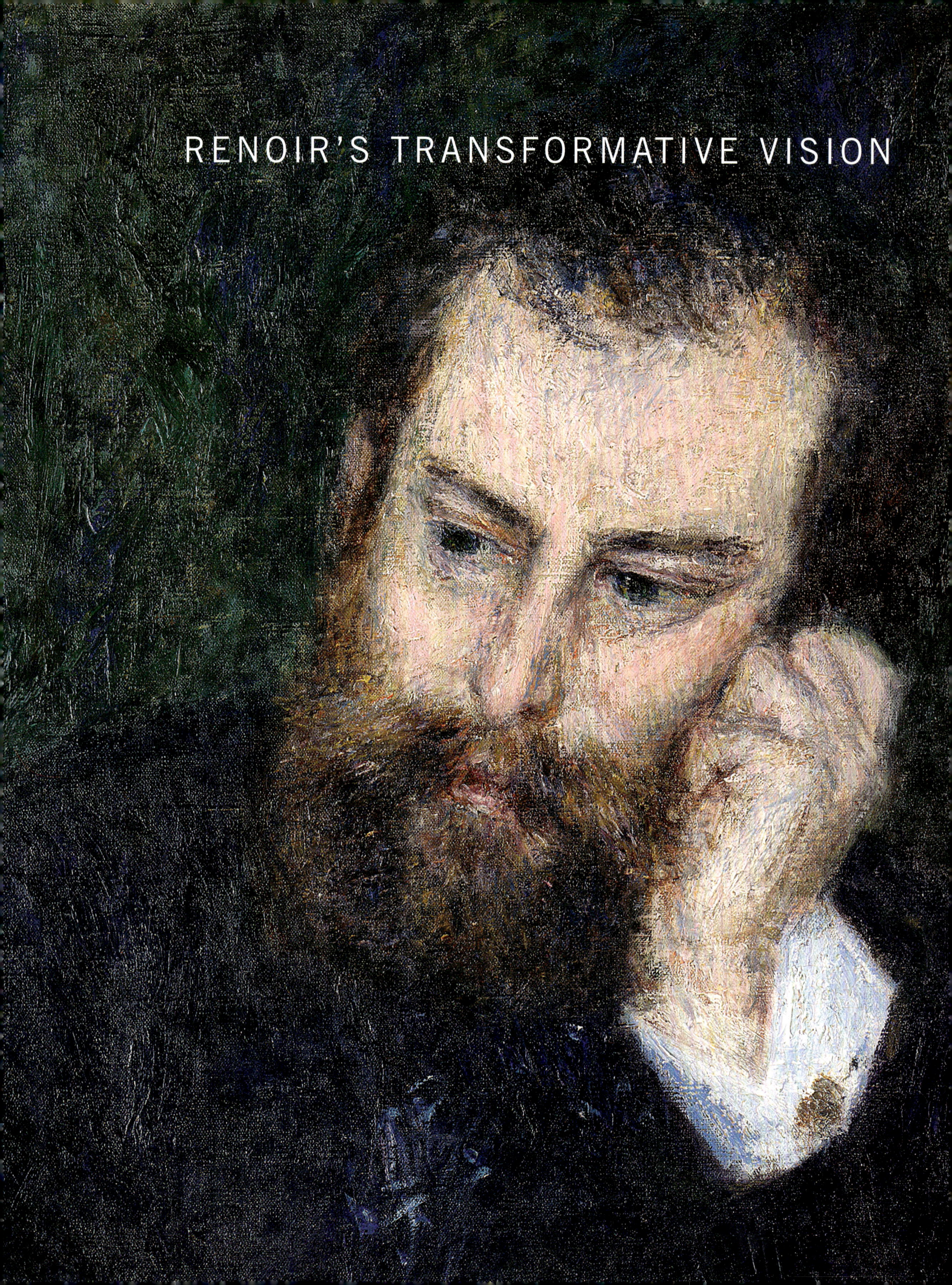

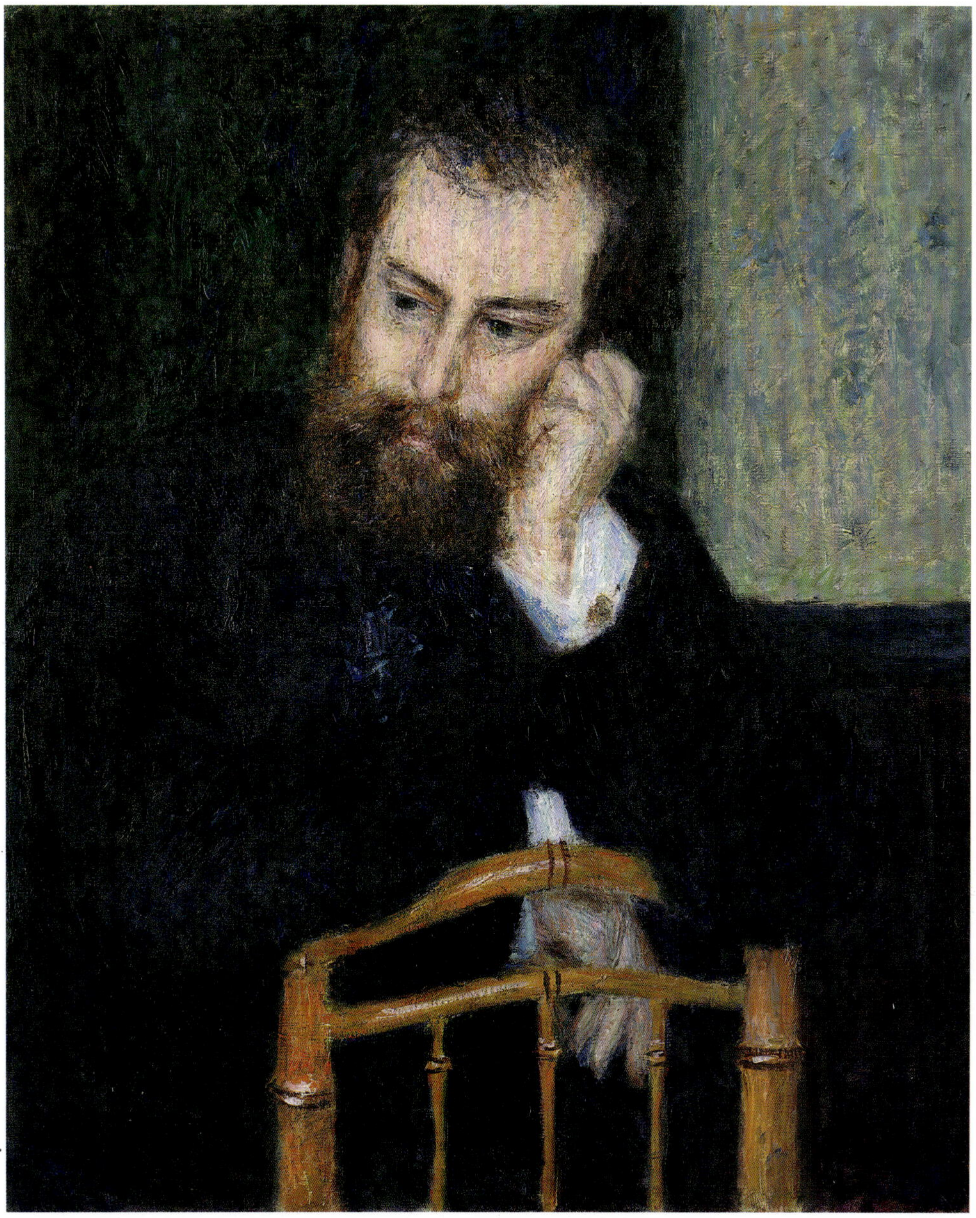

22

Alfred Sisley, 1876

Oil on canvas, mounted on composition board; 66.4 x 54.8 cm (26 1/8 x 21 9/16 in.)
Mr. and Mrs. Lewis Larned Coburn Memorial Collection, 1933.453
Signed lower right: *Renoir.*

Late in life, Claude Monet would recall that Pierre-Auguste Renoir painted this portrait of fellow Impressionist Alfred Sisley at the second house that Monet rented in Argenteuil, which was also the site of Renoir's portrait of Monet, executed in the summer of 1875 (Musée d'Orsay, Paris). Although Renoir exhibited both his depiction of Monet and a self-portrait at the second Impressionist exhibition, in April 1876, it was not until the third group exhibition, held the following year, that his portrait of Sisley was displayed. This suggests that the Art Institute's painting was finished too late in 1876 to be included in the second exhibition.

Sitting casually astride a bamboo-style chair, the handsome and well-groomed Sisley rests his head on his left hand, his eyes lowered and gently averted. It is a pensive and intimate portrayal. Set within a shallow, dark room, illuminated only by a window at the upper right, the sitter appears close to the viewer, his chair pressed against the plane marking the boundary between the viewer's space and the fictive space of the image. Although the composition's dominant tonality is blue, its mood is not one of melancholy; rather, Sisley appears thoughtful and serene, maybe even something of a dreamer. Unlike Renoir's 1875 depiction of Monet holding a palette and brushes, here there are no clues to the subject's vocation. Renoir's rather romantic characterization suggests the gentleness and elegance that impressed Sisley's friends, and speaks less to shared professional goals than to the artists' friendship. Two paintings of Sisley's children that Renoir made in 1875 also testify to this relationship.

One of seven portraits Renoir exhibited in 1877, and the only one fully identified in the catalogue that accompanied the show, *Alfred Sisley* was praised by one critic, who knew the sitter, for being an "extraordinary likeness and [for its] great value as a work of art."

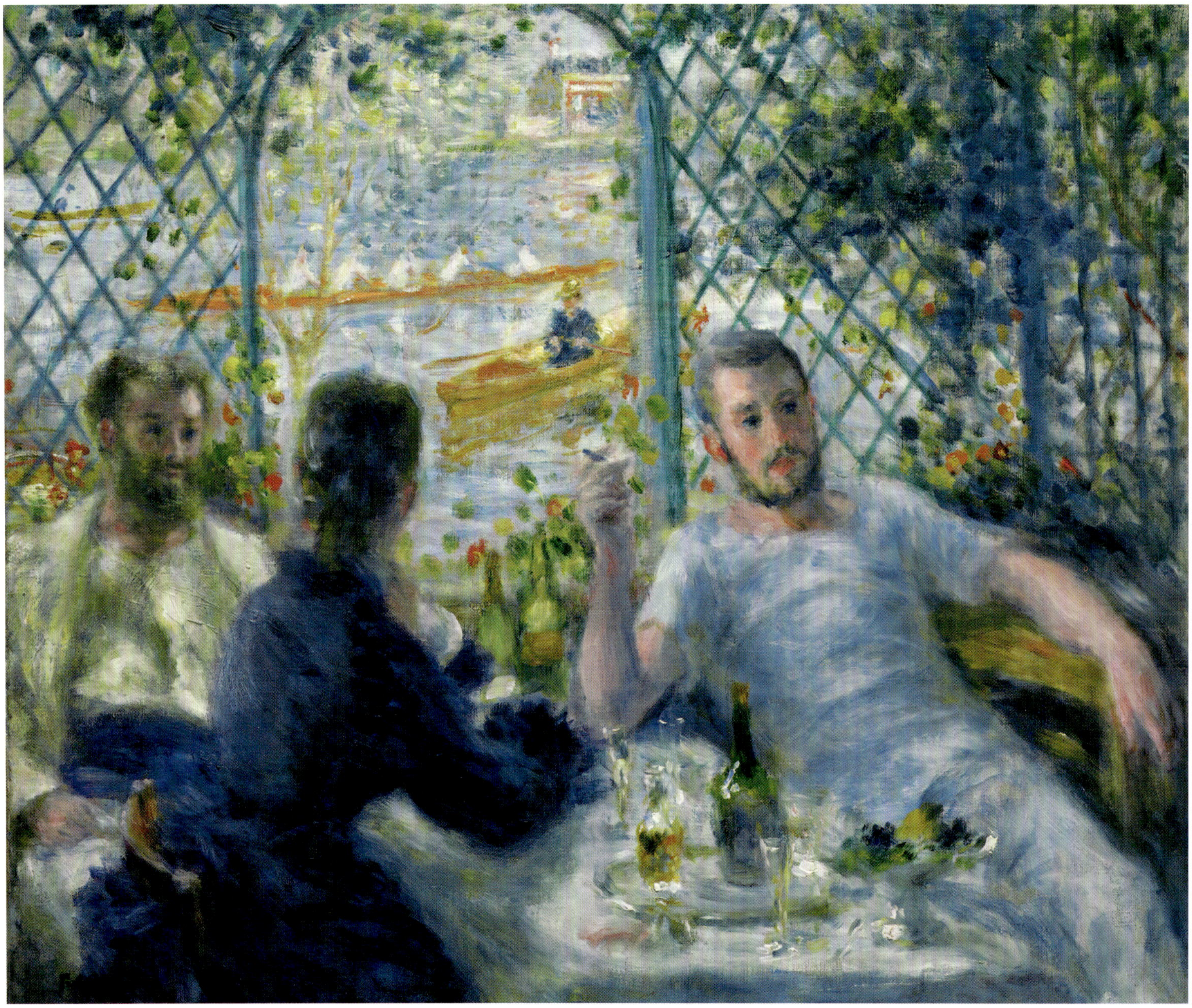

23

Lunch at the Restaurant Fournaise (The Rowers' Lunch), 1875

Oil on canvas; 55.1 x 65.9 cm (21 11/16 x 25 15/16 in.)
Potter Palmer Collection, 1922.437
Signed lower left: *Renoir.*

Pierre-Auguste Renoir painted this canvas—which he first showed at the second Impressionist exhibition, in April 1876, under the title *Déjeuner chez Fournaise*—during the summer of 1875 in Chatou, west of Paris on the Seine River. The town was near Bougival, where in 1869, in Claude Monet's company, he had painted his first pictures celebrating modern bourgeois leisure in the countryside. At Chatou, a popular spot for rowers, the artist befriended the Fournaise family, who owned a restaurant on an island upstream that was a well-known meeting place for oarsmen. Working on one of the terraces of that establishment, Renoir created a vision of middle-class relaxation that fulfills the promise of his earlier work painted alongside Monet.

Lunch at the Restaurant Fournaise is a paean to the joys of youth and summer, a celebration of the rituals of friendship and the bounties of nature, the seasonal rhythms of rest and play. Of the three figures around the table, only one, the young man in a white jacket at left, has been identified. He is M. de Lauradour, a habitué of the restaurant and the nearby bathing resort La Grenouillère. The sunburnt male at right wears white pants and a short-sleeved, collarless shirt—like those of the rowers in the racing boat on the river—which identify him as a boating-club member. Between the two men is a young woman seen from the back, her attention engaged by either the man to her left or the oarswoman near the shore, who is similarly costumed in the blue flannel favored by female boaters. If the interchange between the figures seems unclear, it is because Renoir avoided making the picture overly legible in narrative terms. Rather than recording a specific interaction, he evoked a mood of conviviality. The fruit, wine, and wineglasses on the table, and the way the boater languidly reclines in his chair, casually holding a cigarette, indicate that lunch is over. Pictorially, Renoir's loose brushwork succeeds at banishing narrative specificity and suggests the slightly fuzzy state of torpor that accompanies satiety. Contours blur, merging into one another and the surrounding atmosphere, and immersing the whole scene in soft, shifting light, with whites tinted by reflections and bluish shadows. The resulting dappled effect is echoed in the stricter rhythms of the trellis, which serves as a permeable barrier between the terrace and the river.

Suffused with a warmth that is both social and physical, *Lunch at the Restaurant Fournaise* is a picture of perfect harmony, a vision of a golden age located not in the ancient past but in the present. The focus on people and the lively delicacy with which the softly flickering light is conjured mark Renoir's unique contribution to what we might term classic Impressionism. Indeed, while Monet and Alfred Sisley concentrated almost exclusively on plein-air landscape painting, Renoir remained committed to the human figure, especially to representations of women. He executed several important pictures on the theme of rowing between 1875 and 1881, culminating in the famous *Luncheon of the Boating Party* (1880–81; Phillips Collection, Washington, D.C.; see p. 16). But despite the fact that he frequently worked in the country, Renoir was, unlike his two friends, a visitor there, remaining essentially an artist whose studio and life were in the city.

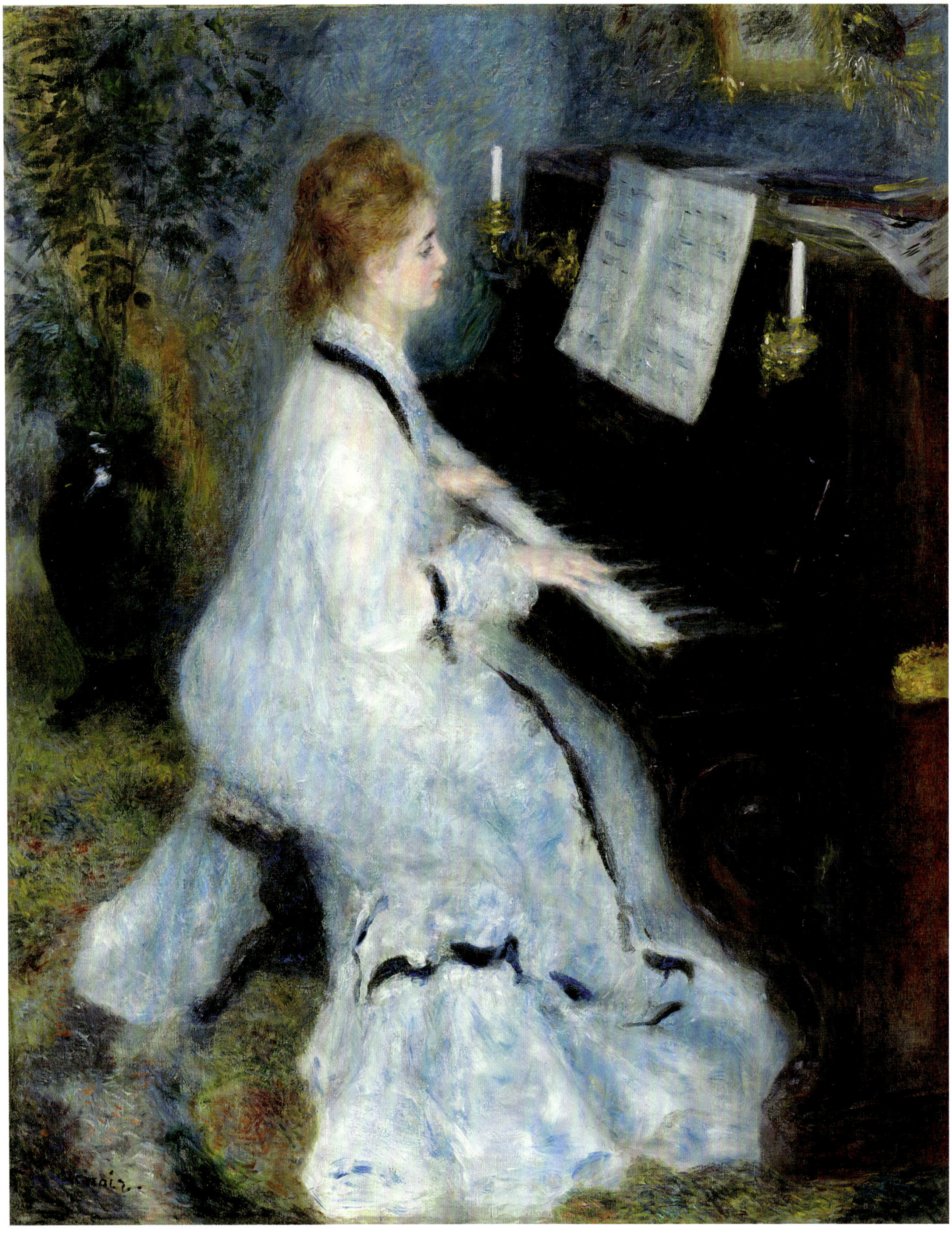

24

Woman at the Piano, 1875/76

Oil on canvas; 93.2 x 74.2 cm (36⅝ x 29½ in.)
Mr. and Mrs. Martin A. Ryerson Collection, 1937.1025
Signed lower left: *Renoir.*

Along with *Lunch at the Restaurant Fournaise* (cat. 23), Pierre-Auguste Renoir showed this canvas at the 1876 Impressionist exhibition. Featuring a woman at a piano, it represents the distillation of the artist's quintessentially Parisian brand of Impressionism, as well as a subject to which he would return frequently in later life. He was not the first of his circle to explore this theme: in the previous decade, Paul Cézanne, Edgar Degas, and Édouard Manet had each treated it, though in ways that were consonant with their own pictorial and expressive aims and thus quite different from Renoir's.

Here the scene is a richly appointed interior with a patterned carpet on the floor; a potted plant placed before a curtain that seems to mark the opening to an adjoining space; and a picture hung on a fabric-covered wall, above a dark, gleaming upright piano, its top piled casually with music. A remarkably pretty young woman, her luminous pink hands caressing the bluish white keyboard, is reading the sheet music open on the stand before her. Her performance seems as effortless as her beauty, as if we are witnessing a totally natural musical extension of the ravishing visual harmony the player embodies. Judging from her at-home dress (*robe d'intérieur*), one might assume her to be alone or in the company of an intimate. A confection of white, diaphanous fabric over a bluish underdress, offset by a winding, dark band, it takes on, through the wizardry of Renoir's brush, a life of its own: its brilliant play of chromatic harmonies and counterpoint of sinuous and cascading rhythms provides more than a match for the sounds produced by the piano's black-and-white keys. Designed to conceal, the garment also reveals, as we see glints of pink flesh, which are picked out on the young woman's shoulder and arm by the light that seems to fall softly over her upper body. Renoir presented the scene from a rather odd vantage point: looking down on the pianist from above, a location coincident not only with the painter's but also with the source of the light that pierces the cool darkness of the interior. Yet neither viewer nor artist obstructs the light, casting a shadow. Are we then meant to be looking in through a window? To ask such a question is to take the picture as a representation of fact, when in fact it is a fantasy.

As the almost insistently striking color harmonies, based on blue, remind us, Renoir is the artist and the performer: the palette is his keyboard, and the woman at the piano is wholly his creation. This is not a portrait of an individual, or even a study of a social type, the skilled bourgeoise; instead it is the depiction of ideal womanhood, uncomplicated by any of the contingencies of the real world. Renoir was in fact uncomfortable with intellectual and educated women, particularly those who nourished professional ambitions. He did not intend, as did Manet, to use the theme of a female pianist to suggest such attributes. His woman at the piano represents the performance of her "natural" function, not the exercise of musical abilities. As Renoir would later write, "In antiquity and among simple peoples, the woman sings and dances. . . . Gracefulness is her domain and even her duty." Eighteenth-century artists might have pictured this ideal as one of the legendary Three Graces, or perhaps as a goddess amid a froth of clouds; Renoir also enveloped his ideal in gossamer, but he transported her from the heavens to a piano stool, from the realm of the gods to the modern drawing room.

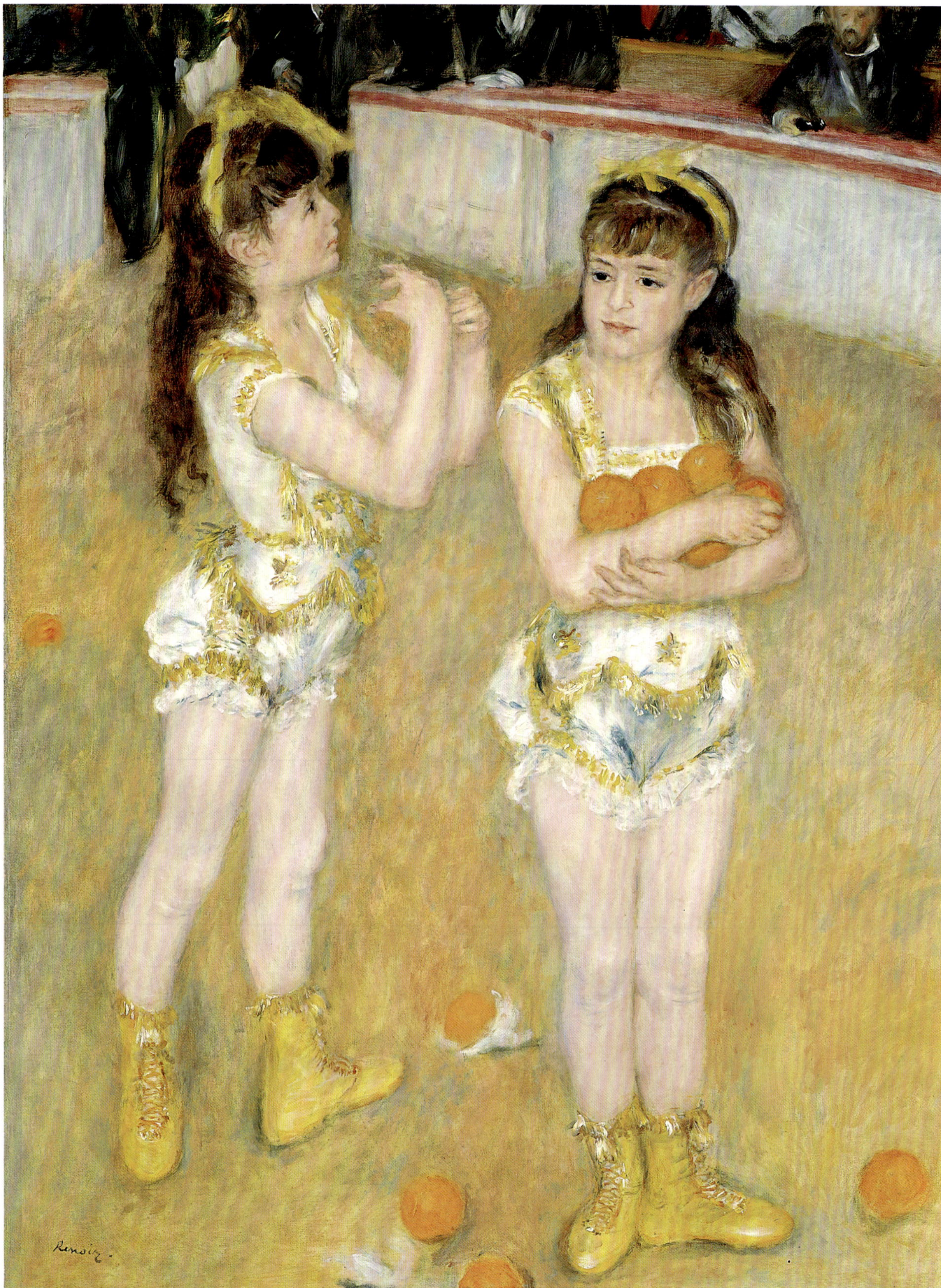

26

Acrobats at the Cirque Fernando (Francisca and Angelina Wartenberg), 1879

Oil on canvas; 131.5 x 99.5 cm (51 3/4 x 39 1/8 in.)
Potter Palmer Collection, 1922.440
Signed lower left: *Renoir.*

One of four permanent circuses in Paris, the Cirque Fernando opened its new circular, brick-and-iron building in Montmartre in June 1875, attracting an enthusiastic following that included Édouard Manet and his friends. Soon the popularity of this entertainment also began to influence the work of the painters and writers who frequented the salon of the publisher and art collector Georges Charpentier. In March 1879, Charpentier published Edmond de Goncourt's *Frères Zemganno*, a novel about two brothers who are circus performers. Just two months earlier, Edgar Degas had attended the Cirque Fernando to make sketches for a painting of the gymnast Miss La La suspended from the ceiling by a rope clenched between her teeth (*Miss La La at the Cirque Fernando*; National Gallery, London).

By this time, Pierre-Auguste Renoir had probably begun his own painting of the Cirque Fernando, featuring Francisca and Angelina Wartenberg, members of an itinerant German acrobatic troupe. The sisters take their bow and gather tributes to their just-completed performance—tissue-wrapped oranges, tossed to them by affluent members of the audience, who are visible at the top of the canvas, seated at ringside in formal attire. Like Degas often did, Renoir represented his subject close-up, as if seen through opera glasses, though in this case from above rather than from below. In part, the foreshortening produced by this viewpoint makes Francisca, who gracefully raises her arms, and Angelina, her arms filled with oranges, appear smaller and younger than their actual ages—seventeen and fourteen, respectively.

Renoir might have conceived this composition for an exhibition of his work held in June 1879 at the spacious offices of the fashionable periodical *La Vie moderne*, which the Charpentiers had launched in April. The fifth in a series held there, Renoir's show, including this work complemented by pastels, occasioned a feature article in the magazine written by the artist's younger brother, Edmond:

> In *Acrobats*, there is really no sense of arrangement. [Renoir] has captured the two children's movements with unbelievable subtlety and immediacy. This is exactly how they walked, bowed, and smiled in the circus ring. . . . [W]hat we have here is real life with all its poetry and all its savor. This absence of the "conventional" . . . gives the impression of nature with all its unexpectedness and its intense harmony; it is nature speaking to me.

Yet Renoir's supposedly natural depiction is, in truth, a fiction. Unlike Degas, Renoir banished from his representation the harsh effects of the gaslight that was used during evening performances, believing, as he stated, that it "turns faces into grimaces." Rather, he painted the sisters as if en plein air, eliminating shadows and building up his forms with thin, diaphanous washes of color, and using delicate, multi-directional brushwork that extends the color of the figures into the space around them and vice versa. To increase this visual harmony, the artist employed a highly arbitrary palette that emphasizes chromatic resonance: the yellows and oranges of the circus floor echo in the girls' costumes, as well as in the delicate reflections on their skin, most apparent in the area of Angelina's neck. Nor do awkward or unseemly poses, like that of Miss La La in Degas's painting of the circus, mar this scene. Renoir captured not the sometimes antic postures that were depicted in a poster advertising the sisters' act, but rather, in the performance's aftermath, a moment of almost balletic grace and dignity.

It has been suggested that in the 1879 *La Vie moderne* article, Renoir, with his brother as his mouthpiece, was claiming for himself the mantle of the alternate Realism that Edmond de Goncourt—like Renoir, a passionate devotee of the art of the eighteenth century—had called for in his preface to *Les Frères Zemganno*: a vision of modern life that emphasizes its poetry rather than its sordidness.

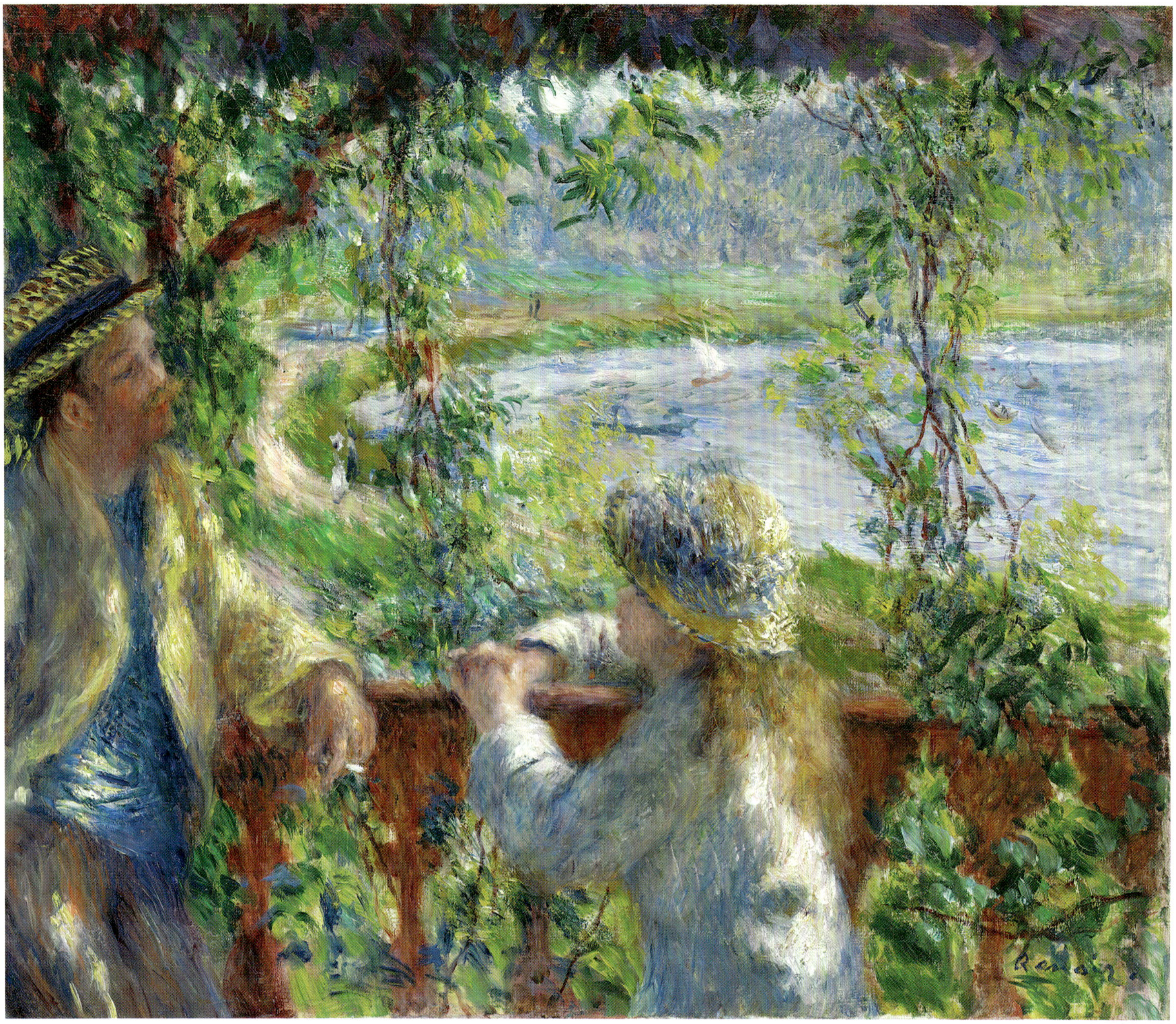

PIERRE-AUGUSTE RENOIR French, 1841–1919

27

Near the Lake, 1879/80

Oil on canvas; 47.5 x 56.3 cm (18 x 22 in.)
Potter Palmer Collection, 1922.439
Signed lower right: *Renoir.*

In the fall of 1879, Pierre-Auguste Renoir returned to Chatou, where he revisited his earlier themes of recreation and leisure (see cat. 23). It may have been at this time that he painted *Near the Lake*, the canvas whose title (which it has carried since at least 1887) makes it difficult to specify its subject and date. There is no record of Renoir visiting a body of water other than the Seine River or the Atlantic Ocean during the years to which, stylistically, this painting must date. Is the setting in fact a bend in the Seine; or did the painter make an undocumented visit to a site such as Lac Enghien, a popular vacation spot fifty minutes by train from Paris via Argenteuil?

Whatever the circumstances of the painting's creation, Renoir here represented a youngish man casually leaning on a balustrade, cigarette in hand, engaged in conversation with a girl depicted in profile, her eyes hidden by the wide brim of a flower-bedecked straw hat. *Near the Lake* hearkens back to the Art Institute's earlier *Lunch at the Restaurant Fournaise*, and, like it, can be seen to anticipate the ambitious work that Renoir would begin in the summer of 1880, when, following a second stay at the vacation estate of the diplomat and banker Paul-Antoine Berard at Wargemont, near Dieppe on the Normandy coast, he wrote to his erstwhile host: "I am at Chatou. . . . I'm doing a painting of oarsmen which I've been itching to do for a long time." The result was Renoir's masterpiece, *Luncheon of the Boating Party* (1880–81).

In *Near the Lake*, we see two figural types that Renoir would recast in this large, multi-figured composition of the following summer. The man in the Chicago painting wears the banded straw hat of a boater, as well as the casual jacket and blue collarless shirt that complete the costume. His companion's pose, as well as her hat, invite comparison with the woman at the left of the large canvas. The model for this figure was Aline Charigot, a twenty-one-year-old seamstress who would soon become the artist's mistress and eventually his wife.

Although there is an obvious thematic continuity from *Lunch at the Restaurant Fournaise* through *Near the Lake* to *Luncheon of the Boating Party*, the three works represent different points in the evolution of Renoir's style. We have only to compare *Near the Lake* with *Lunch at the Restaurant Fournaise* to recognize differences between the two in both touch and palette. Instead of the freely brushed surface and unified atmosphere of the earlier work, Renoir now employed more varied brushwork to differentiate the components of the scene: for example, he used longer, horizontal strokes for the water; shorter, more vertical ones for the hanging vines; and still thinner and more abbreviated hatching marks for parts of the clothing. While the artist again suggested the effects of outdoor sunlight, entering obliquely below the scalloped awning that protects the terrace, he made less of an attempt to absorb everything into an overriding harmony of colored light. Rather, the play of tinted reflections seems confined to individual forms, and the palette itself is more saturated with deeper accents, as in the rich, dark blue of the boater's shirt.

PIERRE-AUGUSTE RENOIR French, 1841–1919

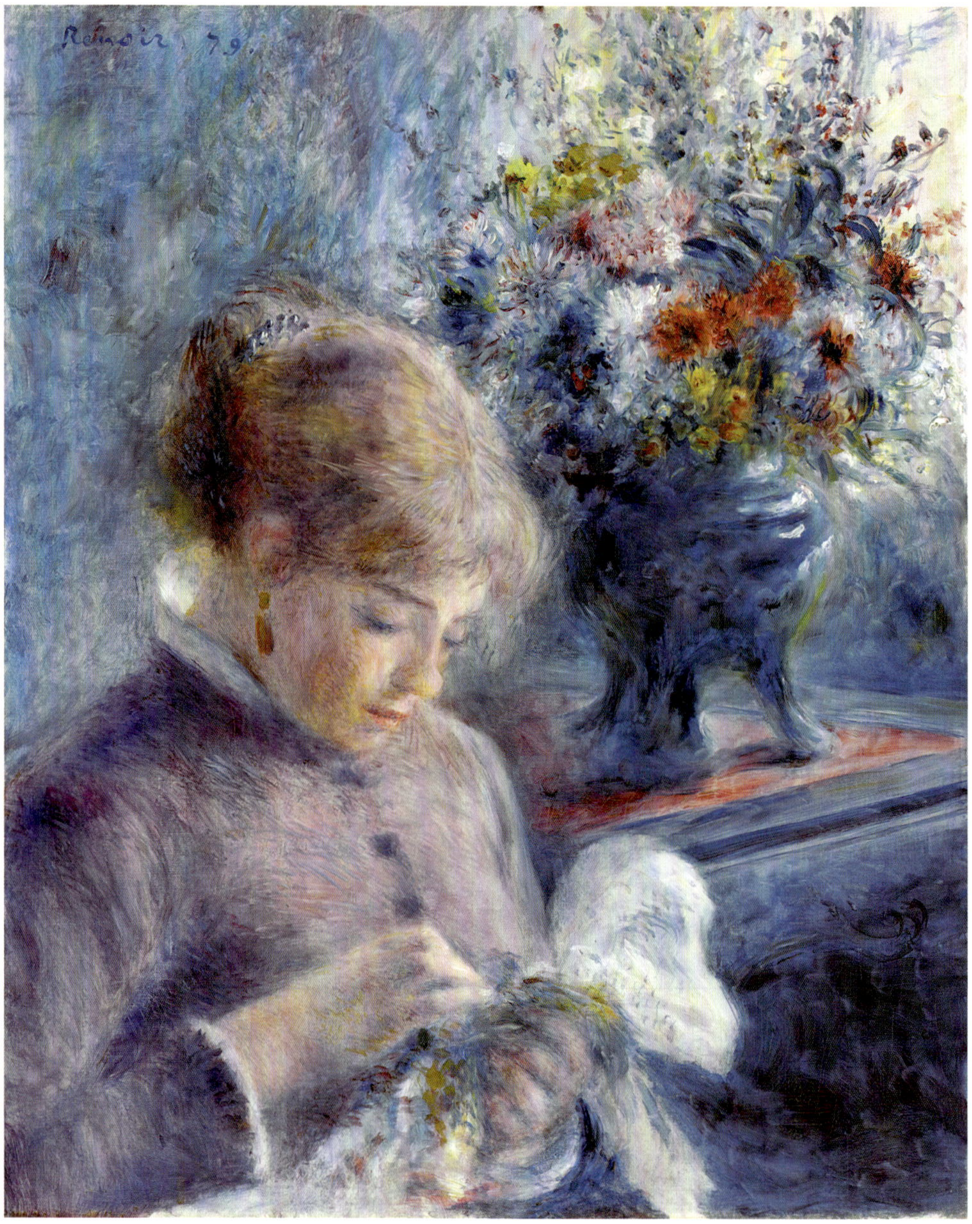

29

Young Woman Sewing, 1879

Oil on canvas; 61.5 x 50.3 cm (24 3/16 x 19 13/16 in.)
Mr. and Mrs. Lewis Larned Coburn Memorial Collection, 1933.452
Signed upper left: *Renoir 79.*

Pierre-Auguste Renoir painted this canvas on his first visit to the estate of Paul-Antoine Berard at Wargemont. The artist had met Berard and his wife at the Charpentier salon. During his stay, he painted a series of individual portraits of Mme Berard and her children, as well as decorations for the château: still lifes of game for the dining room and of flowers for both the library and drawing room. Still-life and figure painting come together in *Young Woman Sewing*, probably one of a number of noncommissioned canvases Renoir painted there.

The flowers—apparently asters and chrysanthemums—suggest that Renoir executed the composition in late summer. His decision to depict the young woman close-up and slightly from above, as if she were unaware of his proximity, resulted in a sense of informality and ease that the social distance between the painter and the members of the Berard family would not have allowed. However, this is not a portrait but a genre scene; the unidentified young woman—simply dressed but wearing jewelry—assumes the role of model rather than sitter. Giving almost equal visual emphasis to the still life and the figure, Renoir joined two representational traditions, establishing a type of equivalence between the transient beauty of flowers in bloom and that of the young female in her physical prime, and thus expressing his unquestioning belief in the traditional gender distinctions that identified women with "nature" and men with "culture."

The young woman's activity underscores this identity. She is engaged in the virtuous pastime of needlework. It seems that she is embroidering, adding colors to the white material she holds in her hands. Her creative efforts offer parallels to those of the painter, who applies color to white prepared canvas; yet her work, unlike his, is confined to the domestic sphere, where, Renoir believed, a woman's true role lay.

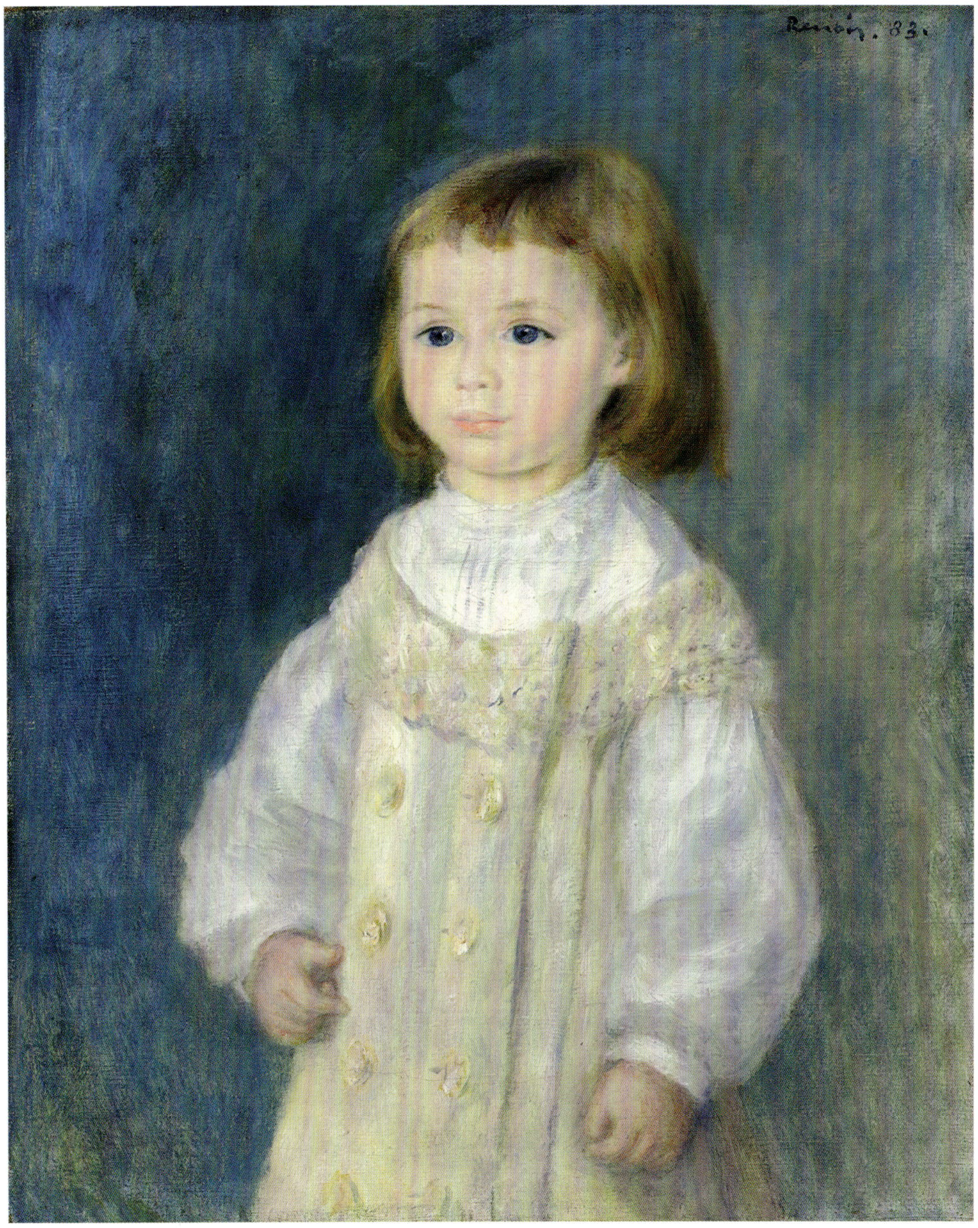

30

Lucie Berard (Child in White), 1883

Oil on canvas; 61.7 x 50.4 cm (24¼ x 19¾ in.)
Mr. and Mrs. Martin A. Ryerson Collection, 1933.1172
Signed upper right: *Renoir. 83.*

By the summer of 1883, Pierre-Auguste Renoir had produced a number of likenesses of Paul-Antoine Berard's four children. The youngest, Lucie, had thus far figured only in a single canvas, an intimate "study sheet" in oil featuring all of the children (Sterling and Francine Clark Art Institute, Williamstown, Massachusetts). In this work, painted in the summer of 1881, the artist showed the one-year-old child asleep as well as awake and a picture of alertness. In the Art Institute's portrait, the three-year-old Lucie is a personification of attentive innocence: dressed in white, with her small, soft hands positioned rather helplessly at her sides and her clear blue eyes unclouded, she looks out past the viewer, as if toward her future. As in his portrait of Mme Clapisson (cat. 31), Renoir apparently fashioned a picture that suited his sitter, but here it was his own vision that dictated its form. While in conception and handling *Lucie Berard* recalls the portrait of the older woman, Renoir's treatment of the young girl is softer. Setting her against a background of violet-blues with touches of yellow that envelops her white smock, he portrayed his sitter with a delicacy that preserves her tentativeness.

Viewers today often find Renoir's depictions of children almost too appealing, but this was not the case at the time they were painted. Lucie's father wrote that although he and his wife "swoon with pleasure in front of [the portrait] . . . unfortunately for Renoir, we cannot get others to derive the pleasure that we do from his work, and this portrait, so different from the type that [is currently fashionable], simply frightens people away." Over the next few years, the artist's aggressive pursuit of a new, linear manner so discouraged potential patrons that, by the mid-1880s, portraiture had ceased to be a major source of his income.

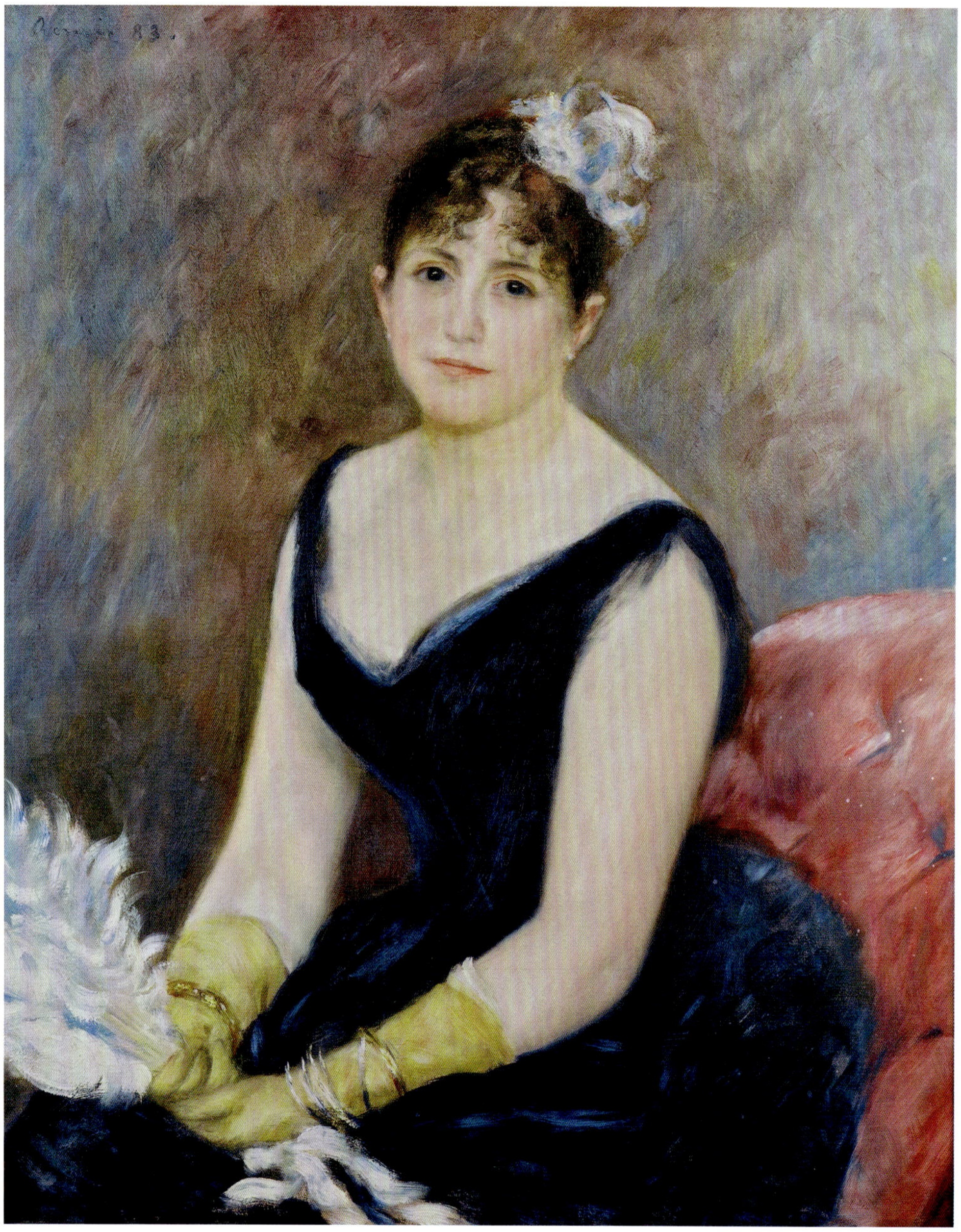

31

Madame Léon Clapisson, 1883

Oil on canvas; 81.8 x 65.2 cm (32⅝ x 25⅝ in.)
Mr. and Mrs. Martin A. Ryerson Collection, 1933.1174
Signed upper left: *Renoir 83.*

This picture, completed early in 1883, is Pierre-Auguste Renoir's second attempt to satisfy the commission from Léon Clapisson to paint his thirty-four-year-old wife, Valentine. Clapisson, a stockbroker, had recently begun collecting the work of the Impressionists, including several of the Algerian paintings that Renoir had just deposited with the dealer Paul Durand-Ruel. Perhaps this is the reason that the artist initially decided to paint Mme Clapisson out of doors, taking tea in a rose garden. But despite his sitter's compliance, the sessions did not go well, and Renoir complained of having difficulty completing the "wretched portrait, which will not work." When, after many sittings and much frustration, he finally finished the canvas, M. Clapisson found it "too audacious." He returned the picture to the painter, who agreed to undertake a more acceptable likeness.

Renoir executed his second portrait very differently from the first, using less diluted, stiffer paint. Representing Valentine indoors, in an evening dress that shows off her shoulders and arms, this portrait found favor with his clients. A fashionable image of a woman sufficiently à la mode to have had her white sauce discussed in the society pages of *La Vie moderne*, it was tailored to satisfy the Clapissons' needs. Yet Renoir's recipe here is not that of the conventional society portraitist of the time. Although he had jokingly proclaimed that he intended to swear off doing "portraits in the sunlight" and instead to adopt the plain, dark backgrounds then in vogue, Renoir in fact set Valentine before a light-filled, abstract design in which he wove together the red, yellow, and blue that he employed with greater concentration in her chair, gloves, and dress.

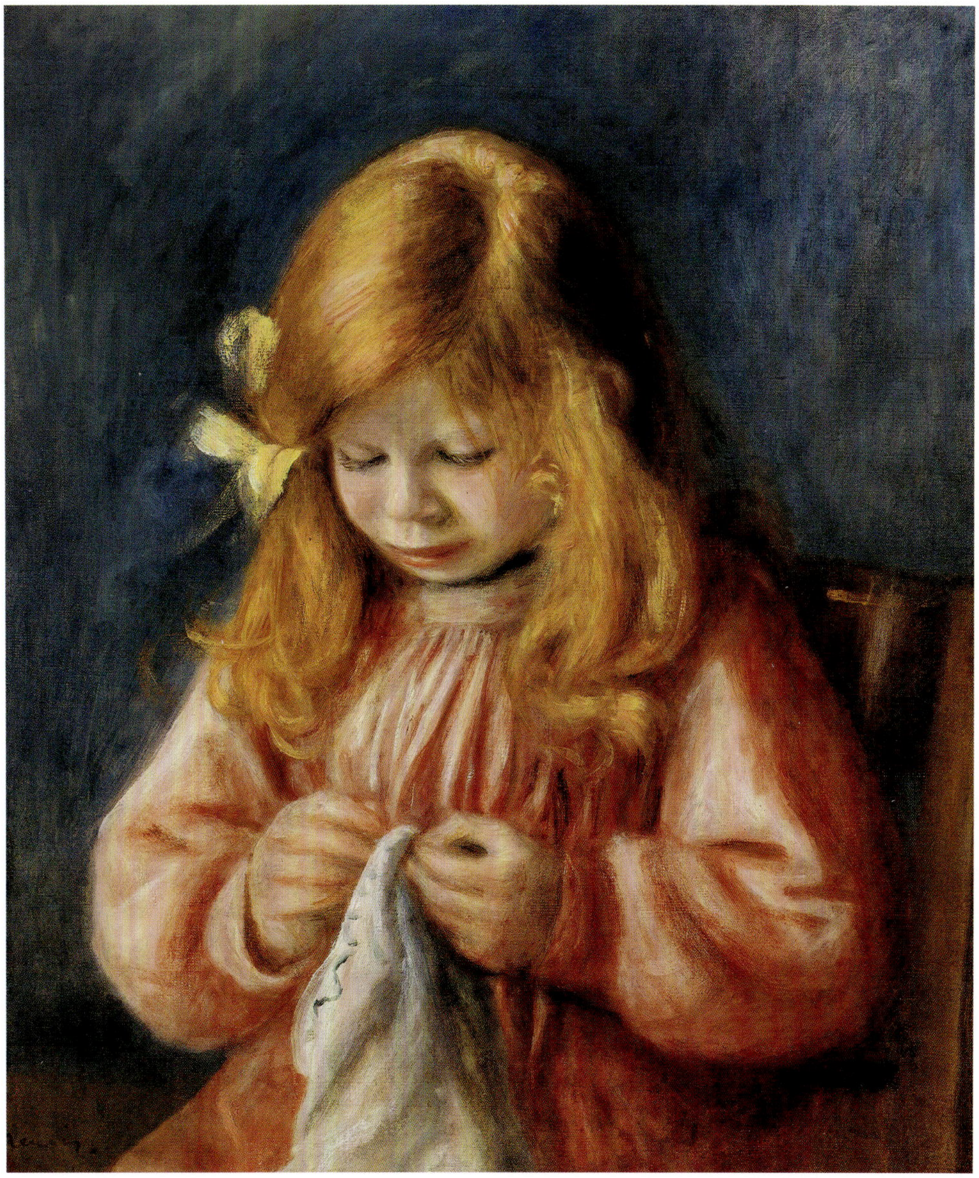

32

Jean Renoir Sewing, 1898/99

Oil on canvas; 55.4 x 46.5 cm (21 3/4 x 18 1/4 in.)
Mr. and Mrs. Martin A. Ryerson Collection, 1937.1027
Signed lower left: *Renoir.*

Like Edgar Degas, Pierre-Auguste Renoir had the Old Masters very much in mind during the 1890s. Although he shared Degas's reverence for the great practitioners of the classical tradition of line, notably Andrea Mantegna and Nicolas Poussin, he was now more focused on the masters of color and broad handling—Rembrandt van Rijn, Peter Paul Rubens, Titian, and Diego Velázquez—and, as he declared, on the art of the eighteenth century in particular.

Renoir's passion for the eighteenth century is reflected in the new importance he gave to the theme of youth, especially after the birth of his second son, Jean, in 1894. "One must be personally involved in what one does," Renoir wrote to a friend when Jean was just seventeen months old. "At the moment, I'm painting Jean pouting. It's no easy thing, but it's such a lovely subject, and I assure you that I'm working for myself and myself alone." Jean later claimed to "remember quite clearly all the preparations for the picture now in the Art Institute of Chicago, showing me sewing." However, although he maintained that he was over five years old at the time, other dated pictures suggest that *Jean Renoir Sewing* actually portrays him about a year younger. The length of his hair is of little help in dating works like this. For while long tresses were in fashion for infant boys, Jean, to his great embarrassment, was forced to wear his hair this way for an unusually long time—until the autumn of 1901, when, at age seven, he went to a school whose regulations required that it be cut. Renoir's love of the "pure gold" of Jean's silken hair, as well as his desire to preserve this attribute of innocence in his paintings of his son, overrode any concern for the relentless taunts that Jean had to endure from other boys.

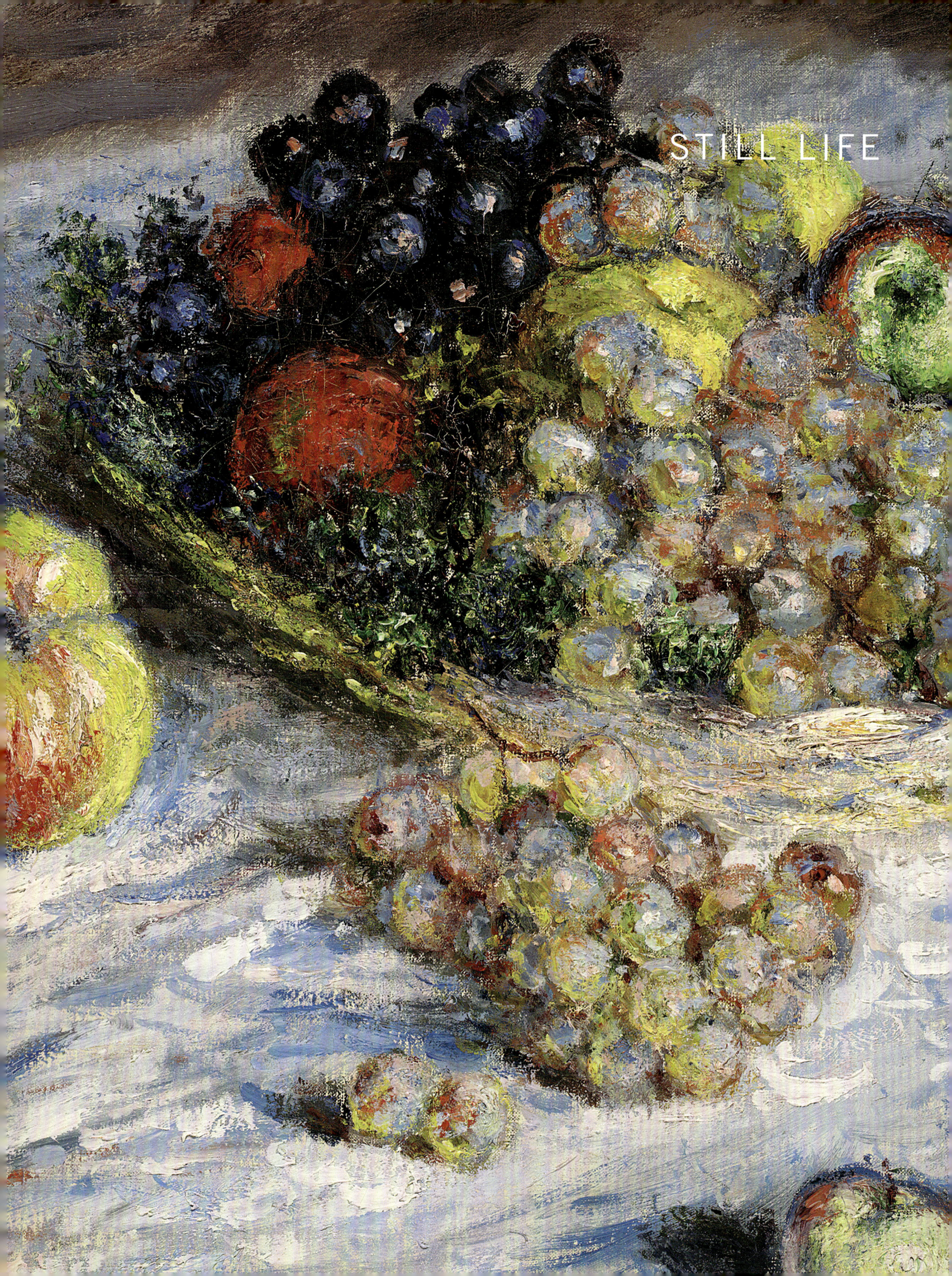
STILL LIFE

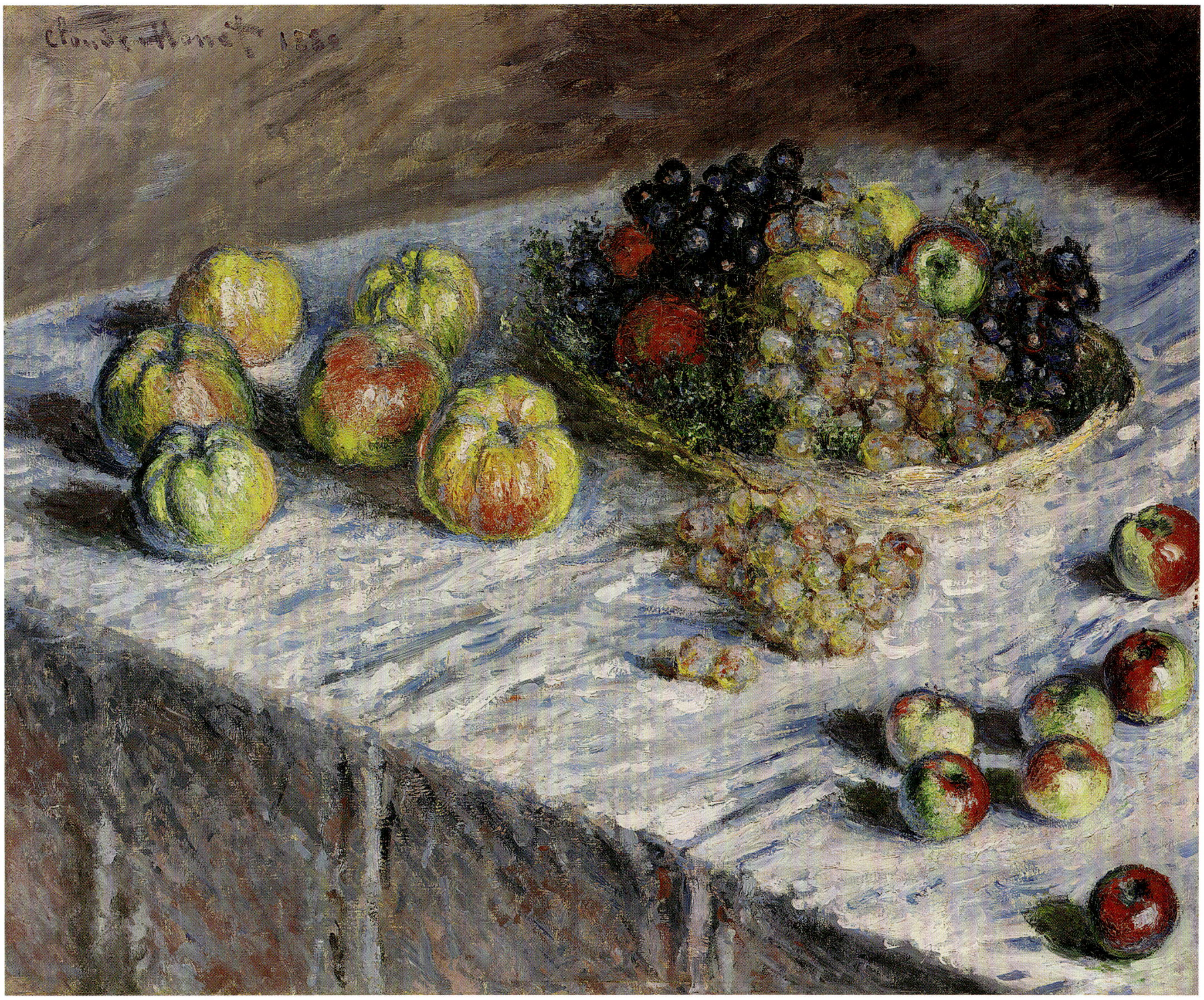

33

Apples and Grapes, 1880

Oil on canvas; 66.2 x 82.3 cm (26 1/16 x 32 3/8 in.)
Mr. and Mrs. Martin A. Ryerson Collection, 1933.1152
Signed upper left: *Claude Monet 1880*

Although he is primarily known as a landscape painter, Claude Monet periodically painted still lifes, which generally found a ready market. In contrast to his earlier still-life compositions, reminiscent of those by Édouard Manet, which showed objects set on gleaming white tablecloths against dark backgrounds (see cat. 1), *Apples and Grapes* embodies the Impressionists' aim to express the textures, colors, and vibrancy found in nature. Monet had several reasons for returning to still-life painting in 1879–80. Having received a mixed response to the twenty-nine works he showed at the fourth Impressionist exhibition, in April 1879, he may have wanted to engage with a theme that was less fraught and more readily accessible. Sales of these images of fruit helped the artist during a time of great financial difficulty following the death of his wife, Camille, in September 1879. Instead of the shortages and strains that he was personally experiencing, Monet's depiction of plump, juicy grapes and shiny red and green apples displayed on a freshly laundered tablecloth conveys a sense of plenitude and well-being. Only the grapes have a translucent fragility (achieved with dabs of white pigment), which the artist used to emphasize the solidity of the apples. They provide a counterweight to the slanting table that fills more than three-fourths of the space, thus eliminating any sense of interior setting or décor. Monet's own viewpoint, looking down at the tabletop from a high, steep angle, anticipates the radical cropping he would use for his later views of Normandy cliffs. Indeed, he treated the extensive cloth surface like a landscape; the play of light on the horizontal brushstrokes, indicating the folds in the tablecloth, recalls other works in which the artist employed similar short, horizontal marks to suggest various terrains or water rippling in sunlight (see cat. 49).

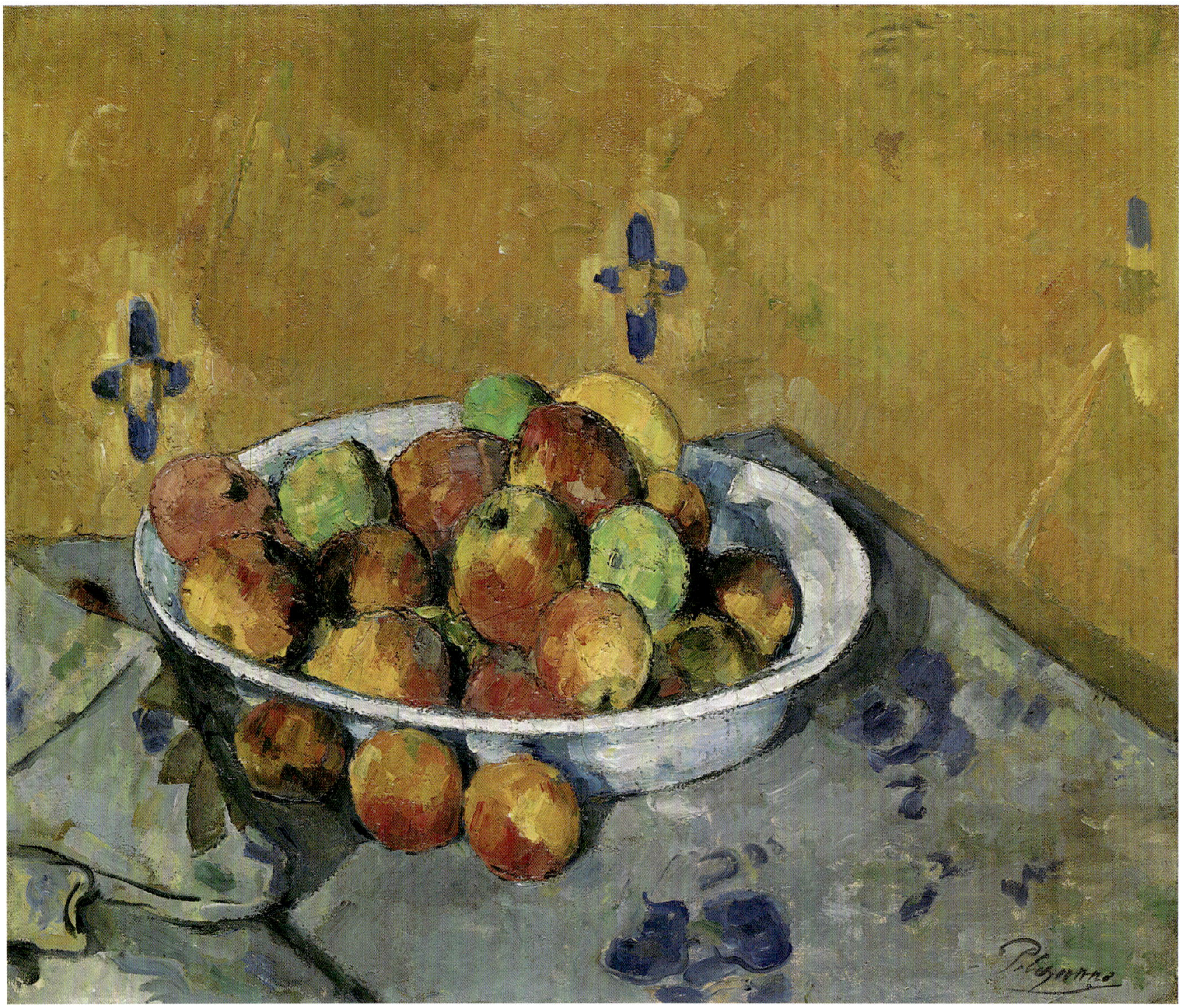

34

The Plate of Apples, c. 1877

Oil on canvas; 45.8 x 54.7 cm (18⅛ x 21½ in.)
Gift of Kate L. Brewster, 1949.512
Signed lower right: *P. Cezanne*

Paul Cézanne was thirty-eight years old when he executed this modest still life, one of several works featuring the ocher wallpaper with blue lozenge-shaped motifs that probably covered the walls of his Paris apartment on the rue de l'Ouest. Although his experience with Camille Pissarro in Auvers and Pontoise in 1872–74 (see cat. 14) had motivated him to paint directly from nature and eliminate the heavy light-dark oppositions that characterize his studio works from the 1860s, Cézanne's approach to still lifes remained very much his own. With its densely pigmented brushstrokes and heavy contours, *The Plate of Apples* is a transitional work—between the thickly "troweled" surfaces of his early paintings and the late compositions in which he applied transparent tones in parallel or blocky strokes. While avoiding the illusionism, modeling, and dramatic chiaroscuro so antithetical to the Impressionist idiom, Cézanne nonetheless sculpted, as much as painted, the surface of this work. His use of a limited range of hues—ocher, blue, and grayish white—underscores the painting's sense of solidity. In some places, the artist employed a palette knife or the end of his brush to incise contours and emphasize dimensionality (around the apples, for example); in others, he created edges by allowing the primed canvas to show between zones of paint, as if he were working from a template that he filled in with color. The diagonal pattern of the decorative wallpaper has been largely painted over; indeed, its encrusted, stuccolike surface may cover an earlier composition. Cézanne's signature, which is stylistically quite different than the painting, is thought to have been added by the artist at a later date. He may have decided not to include this work among the three still lifes he showed in the third Impressionist exhibition, in April 1877, as a result of its reworked and experimental nature.

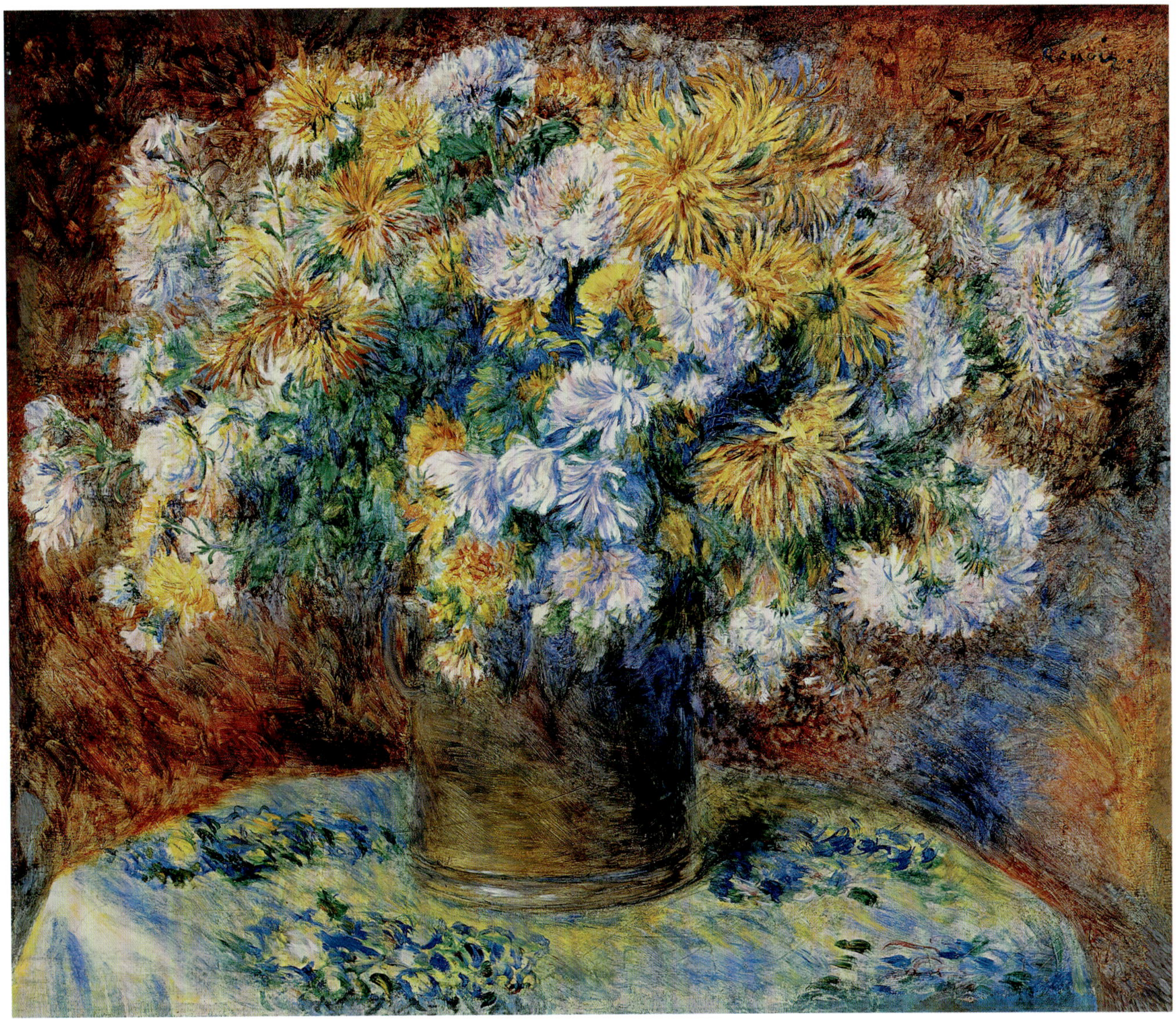

35

Chrysanthemums, 1881/82

Oil on canvas; 54.7 x 65.9 cm (21 ½ x 25 15⁄16 in.)
Mr. and Mrs. Martin A. Ryerson Collection, 1933.1173
Signed upper right: *Renoir.*

It was around the time that Pierre-Auguste Renoir was working on his problematic portrait of Valentine Clapisson (cat. 31) that he painted the glorious still life *Chrysanthemums*, featuring flowers in a simple brown earthenware kitchen crock set on a floral-patterned tablecloth. Renoir had recently produced a number of elaborate flower pieces. Sensitive, like Claude Monet, to the market potential of such works, he also took personal satisfaction in making them. Renoir would later say:

> I just let my brain rest when I paint flowers. I don't experience the same tension as I do when confronted by the model. When I am painting flowers, I establish the tones, I study the values carefully without worrying about losing the picture. I don't dare do this with a figure piece for fear of ruining it. The experience I gain from these works, I eventually apply to my [figure] paintings.

In *Chrysanthemums* Renoir explored effects of transparency and luminosity. Taking a canvas with a commercially prepared white ground, he used a palette knife to lay in another ground of lead-white paint. Although this second layer was thick and took time to dry, it offered particular advantages. Obscuring the grain of the canvas, it resulted in a surface that was much smoother and more capable of reflecting light than one that had not been prepared in this way. Exploiting this technique to maximum effect, Renoir worked very quickly, building up the image with freely applied, thin layers of washlike paint. The remarkable transparency he achieved invites comparison with watercolor—a medium that had not yet attracted Renoir's attention—as well as with the art of overglaze porcelain painting. The artist's early grounding in this craft must have helped to fuel experimentation.

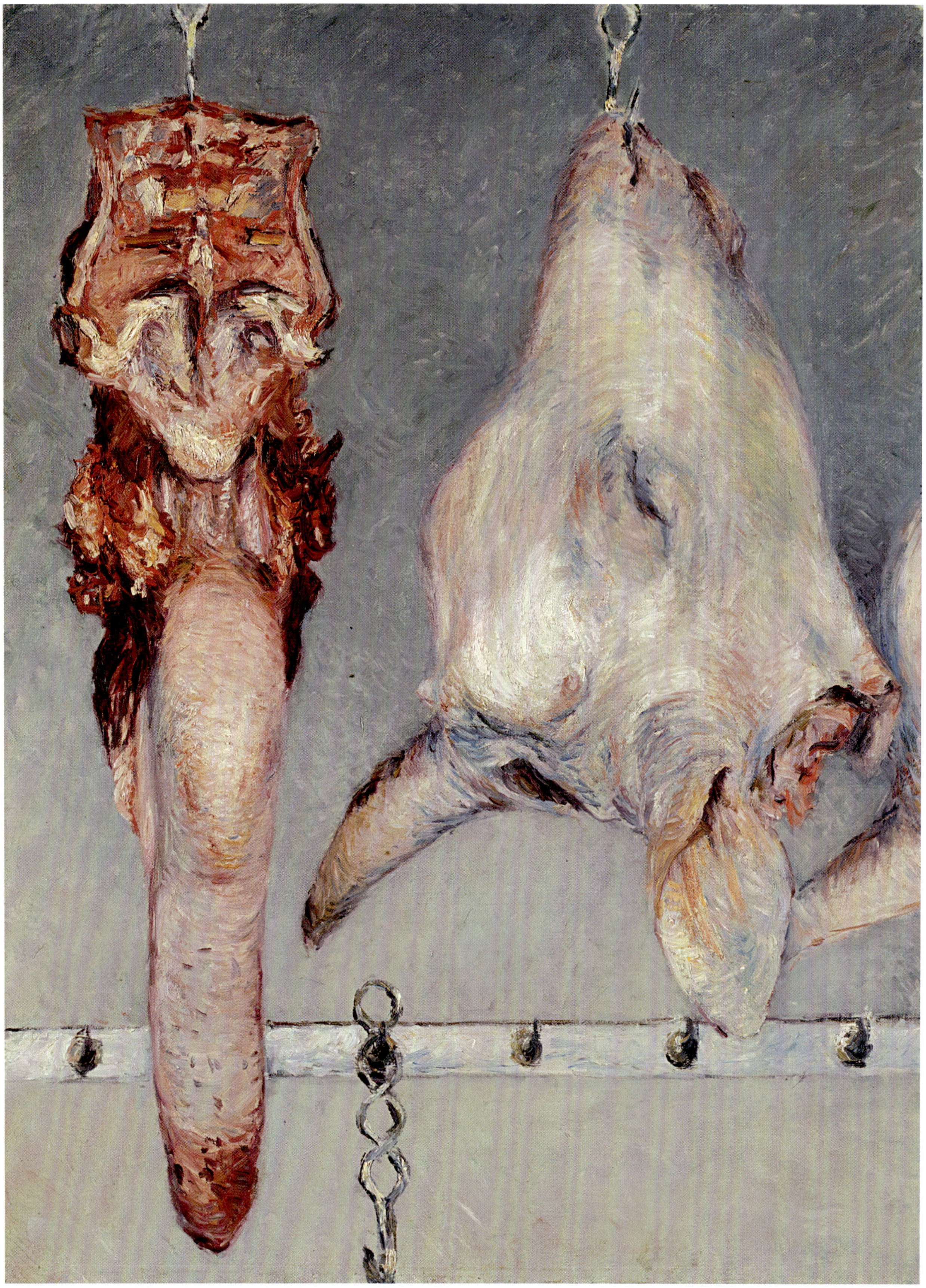

36

Calf's Head and Ox Tongue, c. 1882

Oil on canvas; 73 x 54 cm (29 x 21 in.)
Major Acquisitions Centennial Endowment, 1999.561

Gustave Caillebotte had made only a handful of still lifes—and relatively insignificant ones at that—prior to 1879, when he took up the subject more seriously. The resulting works constitute some of the most provocative and original compositions in his oeuvre, as potent and charged as his most ambitious domestic interiors or representations of street life. Within this series, *Calf's Head and Ox Tongue* is among the most subversive in its challenge not only to the historical tradition of still-life painting but also to the ways his contemporaries approached the genre. With the exception of Paul Cézanne (for whom still lifes played an important role in the development of technique), the Impressionists considered still-life painting to be commercially appealing as well as a kind of artistic "time-out"—a non-demanding break from the exploration of themes of modern life.

Caillebotte's inspiration and intentions were quite different, however. Independently wealthy, he did not need to sell his work. His choice of subject for this painting was not his own creation but an arrangement he came upon in a shop window, similar to the kinds of displays he saw in the butcher and tripe shop below his family home near the Gare Saint-Lazare in Paris. In many ways, *Calf's Head and Ox Tongue* is even more resolutely modern than the street views for which Caillebotte is best known (see cat. 18). This unexpectedly stark composition confronts issues of modern production, marketing, and consumerism. Disassociated from their original sources, isolated, dismembered animal parts are suspended in a kind of commercial purgatory, between death and consumption—dead matter cut off from life and not yet transformed and revalidated as food.

Although he was inspired by the still lifes of seventeenth-century Dutch masters such as Rembrandt van Rijn and others, as well as by the works of nineteenth-century Realist artists such as François Bonvin (who painted bloody slabs of beef hanging in modest interiors), Caillebotte's choices of color and composition distance the raw meat from the brutal reality of its production. In place of the somber chiaroscuro that both Rembrandt and the Realists used to set the stage for such themes, Caillebotte adopted a lively and insouciant near-pastel palette. The fiery red and orange tongue and soft bluish mauve head set against pale blue-gray lend an oddly festive, even seductive, quality to the motif. While the hooks at the top underscore the fact that the meat is lifeless flesh set out for purchase, Caillebotte's decorative palette, soft, caressing brushwork, and elegantly structured composition give new life to "dead nature" and imbue it with a disconcerting ambiguity that invites comparison with works by twentieth-century and contemporary artists, such as Chaïm Soutine and Lucien Freud.

DEGAS: CLASSICAL TRADITION AND MODERN LIFE

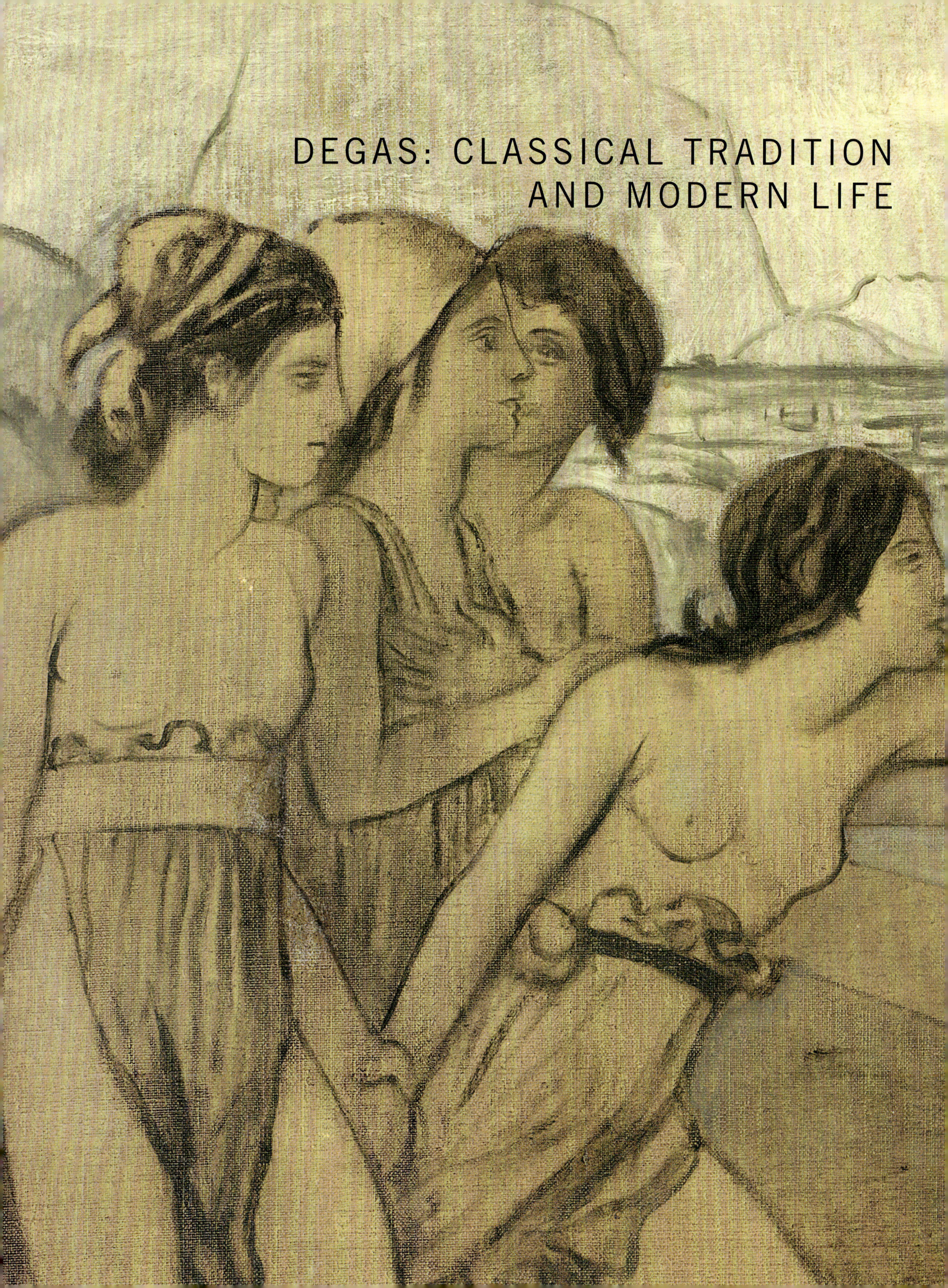

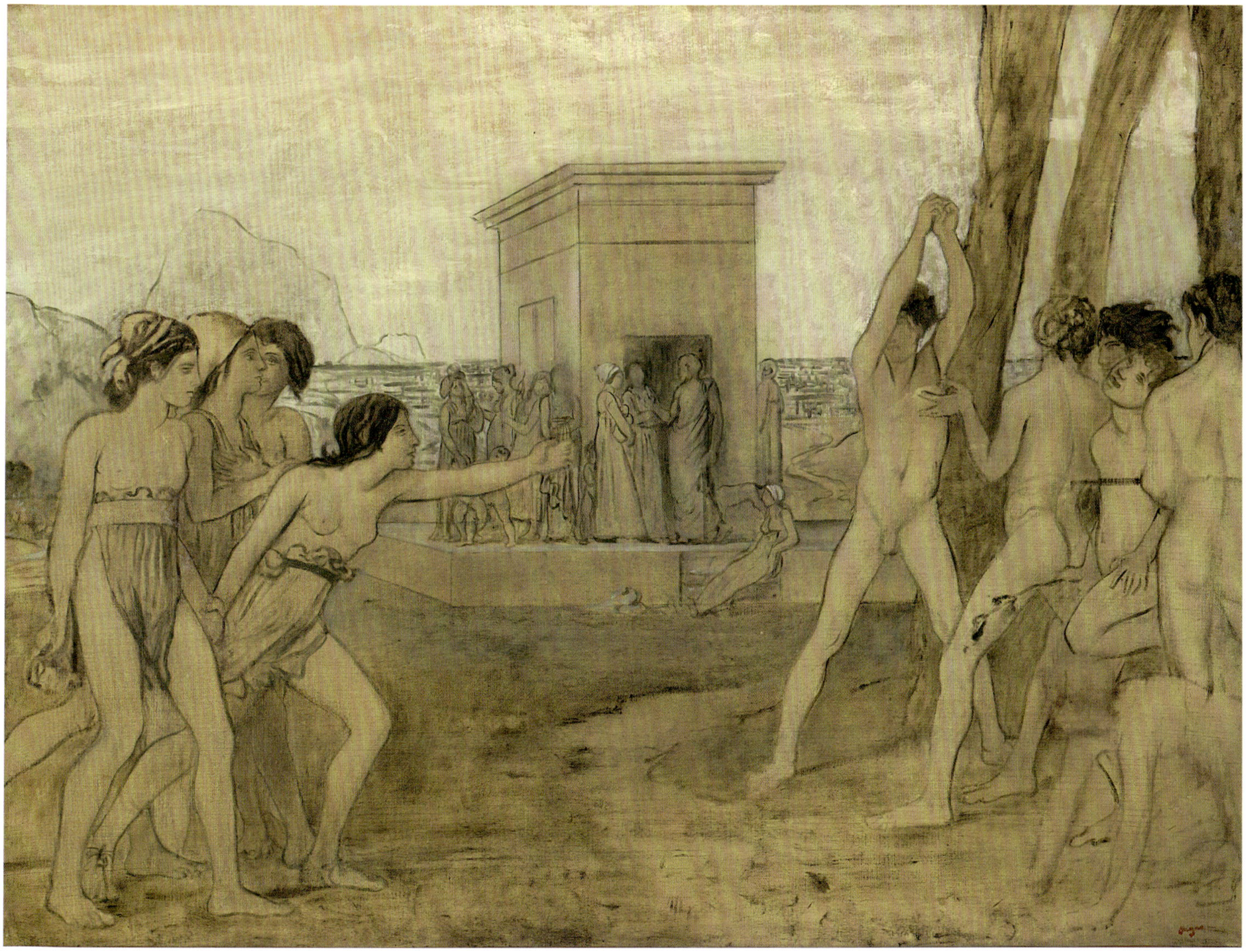

37

Young Spartan Girls Challenging Boys, c. 1860

Oil on canvas; 97.4 x 140 cm (38 5/16 x 55 1/8 in.)
Charles H. and Mary F. S. Worcester Collection, 1961.334
Signed lower right: *Degas*

In 1859 Edgar Degas returned to Paris following a prolonged stay in Italy, where he had visited relatives in Naples and Florence and attended life classes at the Académie Française, Rome. This picture, undertaken around 1860, speaks to the artist's early ambition to realize canvases featuring scenes from the Bible, as well as ancient and more recent history, and thus to compete in the official forum for artistic achievement provided by the state-sponsored Salons. An entry in a contemporary notebook that Degas kept indicates the subject: "young girls and boys fighting in the Plane-tree grove, watched by the elderly Lycurgus and the mothers." His inspiration was the Roman historian Plutarch's account of the life of Lycurgus, a legendary ninth-century B.C. Spartan lawgiver. Lycurgus's social reforms included an unusual egalitarian training whereby female adolescents competed on equal ground with males, exercising publicly in a state of nudity that signified "complete probity, without any . . . corruption whatsoever." Having first explored the idea in both compositional and figure drawings, Degas embarked on this canvas, delineating his composition with considerable detail using brush and diluted oil over charcoal. This initial monochrome stage, resembling a large drawing on canvas, would have been further developed with color layers had Degas continued. But he did not; instead, he started another related painting, removing both the trees and the architecture (National Gallery, London). In the late 1870s, he reworked this second canvas with an eye to showing it in the fifth Impressionist exhibition as *Young Spartan Girls Challenging Boys.* He recast the physiognomies of the youths so that they appear more like contemporary Parisians than do the classicized heads of the figures in the Chicago painting. Although the artist clearly found contemporary resonance in the subject of adolescent sexuality, he never exhibited either picture.

Post-Impressionism

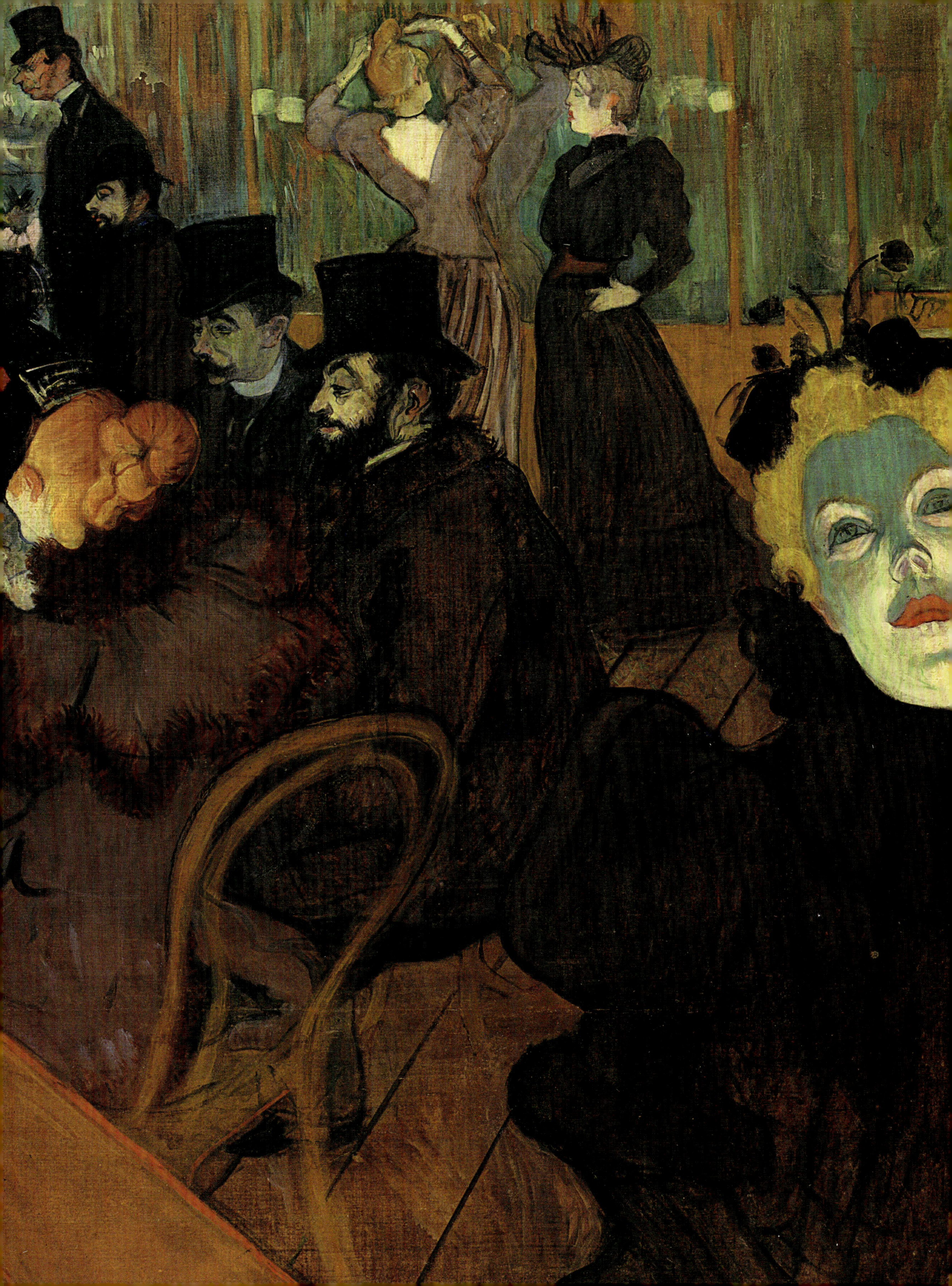

PISSARRO AND MONET: NEW DIRECTIONS

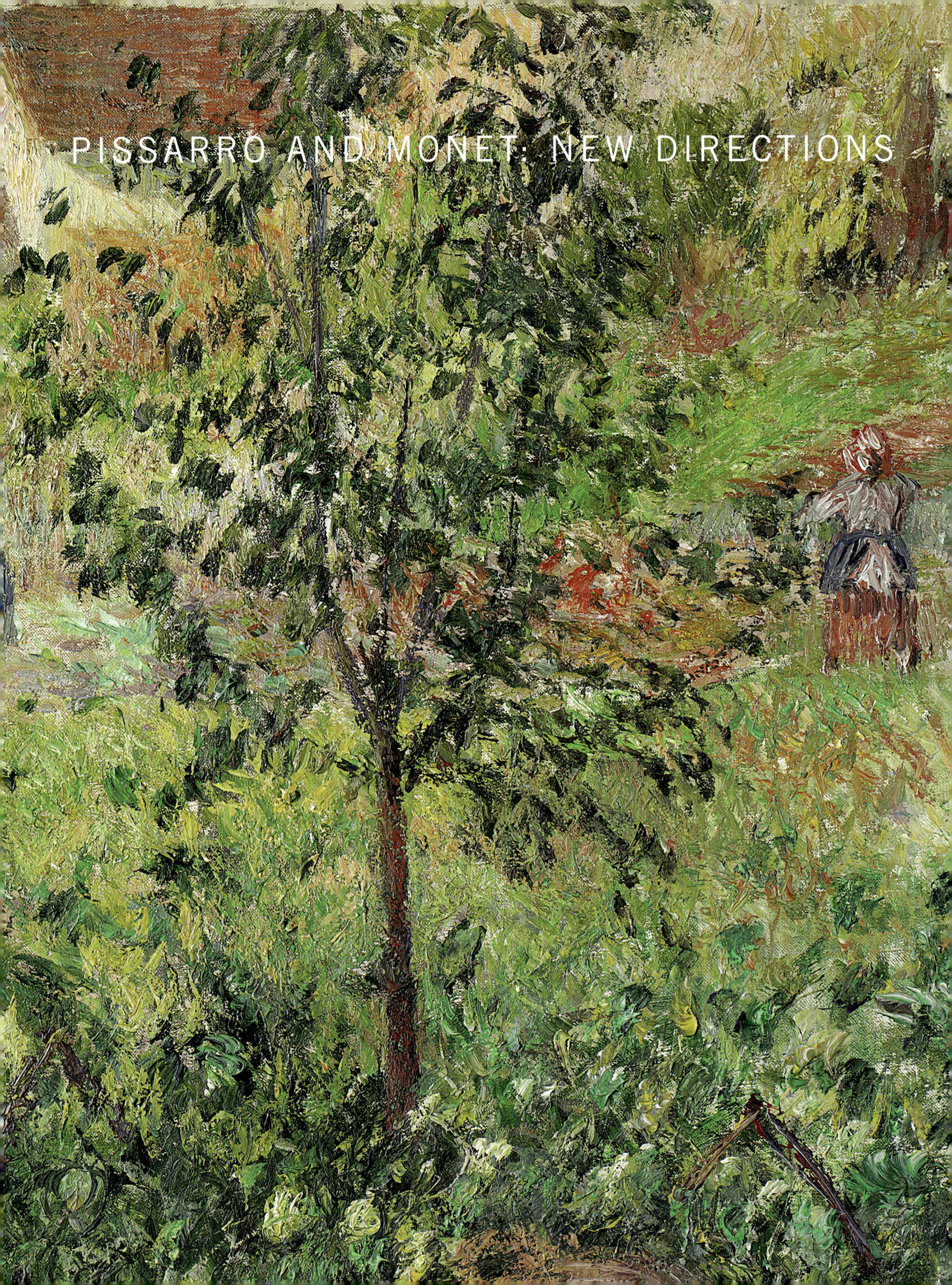

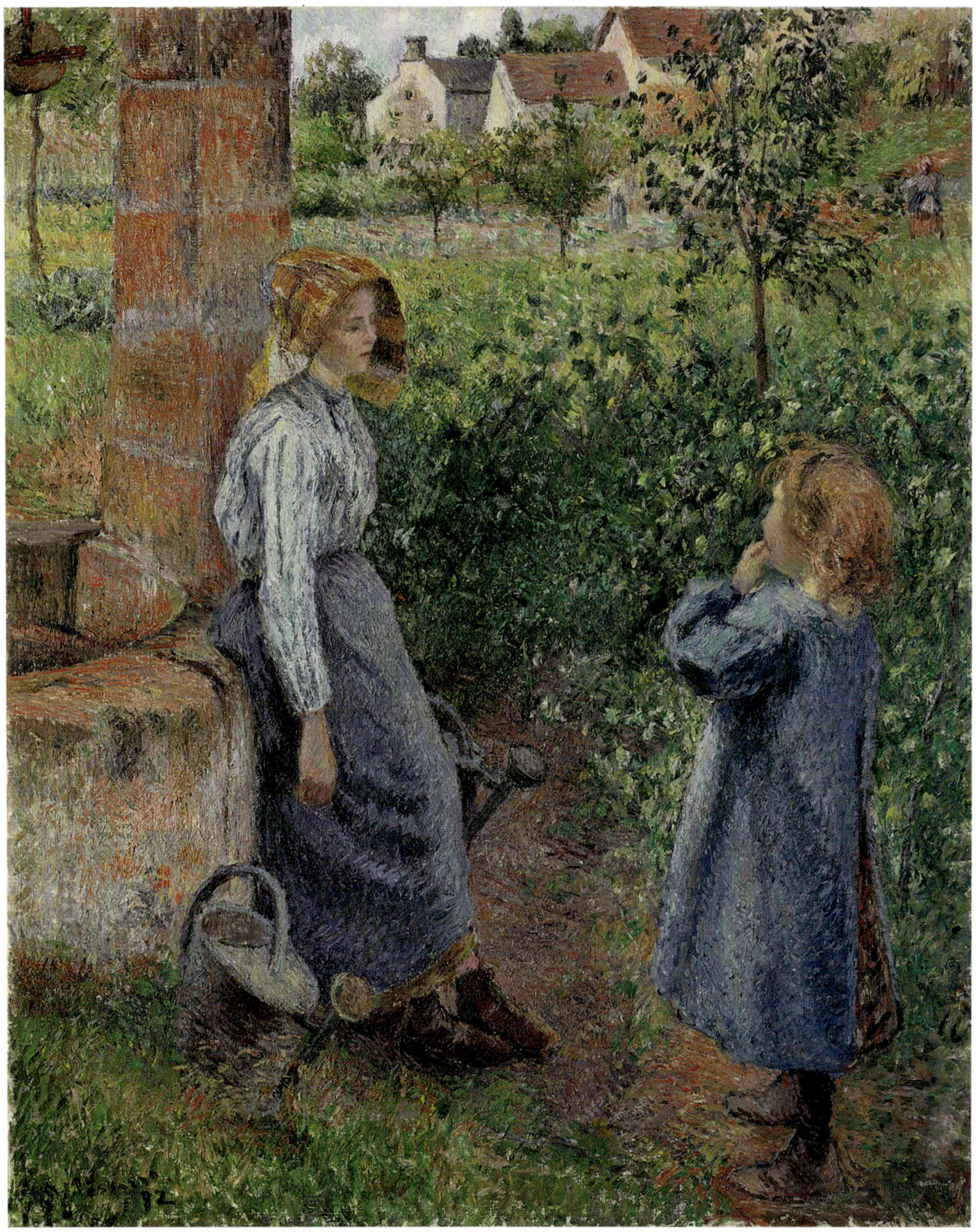

43

Woman and Child at the Well, 1882

Oil on canvas; 81.5 x 66.4 cm (32 1/8 x 26 1/8 in.)
Potter Palmer Collection, 1922.436
Signed lower left: *C. Pissarro / 82*

By the 1880s, Camille Pissarro, like most of his Impressionist colleagues, sought an alternative to the style he had employed over the previous decade. He decided to depict figures rather than landscapes; of the thirty-six paintings he showed at the seventh Impressionist exhibition, in March 1882, twenty-seven were figurative. He probably executed *Woman and Child at the Well* later that summer, since the dealer Paul Durand-Ruel purchased it from him in August. Its format, scale, and technique relate it to a series of paintings showing young peasant girls taking a break from chores, their poses and gestures suggesting narratives that remain ambiguous.

The young girl with a striped blouse in this painting, for example, appears as a domestic servant in other works from the period, including *The Young Country Servant* (1882; Tate Gallery, London). In the Art Institute's canvas, she leans against a well and looks distractedly in the direction of a child identified as Pissarro's fourth son, Ludovic-Rodolphe, who would have been four years old at the time. Raising one hand to his face, which is seen in *profil perdu* (lost profile), Ludovic conveys as little information as the servant girl he confronts.

In many of his compositions of peasant girls from this time, Pissarro set his figures in grassy, horizonless landscapes composed of densely interlocked strokes. Here, however, he included details that recall his earlier landscape imagery: farmhouses, vegetable gardens, and women who diligently irrigate the young sprouts. Many critics saw in Pissarro's works of this period a direct lineage to the art of Jean-François Millet, the Barbizon artist who lived like the peasants that he painted. Pissarro never considered himself a man of the soil. Although he felt strongly that "one must be committed to one's subject to represent it well," he asked, "Is it necessary to be a peasant? Let's be artists above all."

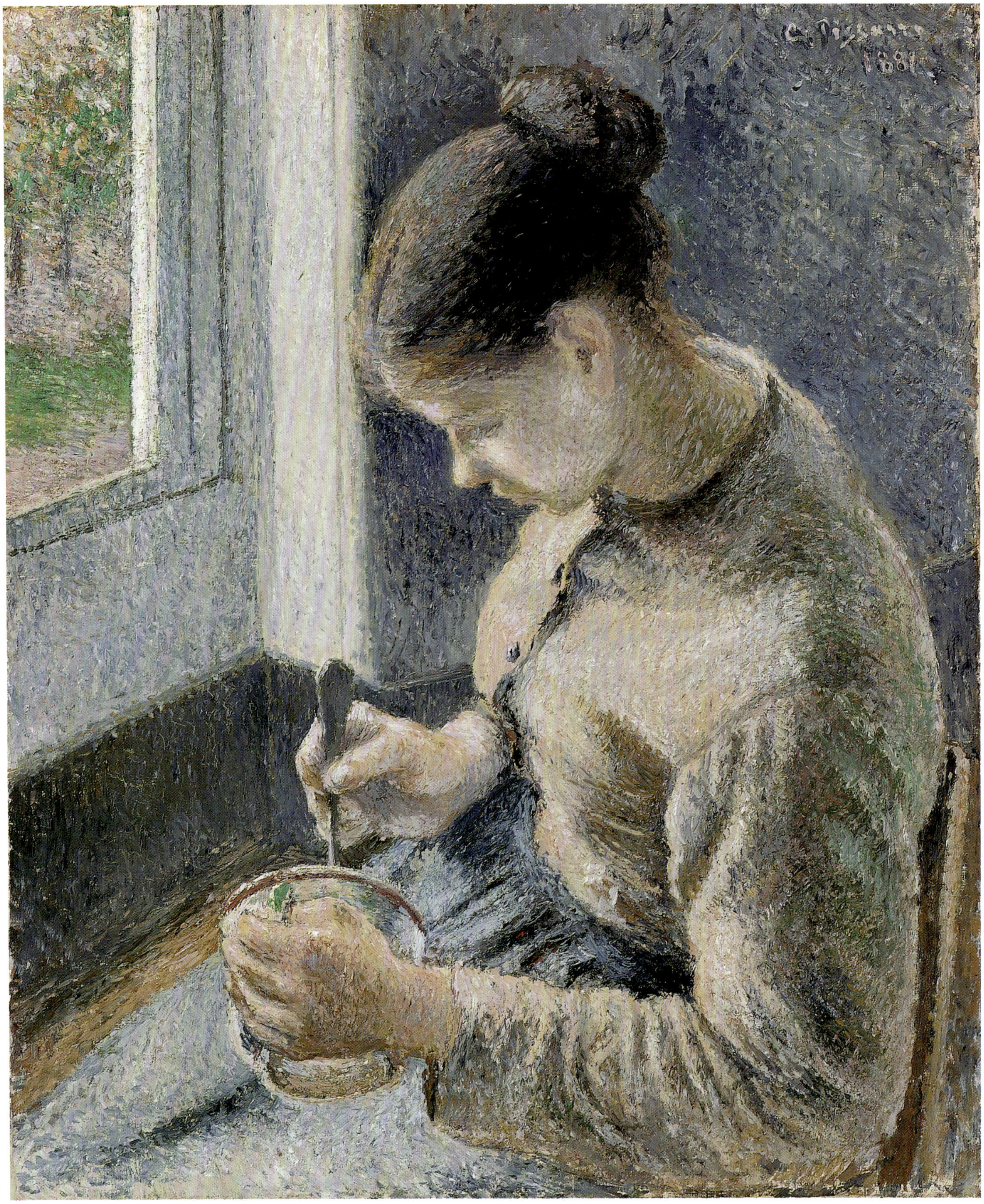

44

Young Peasant Woman Drinking Her Café au Lait, 1881

Oil on canvas; 65.3 x 54.8 cm (25 11/16 x 21 9/16 in.)
Potter Palmer Collection, 1922.433
Signed upper right: *C. Pissarro / 1881*

In the 1880s, at a time when many of the original Impressionist painters had begun to pursue independent styles, Camille Pissarro remained an active proponent of the group. He persuaded Gustave Caillebotte and Claude Monet to take part in the seventh Impressionist exhibition, in March 1882, and was himself particularly visible that year with a number of works showing female peasants—washing, harvesting, weeding, chatting, or sitting, as in this image of a young girl by a window, who tilts her bowl to get the last drops of coffee out of it. Parisian critics admired *Young Peasant Girl Drinking Her Café au Lait*, although many of them were generally unhappy with Pissarro's turn to figure painting.

In this work, the model is bathed in a diffused gray light, her intense focus elevating her action from a morning routine to a quasi-ritual event. Pissarro showed his subject from above and at an oblique angle, so that the large curve of her body dominates the compressed space, while the green tint of her face reflects the grass and trees beyond the window. The small brushstrokes applied one next to the other and sometimes overlaid with dabs of thicker paint result in an irregularly built-up surface, which serves to integrate figure and setting and to evoke the textures of the model's wool clothing. It was this rough, woven paint surface that London critics, who viewed this and other paintings by the artist at an Impressionist exhibition held there from April to July 1883, found objectionable. As Pissarro wrote to his son Lucien, they considered his works offensive to English taste, deeming them "uncouth." Although Pissarro was proud of this work, describing it as among his most "careful" and "finished" paintings, his dealer, Paul Durand-Ruel, may have taken these criticisms to heart. A year later, he urged Pissarro to abandon figure painting and return to "attractive landscapes."

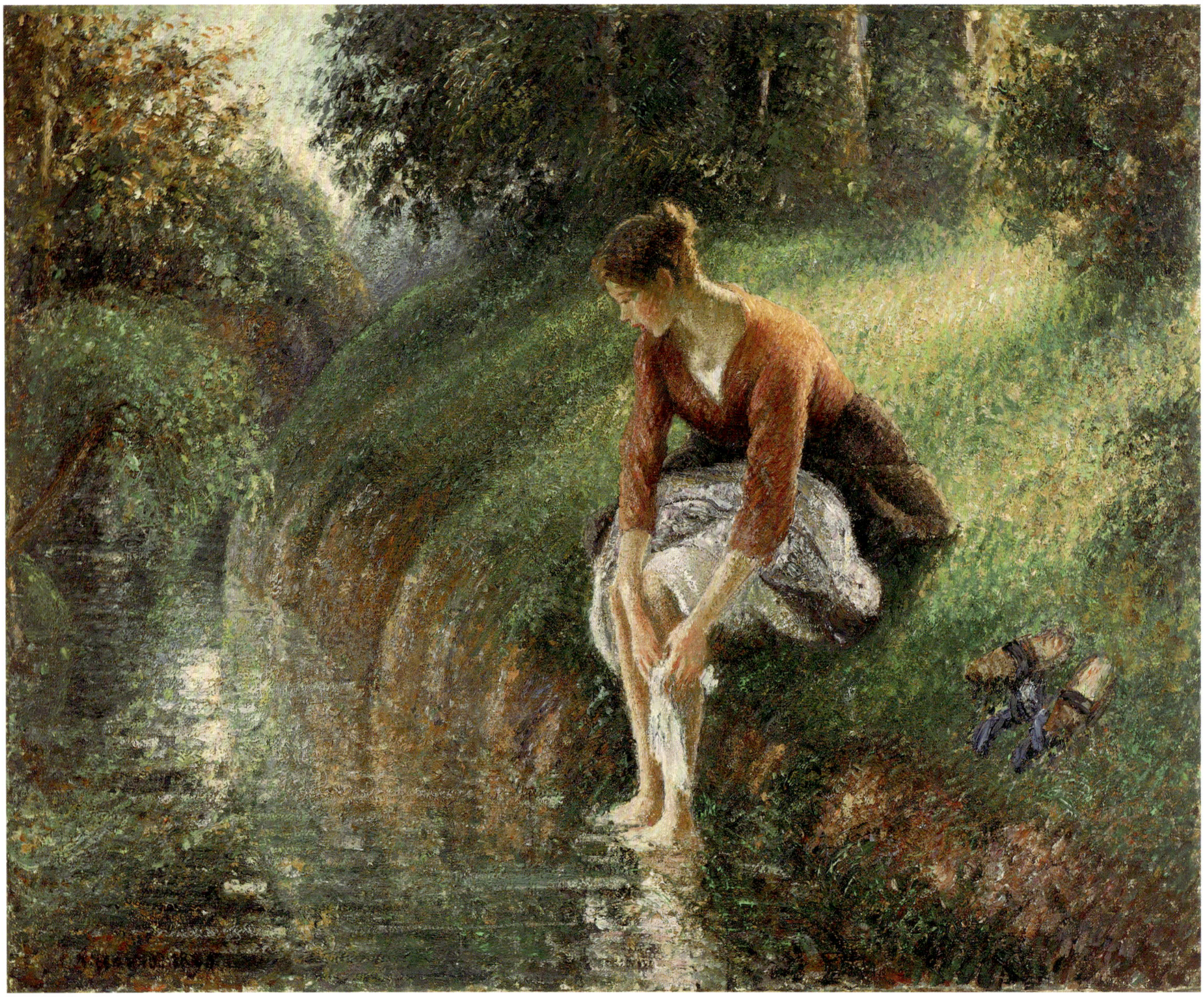

46

Woman Bathing Her Feet in a Brook, 1894/95

Oil on canvas; 73 x 92 cm (28½ x 36 in.)
A Millennium Gift of Sara Lee Corporation, 1999.364
Signed lower left: *C. Pissarro 1895*

During the last decade of his life, Camille Pissarro painted mostly cityscapes and landscapes, often in extended series. His images of bathers, nude and clothed, executed between 1894 and 1896, are exceptions; *Woman Bathing Her Feet in a Brook* is the most ambitious and diligently worked of this group. Pissarro referred to the painting in November 1894, when he wrote to his son Lucien that he wanted to send him a picture of "a little peasant girl dipping her feet in the water, canvas size 30." At the time, Pissarro considered the work finished but still lacking "that little something," although he exclaimed optimistically, "I think I will get it, I feel it!"

His continued ruminations on the composition may explain its heavily encrusted surface and the numerous pentimenti to the model's arm and legs. Pissarro completed the painting by February 1895, when, obviously proud of the picture, he sent it along with three other recent works to be shown at a gallery in Dresden and, a few weeks later, at the Fritz Gurlitt Gallery in Berlin. That same year, he painted *Bather in the Woods* (Metropolitan Museum of Art, New York), a variation of the Art Institute's canvas showing an identically posed nude (a rarity in his oeuvre) in the same setting. Pissarro's interest in this classical theme brings to mind Rembrandt van Rijn's images of Susanna at the bath and the long tradition of representations of bathers by French artists, from François Boucher in the eighteenth century to Pissarro's contemporaries Édouard Manet and Pierre-Auguste Renoir.

In this canvas, and in a smaller one painted in 1894 (*Woman Washing Her Feet in a Brook*; Indianapolis Museum of Art), which may well be a study for *Woman Bathing Her Feet*, however, the model is neither fully dressed nor undressed. She has taken off her wood clogs and cobalt blue stockings and raised her skirt, revealing a cotton underskirt.

For Pissarro this series was a new direction and one that was complicated by the difficulty of engaging models in rural Eragny. Given the even greater challenge of finding women willing to pose in the nude, it seems likely that Pissarro used a fully realized drawing of a seated peasant (*Study of a Young Woman Bathing Her Legs*, c. 1895; Ashmolean Museum, Oxford) for the Art Institute's painting and for the unclothed model in the Metropolitan Museum's version. In both pictures, the surface is thickly textured with a dense overlayer of staccato strokes. These raised dabs catch the light and move the eye around the composition; they also unite the various elements—skin, fabric, water, and vegetation—into a coarse, tapestry-like surface. Although he claimed to have abandoned the Neo-Impressionist style, Pissarro retained the use of complementary colors, as well as the technique of applying pigments in small strokes to achieve maximum luminosity. In this work, he employed variegated, acidic yellows and greens to suggest sunlight striking a patch of grass just beyond the figure and to highlight the back of her neck and the neckline of her bodice. Likewise, in the brook, pinkish yellow dabs applied next to dark moss greens suggest the play of light on the rippling water, which seems momentarily to distract the model from her washing. Despite the outdoor setting, the composition's densely patterned surface creates a sense of airlessness and flattens and distorts the woman's physiognomy. In the end, the painting has less to do with Impressionism than with the tighter, more decorative style of younger avant-garde artists such as Pierre Bonnard and Édouard Vuillard.

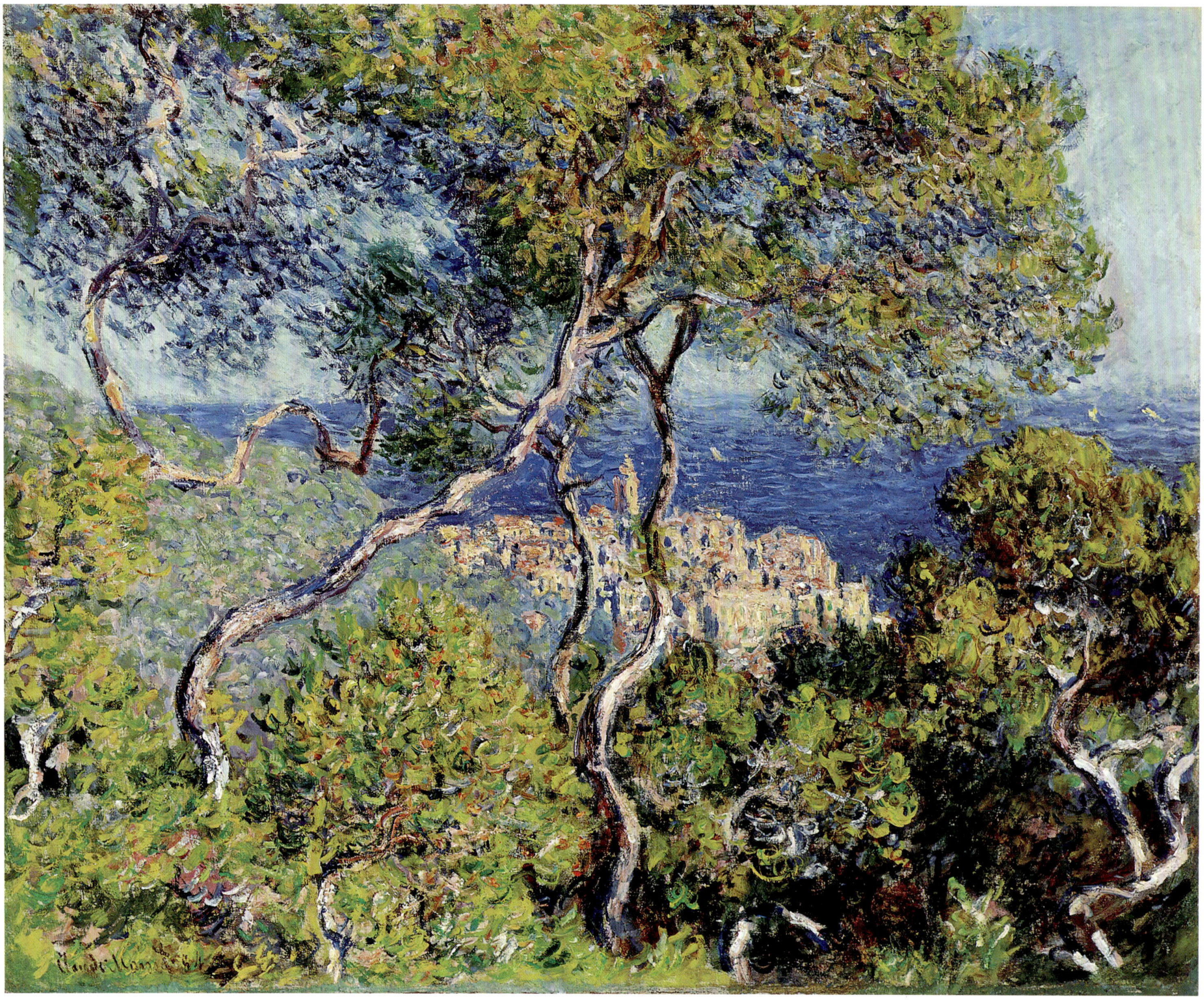

47

Bordighera, 1884

Oil on canvas; 64.8 x 81.3 cm (25½ x 32 in.)
Potter Palmer Collection, 1922.426
Signed lower left: *Claude Monet 84*

After renting a house at Giverny (a village northwest of Paris) in 1883, which he would inhabit for the rest of his life, Claude Monet spent most of the next ten years away from it—traveling to, among other destinations, the Normandy coast in 1883 and, in the first months of 1884, to Bordighera, a town on the Italian Riviera just across the French border. Monet had already visited this picturesque village as a tourist with Pierre-Auguste Renoir in December 1883. Writing to his dealer, Paul Durand-Ruel, he described it as "one of the most beautiful places" that he and Renoir had seen, one he intended to return to alone in order "to bring back a series of new things."

A month later, on January 18, Monet arrived in Bordighera, where he began to work intensely for what he thought would be a period of three weeks, but which instead lasted for nearly three months. In a letter to the sculptor Auguste Rodin, Monet declared that he was "fencing, wrestling with the sun" in order to translate into paint the seductive but blinding light that played tricks on the eye. The artist also equated painting with battle in his near-daily correspondence with Alice Hoschedé, who would become his companion and second wife, as he tried to "rediscover each new day the light and . . . to fight to capture its effect."

The diverse topography and exuberant vegetation of the region also challenged Monet: the artist, who described himself as a "man of isolated trees and large spaces," was frustrated by the difficulty of finding self-contained subjects to paint. Even so important a motif as the Mediterranean seemed impossibly hidden by dense vegetation. In the Art Institute's painting, undoubtedly among the six canvases that he worked on feverishly in the first two weeks of his stay in Bordighera, Monet's solution to these challenges was to set his easel on a hillside, near the Mostaccini Tower on the outskirts of the city, so he could look down on the village and sea.

The real subject of this composition, however, is not that vista, but rather the lush growth that both thrilled and thwarted the artist. Here the interlaced trunks of local pines (interestingly, not the olive and palm trees for which Bordighera is known) create a decorative screen that displays the same mosaic-like touches of pinks, blues, and whites as the houses, church, and bell tower that appear half-concealed in the background. Brilliant blue water cuts across the horizon, creating an exaggerated contrast that Monet worried would upset the "enemies of blue and pink" and would only partially express the sensation of the light, which he termed "fairylike."

Bordighera was one of three paintings of the same subject that Monet showed along with other works at the *International Exhibition of Painting* held at the Georges Petit Gallery, Paris, in May–June 1887. Although not listed in the catalogue, the Art Institute's canvas can be identified as the picture that Gustave Geffroy, Monet's future biographer, singled out for special commendation. In his 1922 biography of the artist, Geffroy was even more effusive in his praise of *Bordighera*, calling it the work that best summarized the visual experience of this Italo-Franco coastal town and an "extraordinary canvas, crammed with an eruption of unimaginable vegetation ablaze with light that bursts forth like the sudden appearance of the sun, making everything around it fade."

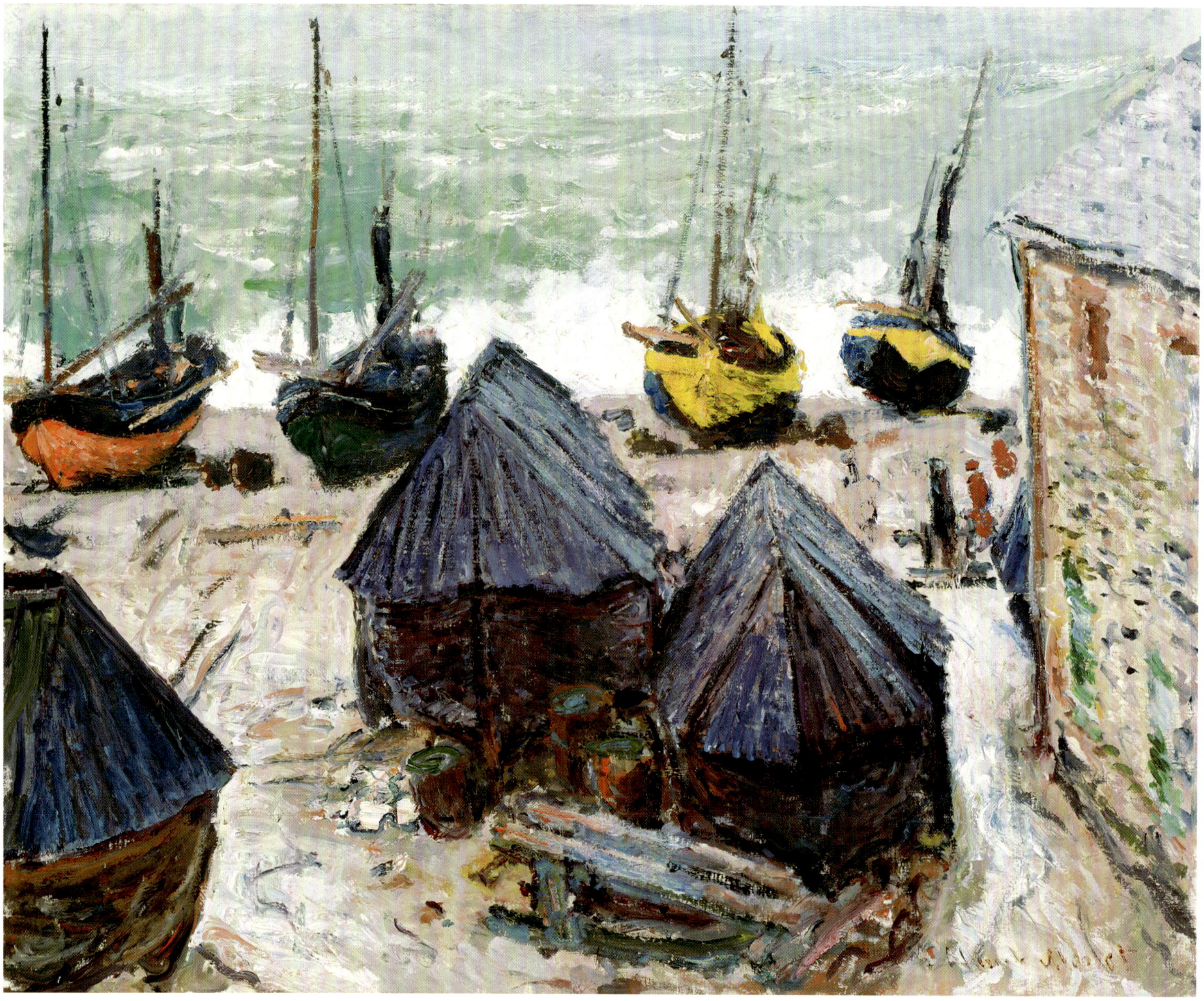

48

Boats on the Beach at Étretat, 1885

Oil on canvas; 65.5 x 81.3 cm (25 ¾ x 32 in.)
Charles H. and Mary F. S. Worcester Collection, 1947.95
Signed lower right: *Claude Monet*

By the mid-1880s, Claude Monet had distanced himself from the modern city, seeking challenging, inaccessible landscapes to paint. One of these sites was the Norman town of Étretat, famous for its monumental cliffs, dramatic coastal rock formations, and fashionable summer homes. *Boats on the Beach at Étretat* depicts none of these familiar views, however, focusing instead on a narrow patch of beach devoid of holiday travelers, below a stormy sky. Forced indoors by inclement fall weather, Monet framed his subject from the window of his room in the Hôtel Blanquet, where he stayed from mid-October to mid-December 1885. In one of his daily letters to Alice Hoschédé, dated November 24, he noted that he spent the afternoon in his room, "painting the *caloges* [retired fishing boats covered with tarred planks and used for storage] in the rain, and then still at my window I tried to paint the departure of the boats." Both of the works he described are in the Art Institute's collection: the first is *Boats on the Beach*; the second, the slightly larger canvas *Departure of the Boats from Étretat*, illustrates a break in the weather and the resumption of fishing-related activities. In each painting, Monet centered his composition on the *caloges*. By contrasting their dark, massive forms with the orange and yellow fishing vessels on the shore, he underscored their lowly status and the increasingly obsolete role of fishing in coastal villages that were being transformed by tourism. However, Monet was undoubtedly also interested in the *caloges* as forms that evoke solidity and shelter, a theme to which he would return in his series *Stacks of Wheat* (see cats. 75–80).

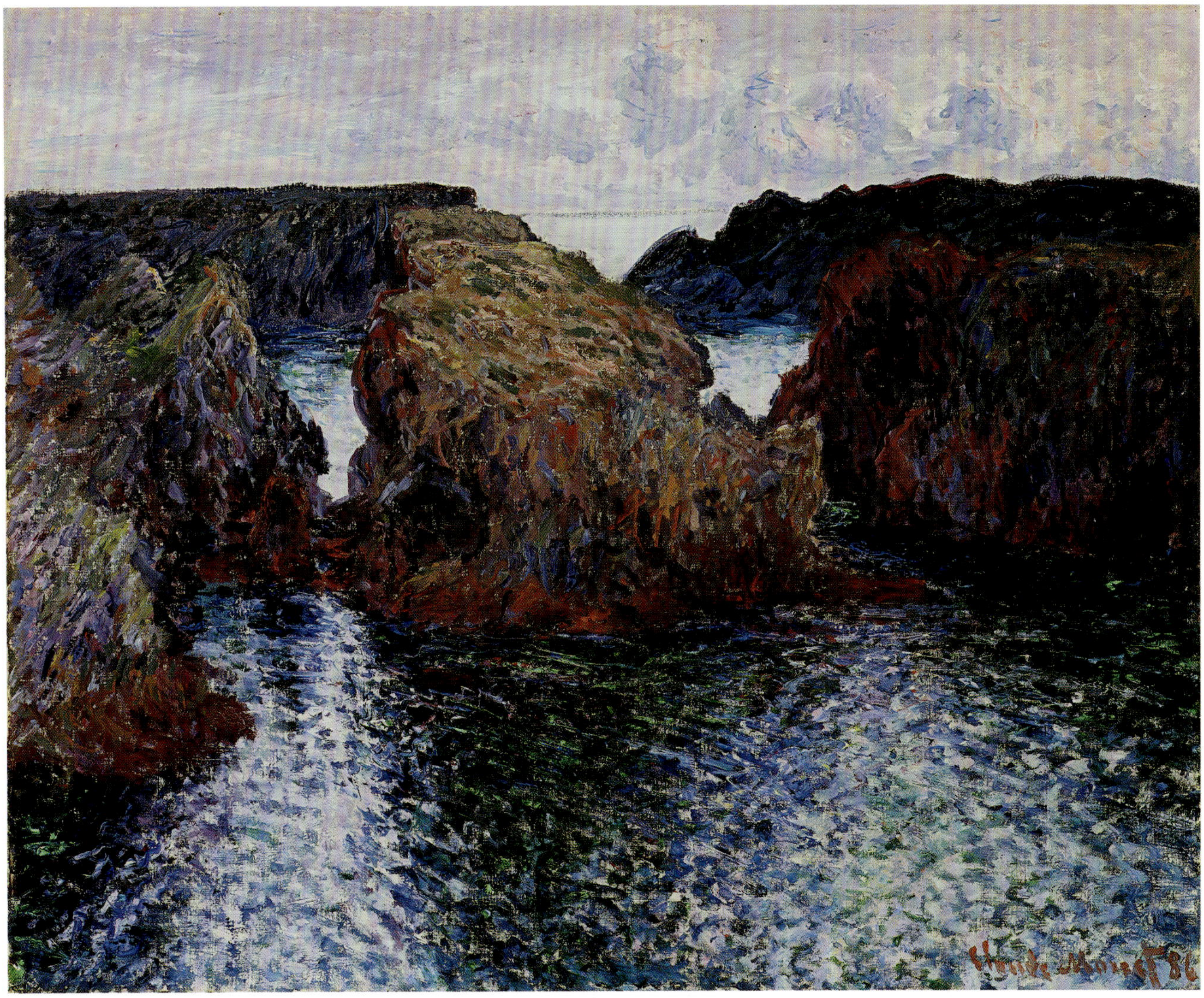

49

Rocks at Port-Goulphar, Belle-Ile, 1886

Oil on canvas; 66 x 81.8 cm (26 x 32 3/16 in.)
Gift of Mr. and Mrs. Chauncey B. Borland, 1964.210
Signed lower right: *Claude Monet 86*

Claude Monet's quest for unknown and compelling landscapes led him to Belle-Ile-en-Mer, a small island off the southern shore of Brittany known for its "savage coast" of fantastic grottoes, needles (sharp rocks), reefs, and cliffs. As he often did, the artist misjudged the time he would need to explore and capture the beauty of the place, which he called "lugubrious," "terrifying," and "very beautiful"; he stayed for more than two months, rather than the two weeks he had initially planned.

This canvas is one of a group depicting the frieze of rock configurations known as Port-Goulphar. It may have been among the first works that Monet executed after arriving at Kervilahouen, the village nearest to Port-Goulphar, on September 15, 1886. Since the painting clearly depicts fair weather, he may have made it before the tempest that overtook the island from October 9 to 15. Monet painted *Rocks at Port-Goulphar* from a cliff top, providing no indication of the ground on which he stood; instead, the triangular patterns of light on the rippling waters pull the viewer vertiginously up and down. Anchoring the composition are the firm silhouettes of massive, dolmenlike rock formations, described with dense brushwork and kaleidoscopic colors that suggest their craggy surfaces. Throughout his Belle-Ile campaign, Monet continually reworked his compositions. For this reason, he refused to send any of the works to his dealer, claiming that he needed to reassess the effect of the group back in his Giverny studio. Less than a month later, however, he was still working on nearly forty canvases, a number of which were not shown until the following spring at the Georges Petit Gallery, Paris. Despite their apparently direct touch, the Belle-Ile paintings mark the beginning of Monet's move to a more deliberate technique, palette, and concern for decorative unity, which he would develop further in his series.

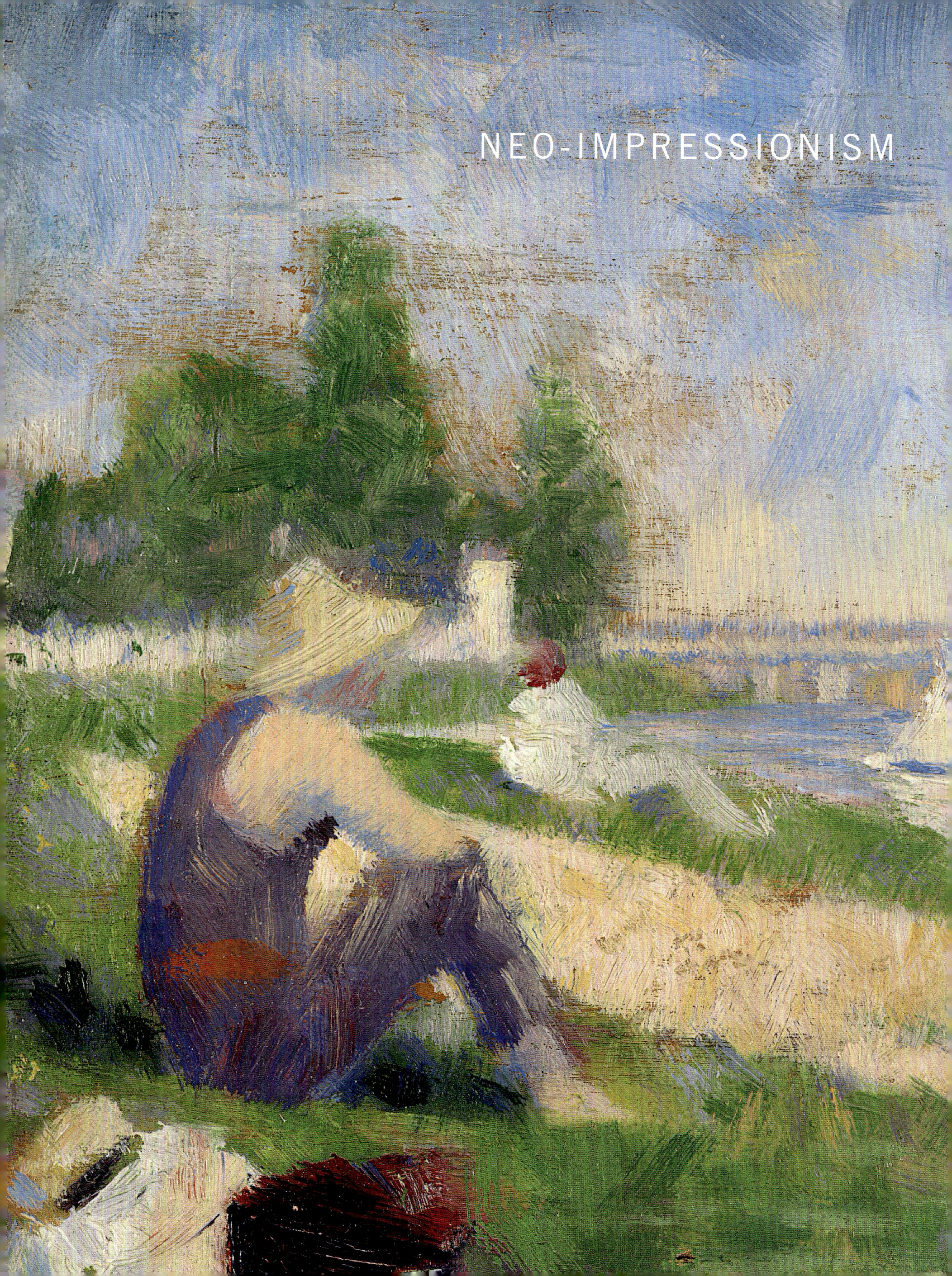
NEO-IMPRESSIONISM

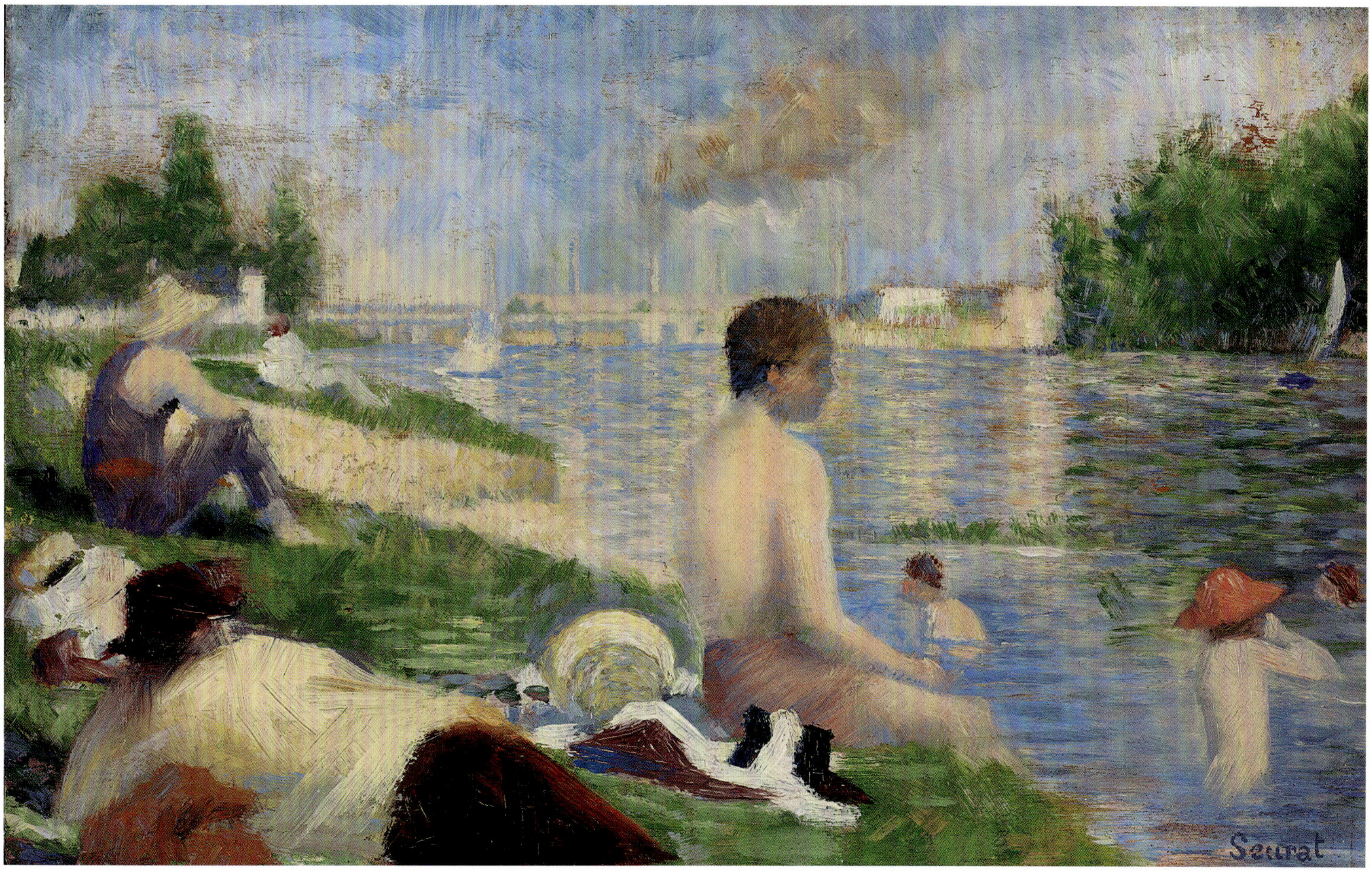

50

Final Study for "Bathers at Asnières," 1883

Oil on panel; 15.8 x 25.1 cm (6¼ x 9⅞ in.)
Gift of the Adele R. Levy Fund, Inc., 1962.578
Signed lower right: *Seurat*

Having received traditional instruction at the École des Beaux-Arts in Paris, Georges Seurat set himself the daunting task of creating a new classicism, one that employed forms that embody an art of enduring ideals, while preserving the vitality of the Impressionists' exploration of modern life. Seurat revealed the full extent of his ambition in *Bathers at Asnières* (1884; National Gallery, London), on which he began working in 1883. Monumental in scale, it exhibits affinities with the Impressionists' modern-life themes and lightened palette, although its subject—men and boys on the bank of the Seine River in the working-class suburb of Asnières—differs greatly from Claude Monet's and Pierre-Auguste Renoir's sparkling depictions of leisure activities in attractive outdoor settings (see cats. 13 and 23). In Seurat's compositions, Impressionist spontaneity yielded to a more academic approach; to prepare for this and other major projects, the artist made careful drawings of models in his studio, as well as numerous small oil-on-panel studies (*croquetons*) at the site. The Art Institute's oil sketch is considered closest to the final picture, but the multi-directional, free brushstrokes of the former distinguish it from the latter, with its meticulously worked surface. Seurat exhibited the nearly seven-by-ten-foot *Bathers* in May 1884 at the new artist-run, non-juried Salon des Indépendents in Paris; he must have been equally pleased with the Art Institute's final study, which he signed prominently and may have shown at a smaller exhibition that same year. In both canvas and panel, the firmly contoured and rhythmically balanced figures underscore the overall stillness and solemnity of a composition that was intended to bring together classical tradition and contemporary innovations. This synthesis would be fully realized in the artist's next big project, *A Sunday on La Grande Jatte—1884* (see p. 14 and cat. 51), which is set across the river from Asnières, on the island just visible as a clump of green foliage in the upper right of *Bathers*.

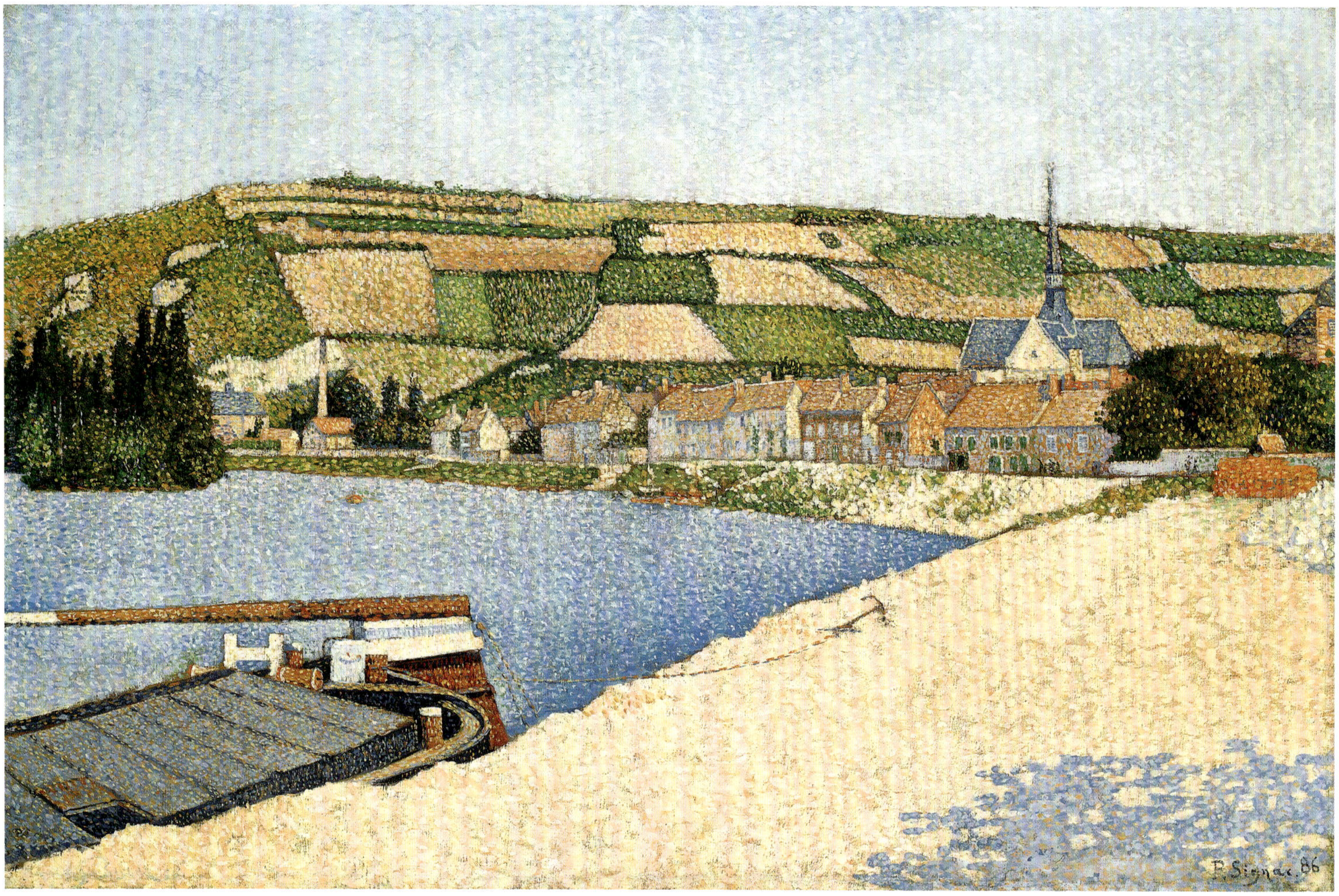
P. Signac. 86

52

Les Andelys, Côte d'Aval, 1886

Oil on canvas; 60 x 92 cm (23 5/8 x 36 1/4 in.)
Through prior gift of William Wood Prince, 1993.208
Signed lower right: *P. Signac. 86*

This luminous image shows the harbor of Les Andelys, a village on the curve of the Seine River near Giverny, about sixty miles from Paris. It is one of a suite of ten works that Paul Signac made in the summer and early fall of 1886, and it marks the first time that he painted a series using Divisionist or Neo-Impressionist techniques. Signac chose Les Andelys as the setting for this composition not only because it was among the loveliest villages along the Seine, but also because of its relative proximity to Paris, where he was in charge of preparing for the August opening of the Salon des Indépendents. Two years earlier, at the inaugural exhibition of that group, he had met Georges Seurat. This encounter proved to be a turning point for Signac's art, which until then had consisted largely of landscapes painted in the Impressionist style and palette.

After meeting Seurat, Signac transformed his style from what Camille Pissarro (himself a recent convert to Divisionism) called "romantic Impressionism," an art associated with the spontaneous capturing of nature, to "scientific Impressionism," which was based on technical innovations grounded in optical and color theory. Although entirely different in temperament—Seurat was laconic and introverted, while Signac was jovial and sociable—the artists found their friendship to be mutually beneficial. As Signac adopted the Divisionist technique to obtain more luminous and vibrant color effects, he awakened Seurat to the Impressionists' use of pure colors. Unlike Seurat, whose stylistic innovations sprang from his training at the École des Beaux-Arts, Paris, and his deep-seated belief in classical structure, Signac, a basically self-taught artist, embraced Seurat's method as a refinement and modification of Impressionism, rather than a complete break with it.

Les Andelys, the largest and most radically synthesized of the series that Signac undertook, exhibits his mastery of the new style. A study for the same canvas (1886; Norton Simon Museum, Pasadena) displays more spontaneous Impressionistic brushwork and a greenish blue palette that captures the look of the small harbor and surrounding hills. From study to final canvas, the artist simplified forms and created a geometric structure of two triangles—one blue, one yellow—that intersect at the composition's center. In the distance can be seen farmland, or what one critic described as a "sparkling [patchwork] of cultivated fields." To the Art Institute's canvas, Signac added a small boat, its dropped mast perfectly aligned with the thicket of pines on the small island directly opposite it. Using these geometries, as well as zones of complementary colors, he played with notions of near and far, of surface and depth, emulating the spatial innovations that Seurat had used in his monumental painting *A Sunday on La Grande Jatte—1884*. The lacy blue pattern at the lower right, which evokes dappled sunlight appearing through overhead foliage, and the broadly brushed sky suggest that Signac had not yet fully relinquished the Impressionist focus on color and handling. In a few years, he would abandon these concerns for a consistently decorative style that relied increasingly on primary colors.

Signac showed *Les Andelys* and other canvases from the series within a year of their completion at the Salon des Indépendents and the avant-garde Théâtre Libre d'Antoine, Paris, before presenting this painting to Alexandre Charpentier, a sculptor friend also involved in the Théâtre Libre. The fact that Signac gave most of the works in the series to family and friends suggests that he wanted to keep these paintings—his first concerted effort in the Neo-Impressionist technique—close at hand, out of the marketplace, and perhaps among those who were favorably predisposed to his new style.

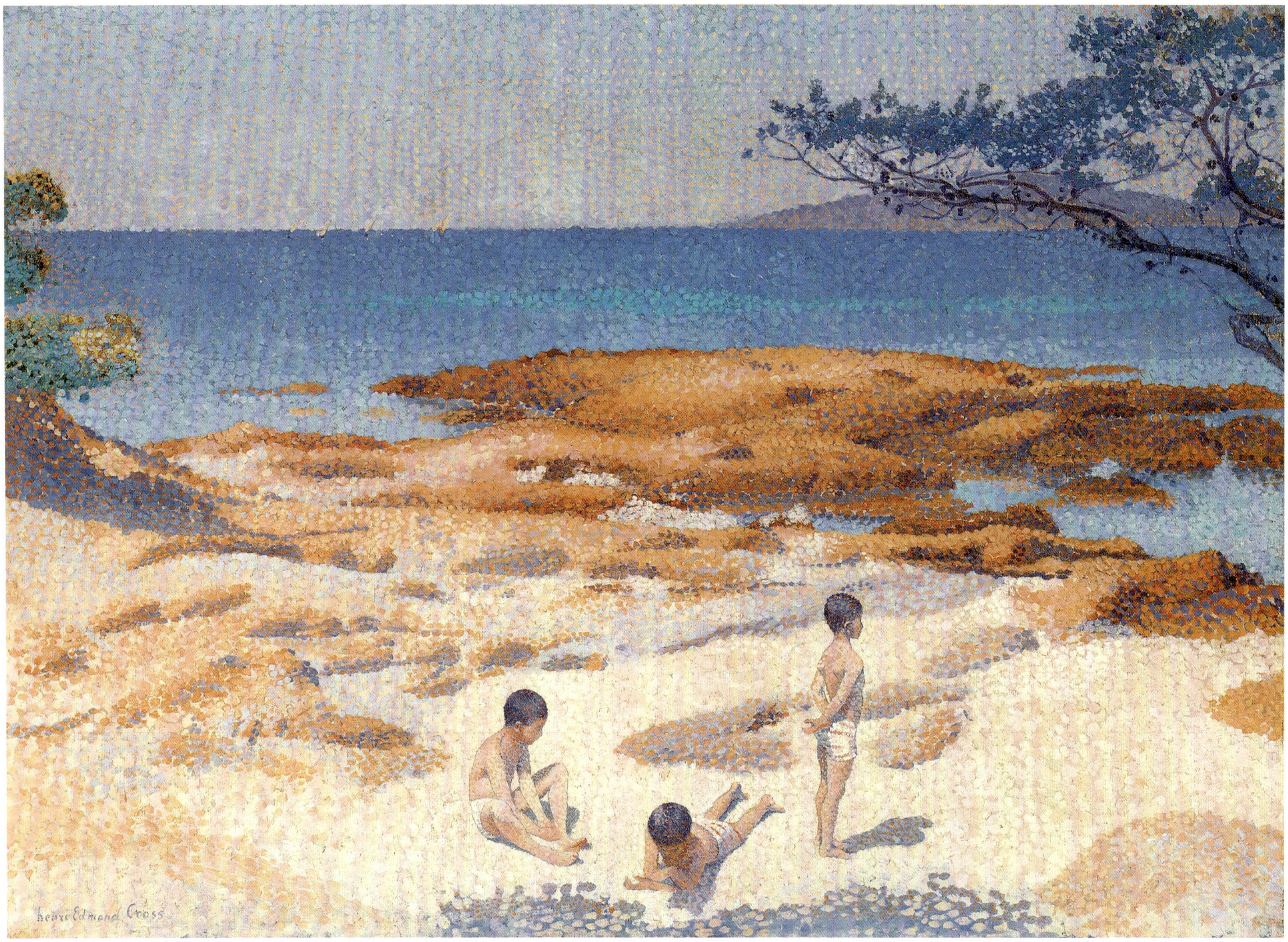
henri Edmond Cross

53

Beach at Cabasson (Baigne-Cul), 1891–92

Oil on canvas; 65.3 x 92.3 cm (25¾ x 36⅜ in.)
L. L. and A. S. Coburn, and Bette and Neison Harris funds; Charles H. and Mary F. S. Worcester Collection; through prior acquisition of Kate L. Brewster Collection, 1983.513
Signed lower left: *henri* [sic] *Edmond Cross*

In October 1891, Henri-Edmond Cross, seeking relief from his rheumatoid arthritis, moved to Cabasson, a small hamlet in the Var region on the Côte d'Azur. There he painted this sun-drenched beach scene, one of his first completely realized Neo-Impressionist works. Like Paul Signac, who introduced Cross to the region (and who would move a year later to nearby Saint-Tropez), Cross became acquainted with Georges Seurat and his innovative color theories in 1884, at the newly founded Salon des Indépendents.

Unlike Signac, however, Cross did not immediately assimilate the theories of complementary colors and optical mixture. In 1884, when Signac was still a fledgling painter working on the margins of the Impressionist movement, Cross was an established artist, known for the somber, sensuous portraits and still lifes he exhibited at the official Salon. Although he became friends with Charles Angrand, Camille Pissarro, Seurat, Signac, and other Neo-Impressionists, it was only after settling on the Mediterranean coast that he embraced the divided brushwork and color gradations of "scientific Impressionism" (see cat. 52) as a means to express the region's radiant heat and vibrant hues.

Despite his residency in Cabasson and the neighboring village of Saint-Clair, where he lived from 1892 until the end of his life, Cross continued to be involved with Signac's group and to exhibit with the Indépendents. In the spring of 1892, he showed *Beach at Cabasson* and *Coast near Antibes* (1891–92; National Gallery of Art, Washington, D.C.), the two important paintings he had begun in the fall of 1891 and finished in the winter of 1892. Although one reviewer of the exhibition felt that the artist's new style "irritates the eye," he singled out four works, including the Art Institute's, for their "luminous charm." Cross felt strongly about both the *Cabasson* and *Antibes* canvases, showing them in at least five different exhibitions between March 1892 and May 1893, including at the important venue for avant-garde art Les Vingt (The Twenty), Brussels.

Writing to Signac about *Cabasson* in particular, Cross noted that he had worked "in harmonies of oranges and blues." To achieve these colors, he added light orange, dotlike touches over blue in precise rows for the sky and used thick impasto strokes made with a small, flat brush for the beach. For the boys (whose close resemblance to one another suggests that the same model posed for all three), he employed a different technique entirely, outlining them in thin blue paint filled in with cream-colored pigment. To punctuate the expanse of orange and yellow sand, Cross painted a blue and lavender patch over the orange that suggests the dappled shadow of a Mediterranean pine, recalling Signac's own decorative motif-cum-shadow in the river scene *Les Andelys*. But whereas Signac's canvas evokes a specific place and moment, only the title elucidates the setting for Cross's depiction of a timeless arcadia. Like Seurat, who wanted to make permanent expressions of modern-life subjects, Cross here conveyed a feeling of repose and quietude, mitigated only by the standing youth shown looking out to sea.

In his later Mediterranean visions, Cross would reject the soft palette and carefully determined structural zoning (sand, sea, and sky) of this and other early works made in the Neo-Impressionist style. By 1896 he had adopted more forceful compositions and a brilliant palette that would appeal to the future Fauves, especially Henri Matisse, who owned paintings by the older artist and worked closely with him in 1904.

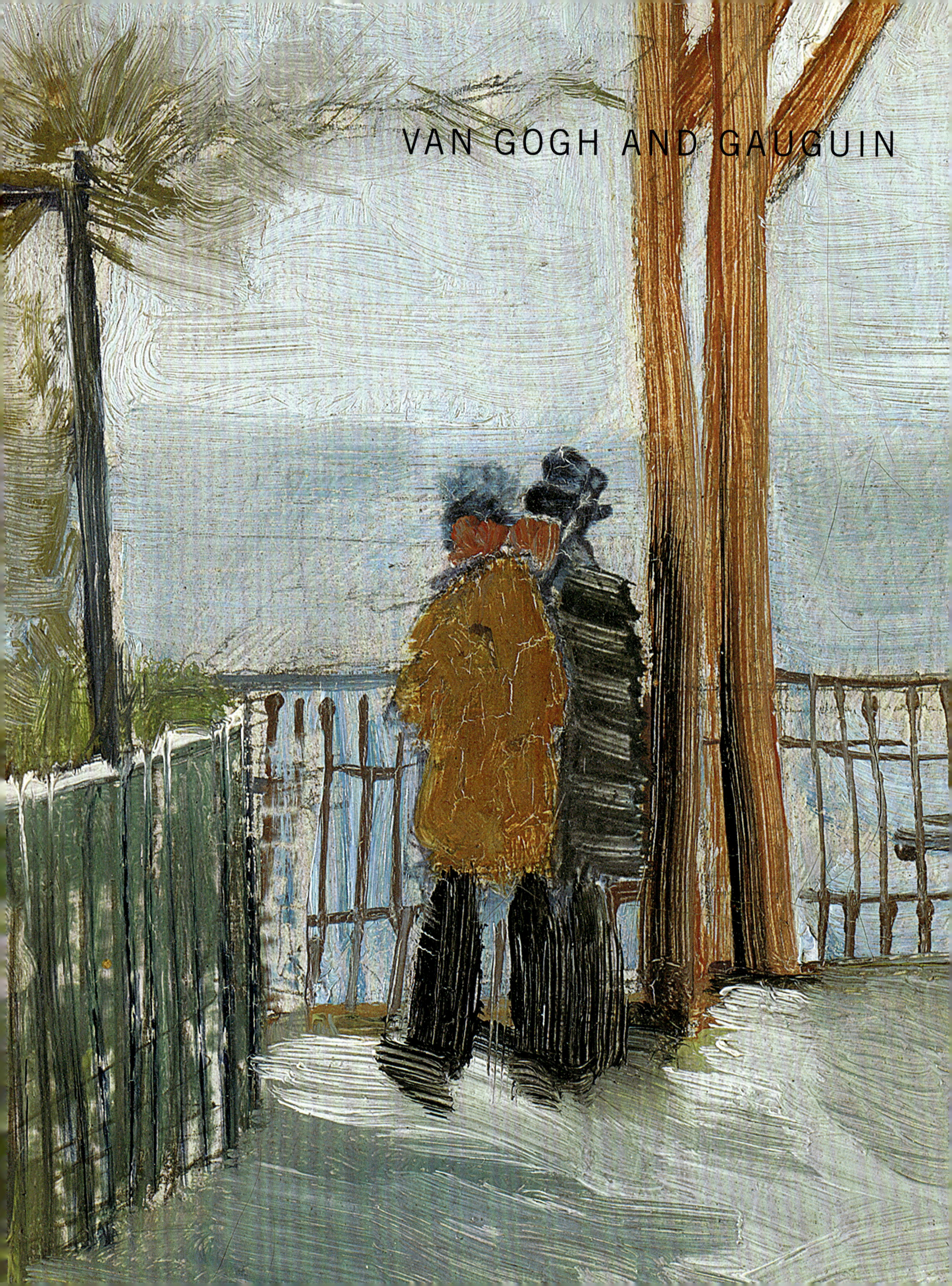
VAN GOGH AND GAUGUIN

54

Terrace and Observation Deck at the Moulin de Blute-Fin, Montmartre, 1887

Oil on canvas, mounted on pressboard;
43.6 x 33 cm (17 1/8 x 13 in.)
Helen Birch Bartlett Memorial Collection, 1926.202

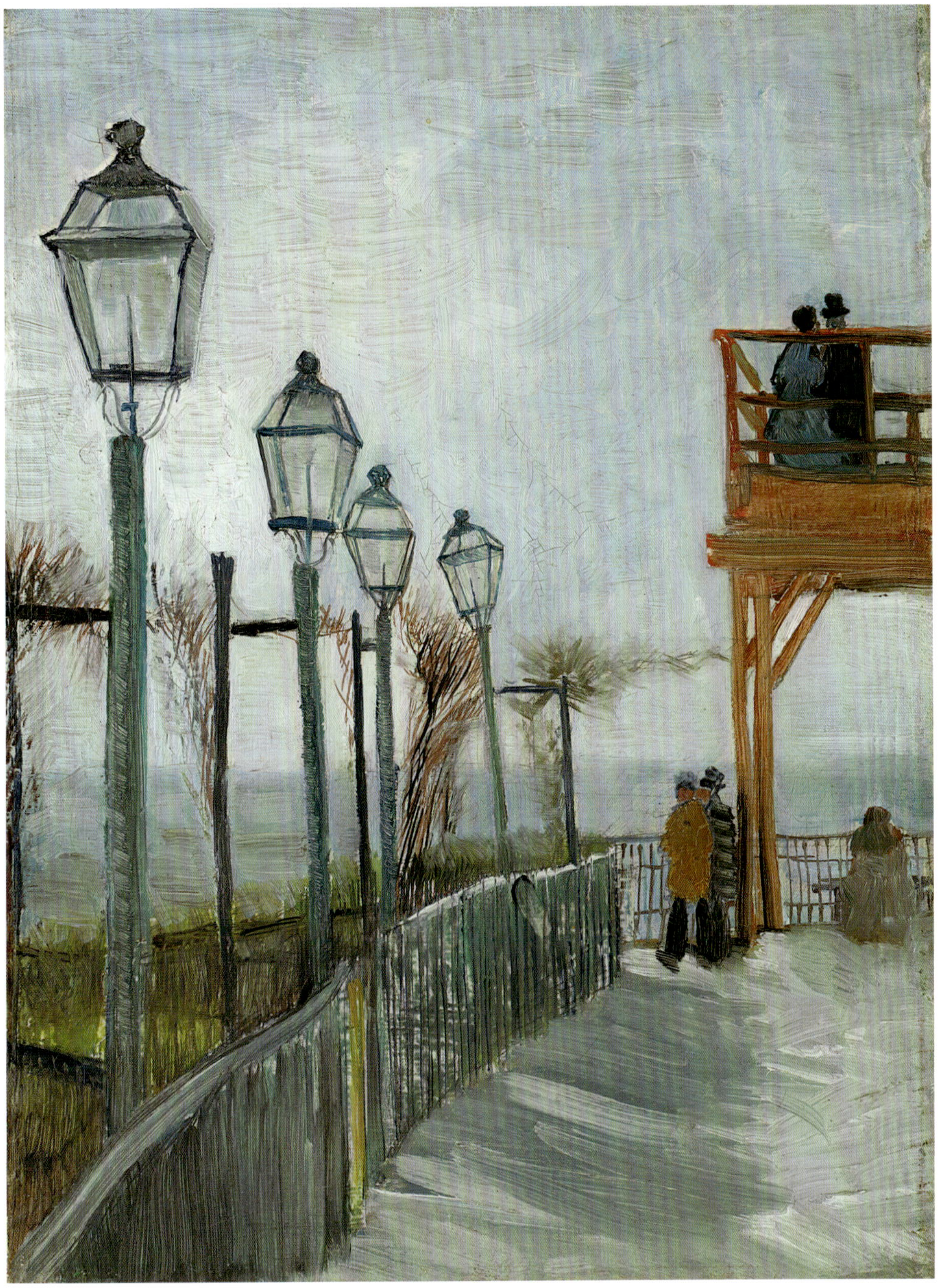

This picture dates to the winter of 1887, roughly one year after Vincent van Gogh arrived in Paris to join his brother the art dealer Theo van Gogh. He had traveled from Antwerp, where he worked for several months after leaving his native Holland in late 1885. An infrared reflectogram of the canvas recently revealed that the artist painted this Paris view over an earlier Antwerp study that he had described in a letter of December 1885 as "backs of old houses, seen from my window."

Reflecting his new Parisian neighborhood, *Terrace and Observation Deck* is one of a sizeable group of landscapes featuring the Butte Montmartre, a short climb from the apartment on the rue Lepic where Vincent and Theo had moved in June 1886. Situated on Paris's northern edge and rising high over the city, Montmartre was dotted by traces of its quickly receding rural past—abandoned quarries, kitchen gardens, and three surviving windmills, including the Moulin de Blute-Fin, virtually at Vincent's doorstep. The nonfunctional mill had become a tourist attraction, affording spectacular panoramic views over Paris from the observation tower erected beside it. It was also part of the dance-hall complex known as the Moulin de la Galette. Although Henri de Toulouse-Lautrec would later treat the somewhat sordid goings-on of the dance hall (see cat. 61), Van Gogh focused on the exterior, here excluding the mill altogether in favor of the terrace and observation deck with visitors contemplating the haze-wrapped city below. The underlying charcoal drawing, also revealed by infrared reflectography, shows that the artist established the rapid spatial recession marked by the line of slightly tipsy lampposts by using the threaded perspective frame that he had had made in The Hague in 1882 to help him master relative proportions in his depictions of deep space.

TOULOUSE-LAUTREC AND MONTMARTRE

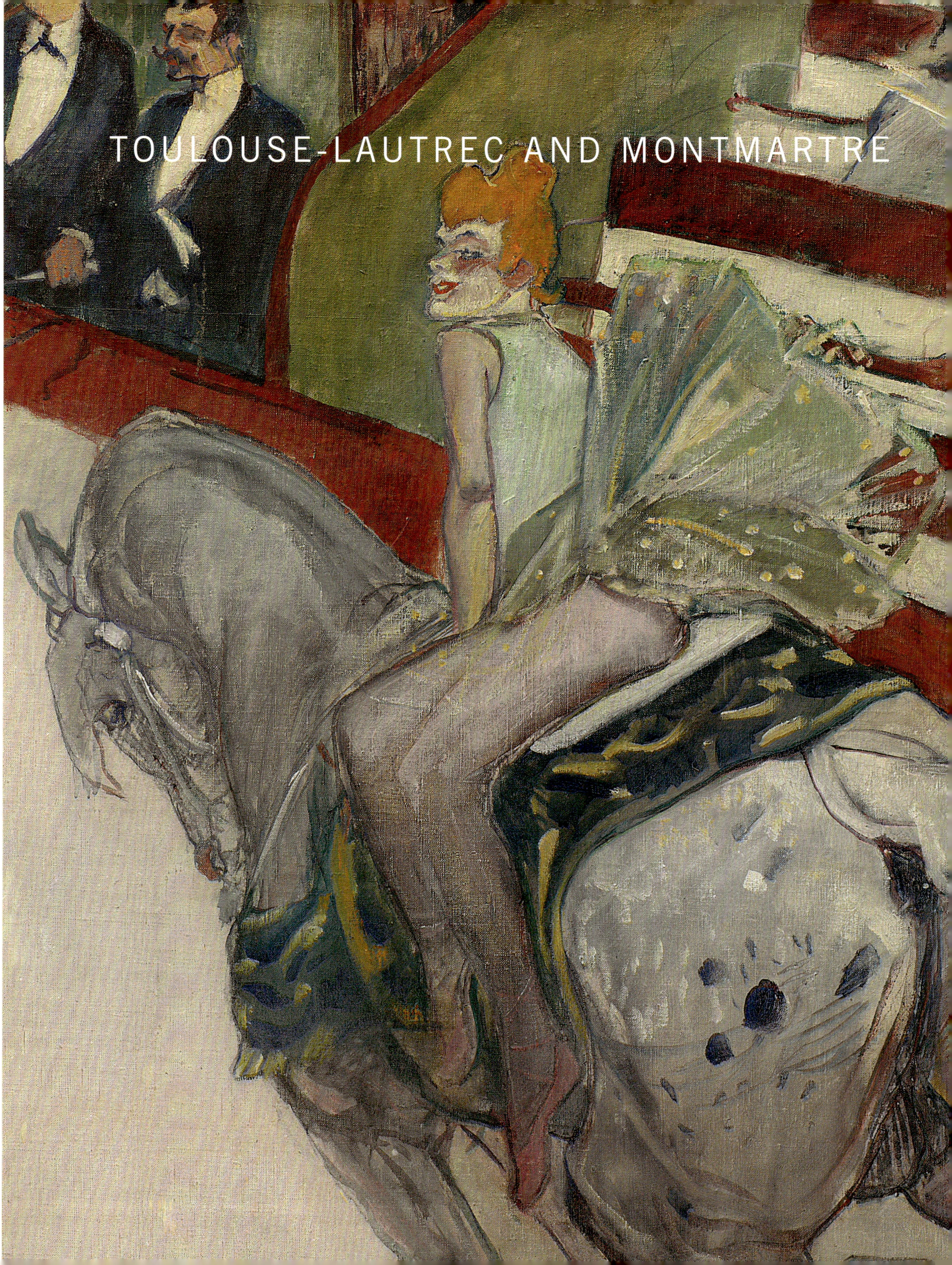

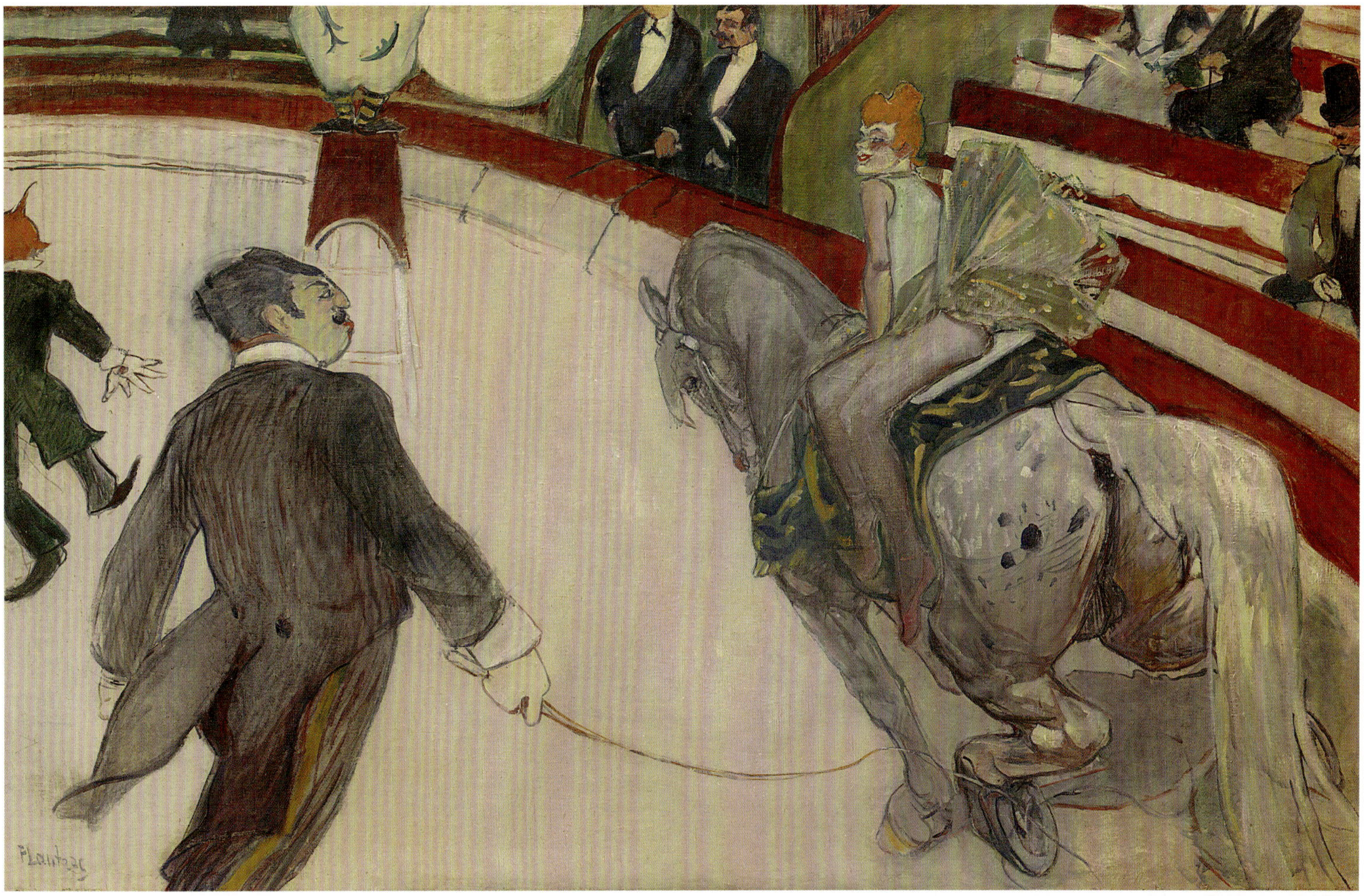

60

Equestrienne (At the Cirque Fernando), 1887–88

Oil on canvas; 100.3 x 161.3 cm (39 ½ x 63 ½ in.)
Joseph Winterbotham Collection, 1925.523
Signed lower left: *HT Lautrec*

In the late nineteenth century, the circus—whether in the open air, temporary tents, or, like the Cirque Fernando (after 1875), in an enclosed permanent structure—appealed to Montmartre artists and writers both for its perpetual activity and for the colorful spectacles it provided (see cat. 26). Henri de Toulouse-Lautrec became fascinated with the ambiguous nature of such Montmartrois entertainments, which he would continue to explore throughout his short career. Although it is unclear whether *Equestrienne* was a study or later version of a mural-size vertical painting (now lost) also showing a ringmaster and rider, the picture was publicly exhibited in the Moulin Rouge dance hall after it was purchased by the owner of that establishment to decorate the foyer. In the unconventionally cropped, semi-circular arena, elongated to fit the horizontal format of the painting, Lautrec captured the frenetic and potentially dangerous moment when the brawny stallion, whipped on by M. Loyal, the circus's well-known ringmaster, gathers sufficient momentum for the rider to stand up and leap through the paper hoop held by a clown.

The model for the garishly made-up rider, who is dressed in a ballet tutu of gauze and sequins, may well have been Suzanne Valadon, a former circus performer, model, and aspiring artist with whom Lautrec would have a nearly three-year relationship. She snarls at M. Loyal, who glares back at her. Indeed, the painting has been titled both *Écuyère* (*Bareback Rider*) and *The Ringmaster*, underscoring these figures' primacy in the somewhat sadistic duet that electrifies the act. Against their coarse, but impassioned performance, Lautrec contrasted the well-dressed, yet seemingly unresponsive bourgeois audience seated at ringside. Given the artist's own aristocratic background, in which horsemanship was considered a privileged gentleman's sport, *Equestrienne*, his first important canvas on a Montmartrois theme, seems an ironic comment on the society he had rejected and on the gritty urban world he had embraced.

CÉZANNE'S CLASSICISM

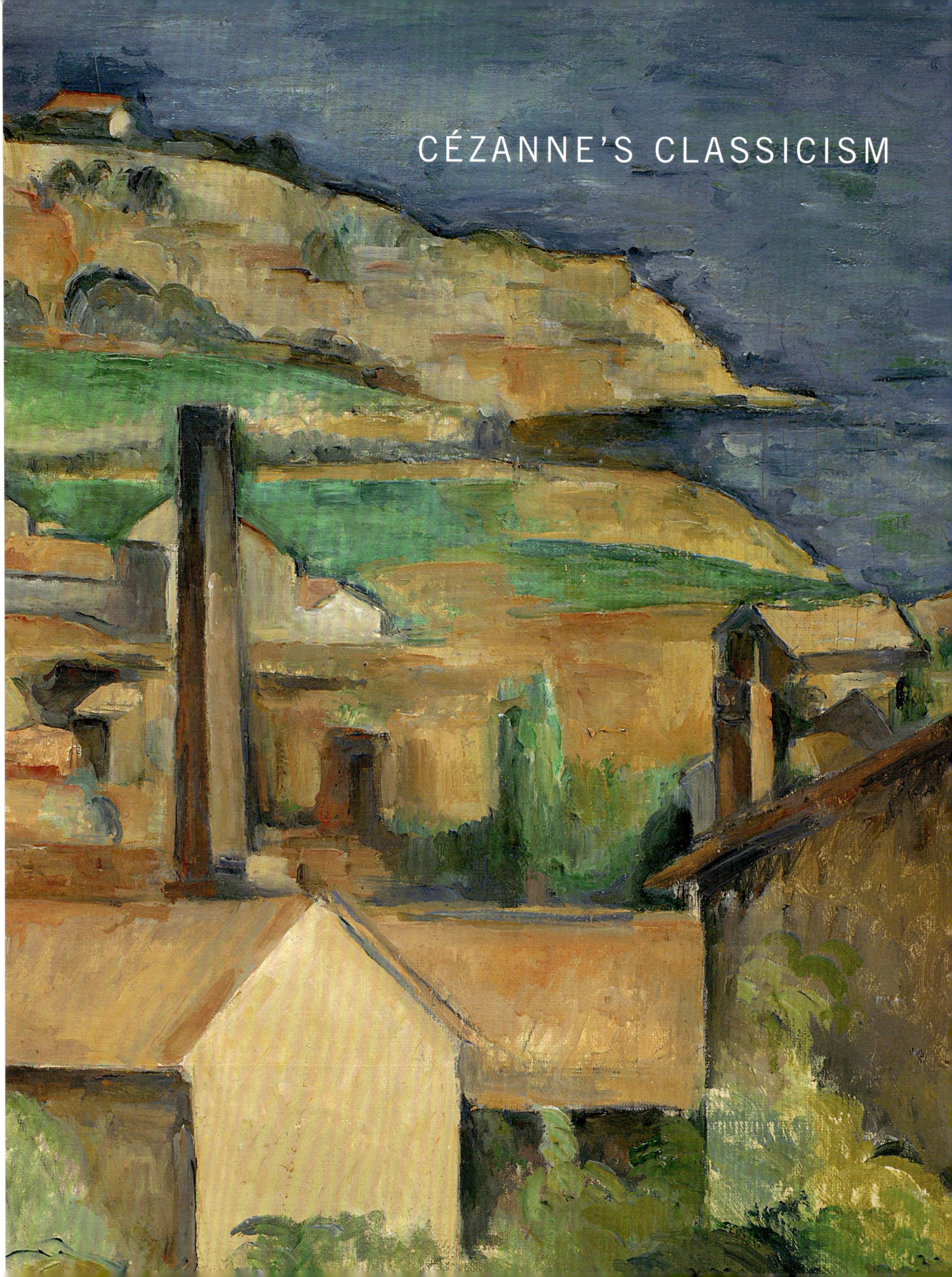

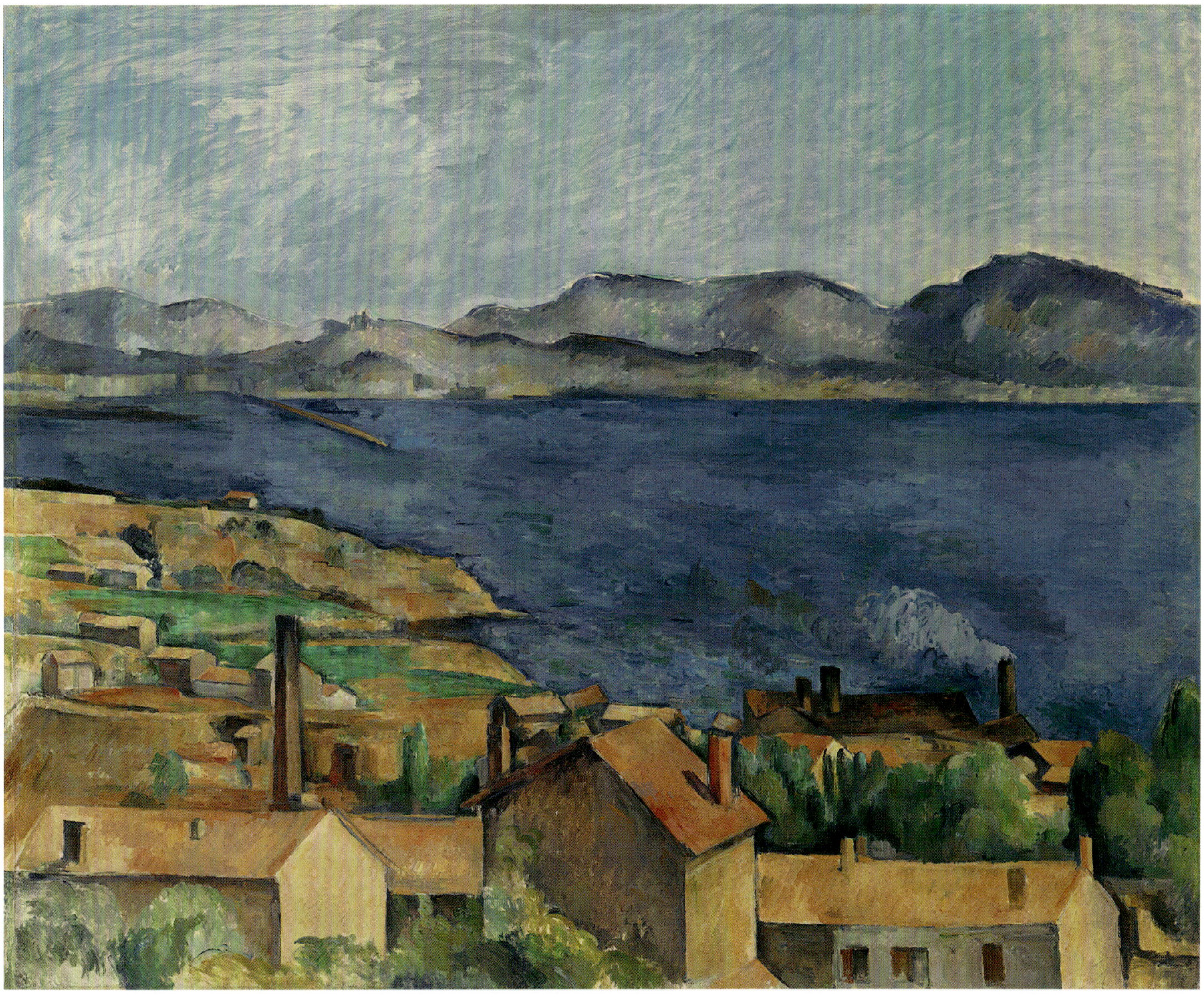

63

The Bay of Marseilles, Seen from L'Estaque, c. 1885

Oil on canvas; 80.2 x 100.6 cm (31⅝ x 39⅝ in.)
Mr. and Mrs. Martin A. Ryerson Collection, 1933.1116

In scale and resolution, *The Bay of Marseilles, Seen from L'Estaque* can be considered the culminating work of a group of landscapes that Paul Cézanne painted in the 1880s at L'Estaque, a picturesque fishing village a few miles from the port city of Marseilles. The artist first visited L'Estaque, where his mother had long rented a summer home, in 1864, and he returned to the village a number of times, including during the Franco-Prussian War (1870–71), when he stayed there to escape being drafted. In the early 1880s, he needed to be near his mother and sister in Aix-en-Provence as well as his mistress, Emélie-Hortense Fiquet, and their school-age son, Paul, in Marseilles. L'Estaque provided a geographical and emotional refuge; it also served as the setting for some of his grandest landscapes, second only to his views of Mont Sainte-Victoire. Writing to his childhood friend the author Émile Zola in 1883, Cézanne remarked that he was renting a house and had found some beautiful views, although he was still looking for "motifs." He would eventually discover one in the view seen in this painting, from a hillside adjacent to the village, looking down on its irregular coastline and toward Marseilles. Across the bay, at the bottom right, he depicted a chimney whose unexpected puff of smoke does not so much rise as blow sideways in the direction of the jetty at the upper left, suggesting an imaginary diagonal that divides the composition into sea, mountains, and sky on one side, and sea and houses nestled among trees and rocks on the other. Cézanne used a variety of brushstrokes—from the thickly banded marks of the sea to the wispy brushing in of the sky—and a palette of subtly modulated ochers and blues to convey what the scholar Meyer Schapiro deemed "a marvelous peace and strength . . . the true feeling of the Mediterranean."

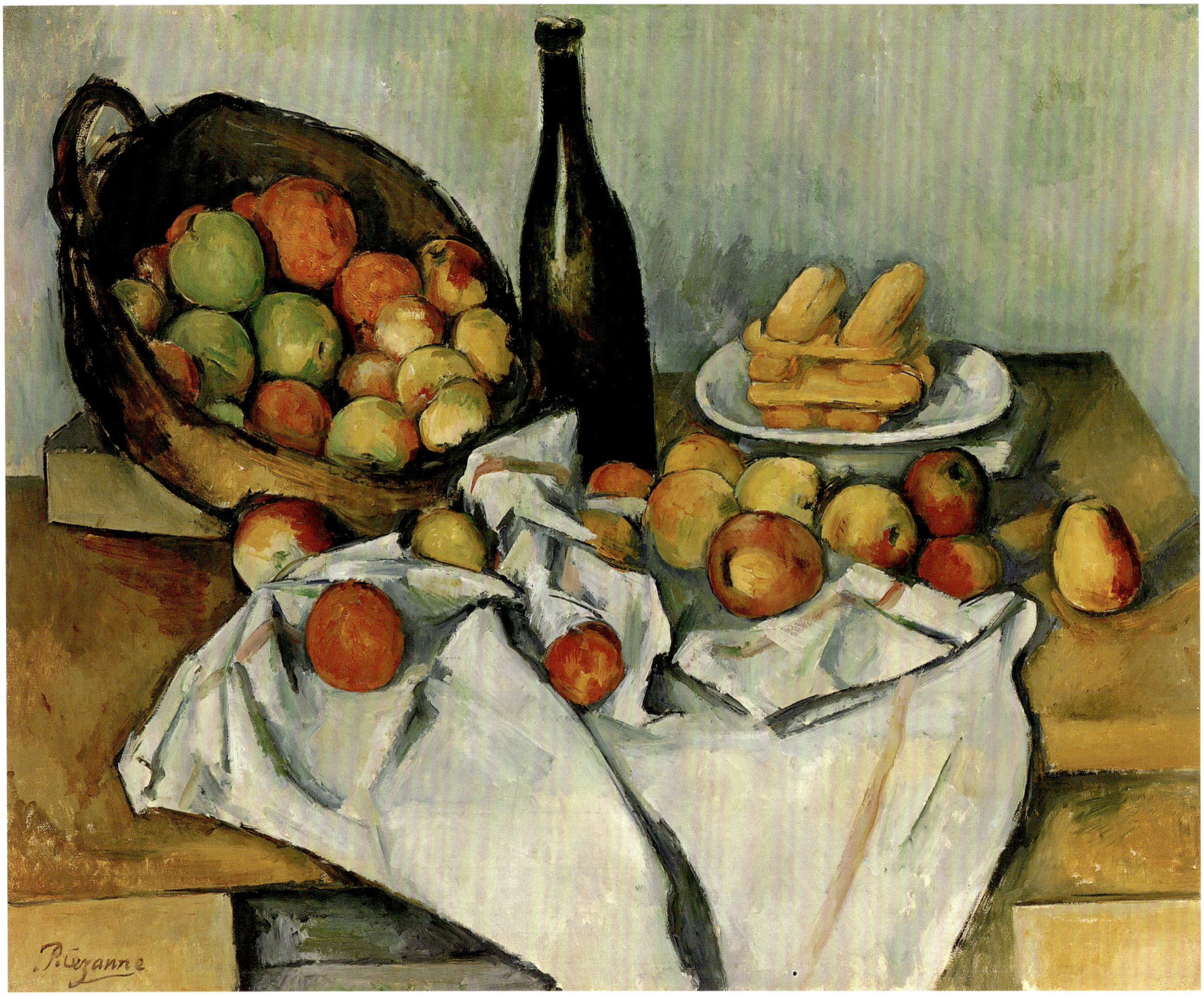
P.Cezanne

67

The Basket of Apples, c. 1893

Oil on canvas; 65 x 80 cm (25 7/16 x 31 1/2 in.)
Helen Birch Bartlett Memorial Collection, 1926.252
Signed lower left: *P. Cézanne*

Paul Cézanne probably signed this still life before sending it to his first one-man exhibition, in November 1895, which was organized by the fledgling art dealer Ambroise Vollard. The show provided artists and collectors with their first opportunity to appreciate the development of the reclusive artist working in Provence, who, for the most part, had turned away from the Paris art scene nearly twenty years earlier and whose works were only known through a few select collections. Even Cézanne's former colleagues, like Camille Pissarro, who owned a number of his paintings from the 1870s, found the show revelatory. Pissarro referred in particular to the "astonishing" and "irreproachable" perfection of the still lifes.

In *The Basket of Apples*, Cézanne's fascination with apples as three-dimensional forms is his true subject. The publisher, journalist, and collector Thadée Natanson probably had this work in mind when he reviewed the exhibition and noted that "[Cézanne] is and remains a painter of apples—apples that are smooth, round, fresh, ponderous, dazzling, of shifting color, not the ones you'd like to eat . . . but rather of forms that ravish. . . . He has made apples his own." No less than thirty of these seemingly uncontrollable geometric spheres populate the composition, beginning at the upper left and cascading down to the lower right, where a sole apple with a flattened side abruptly halts the diagonal movement.

The pieces of fruit appear to fall out of the tilted basket, which sits precariously on a wood slab or book, only to be checked and held in suspension by the deep valleys and peaks of the dish cloth crumpled on the slanting tabletop. Although this stiff, sculptural piece of fabric blocks movement and conveys a sense of permanence, it does little to counteract the overall implication of shifting and descending forms. Even the wine bottle, which appears at first to serve as a vertical axis that anchors the composition, lists slightly; it recalls the odd tilt of Mme Cézanne in the Art Institute's portrait of her (cat. 64) and contributes to an overriding sense of instability, of things momentarily suspended in place.

The precarious balance of elements in this not-still still life is particularly apparent in the ladyfinger biscuits, carefully layered on the plate at the right and set against a darker blue patch that distinguishes them from the turquoise background. Their shadow appears to connect with the wine bottle (already a tilting object), and their ability to maintain the latticelike arrangement seems physically impossible outside of art. Cézanne's balancing act of contradictories extends to the palette, which is dominated by blues and oranges.

His use of pronounced contours in some places and sketchy and "broken" ones in others, along with the fact that the tabletop emerges on the right side at a different level than on the left, adds to the quality of impermanence and, most importantly, underscores the deliberative nature of art making. It is clear that here, and in other compositions of this time, Cézanne was involved in a critical rethinking of form, space, and perception. It was these experimentations with fragmenting reality that led Pablo Picasso to declare that the older artist was "my one and only master . . . the father of us all."

The Basket of Apples was the first work by Cézanne to enter to the Art Institute's collection. It was also singled out early on as one of the artist's masterpieces when Maurice Denis included it, along with a portrait of Cézanne, in his mural decoration *History of the Arts in France*, for the Dutuit dome in the Petit Palais, Paris (1924/25).

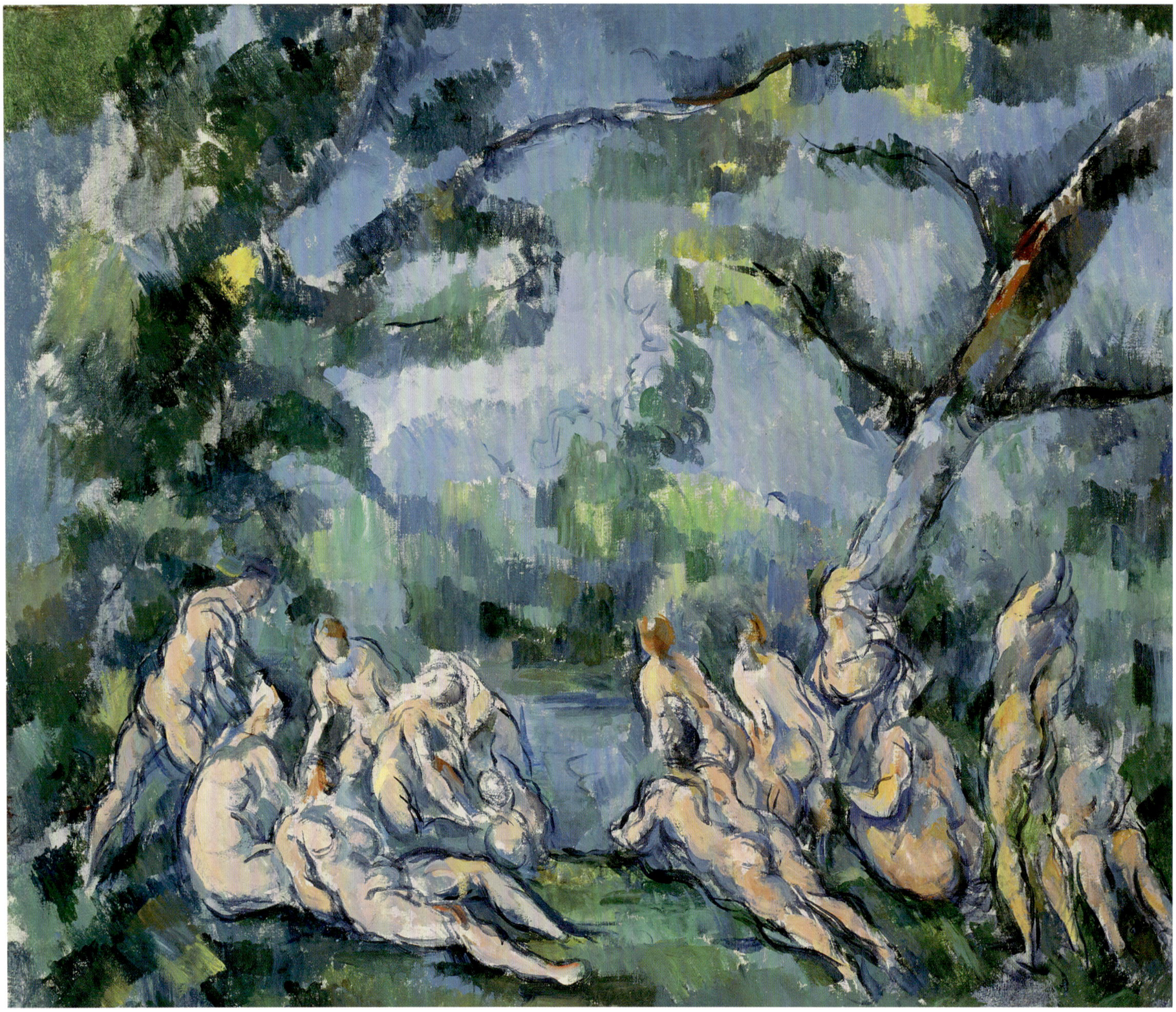

68

The Bathers, 1899/1904

Oil on canvas; 51.3 x 61.7 cm (20 3/16 x 24 1/4 in.)
Amy McCormick Memorial Collection, 1942.457

In the 1870s, Paul Cézanne made his first attempts to depict nudes out of doors, initiating a meditation on this traditional subject that would preoccupy him on and off over the next three decades. Although he painted a few mythological scenes with nudes, he dealt with this theme primarily in his *Bathers* canvases, which rarely show figures actually bathing. Instead, he struggled to achieve a pictorial resolution—based on composition, construction, and palette—between classical iconography and his modernist viewpoint.

The Art Institute's *The Bathers* belongs to the last of Cézanne's three chronological phases of work on the theme: the first focused on single figures; the second, on male or female figures grouped closely together; and the third, beginning in the 1890s, included large and complex multifigure compositions. Among the paintings from this last phase are two monumental canvases that were considered unfinished at the artist's death in 1906: *Large Bathers*, in the National Gallery of London (1894–1905); and an even larger canvas of the same title in the Philadelphia Museum of Art (1906). Both include several of the female figures that appear in the much smaller and sketchier Chicago painting.

Although this canvas has been described as an intermediary study for the larger compositions, it is also very much an independent picture, with freer and more lighthearted brushwork that sets it apart from the laboriously worked larger versions. It shares with them the general setting and the group of females lying, bending, stooping, and standing in the foreground, but it has none of their ponderous gravitas. It is as if the artist lightly skipped his brush over the surface, patching in areas of foliage in parallel strokes and dabbing the flesh tones for the female figures, whose contours are barely indicated by the agitated, broken blue lines. Indeed, in some cases, the gender of these figures would be difficult to determine were it not for the comparison with the other larger canvases, which show the women's cascading hair and solidly defined torsos. Common to all three compositions are the lunging female at the left, two red-haired figures just right of the center, who seem ready to plunge into the water, and a woman lying on her belly to the right of the center.

Only the Chicago picture, however, includes the sprawling female third from the left, who does not fit into the iconography of any of the other *Bathers* paintings. She holds herself up on her forearms in a pose recalling Édouard Manet's *Olympia*—the highly charged depiction of a prostitute that had already inspired earlier paintings by Cézanne. The woman's pose could also have been drawn from any number of reproductions the artist owned or drawings he had made in the Musée du Louvre, Paris, as a student. For, unlike his still lifes, portraits, and landscapes, Cézanne conceived of and created his *Bathers* from his mind and memory, treating them as pictorial symbols evoking the Old Masters he so admired, to be integrated and harmonized into the familiar landscape of Provence.

The Chicago painting, for all its compositional complexity, evokes the lightness of a watercolor, especially in the thin parallel strokes and dashes and the ample areas of white-primed canvas that Cézanne allowed to show through. Although clearly related, it is not a study for either monumental composition but rather an exploratory work, similar to Georges Seurat's small oil on panel studies (see cats. 50–51). In Cézanne's case, he was still working on the final resolution at his death, so it is in his small oil paintings and watercolors, conceived en route to the large *Bathers* canvases, that one can appreciate the artist's quest to rethink classical iconography in a modern visual idiom.

GAUGUIN AND THE SOUTH SEAS

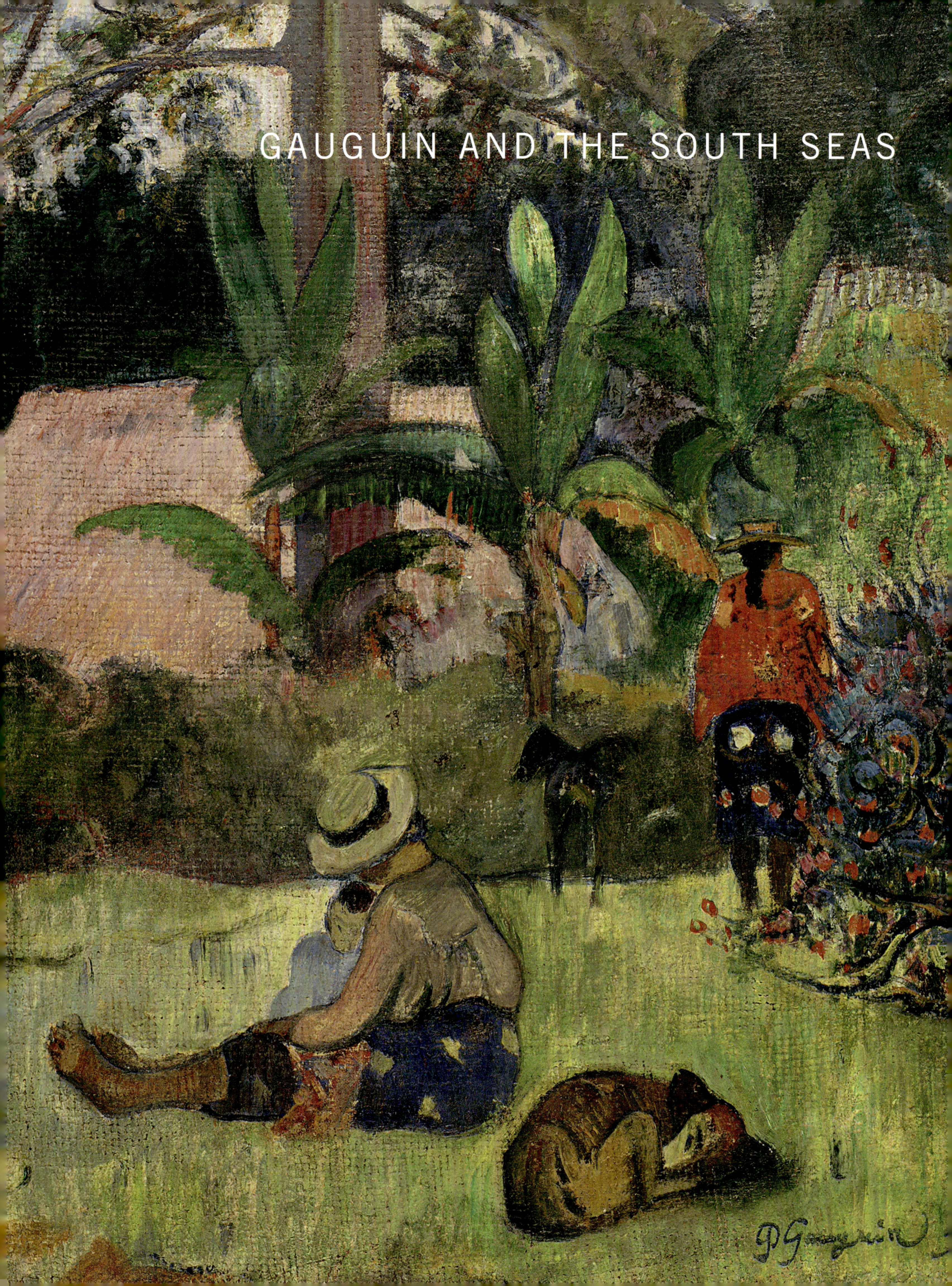

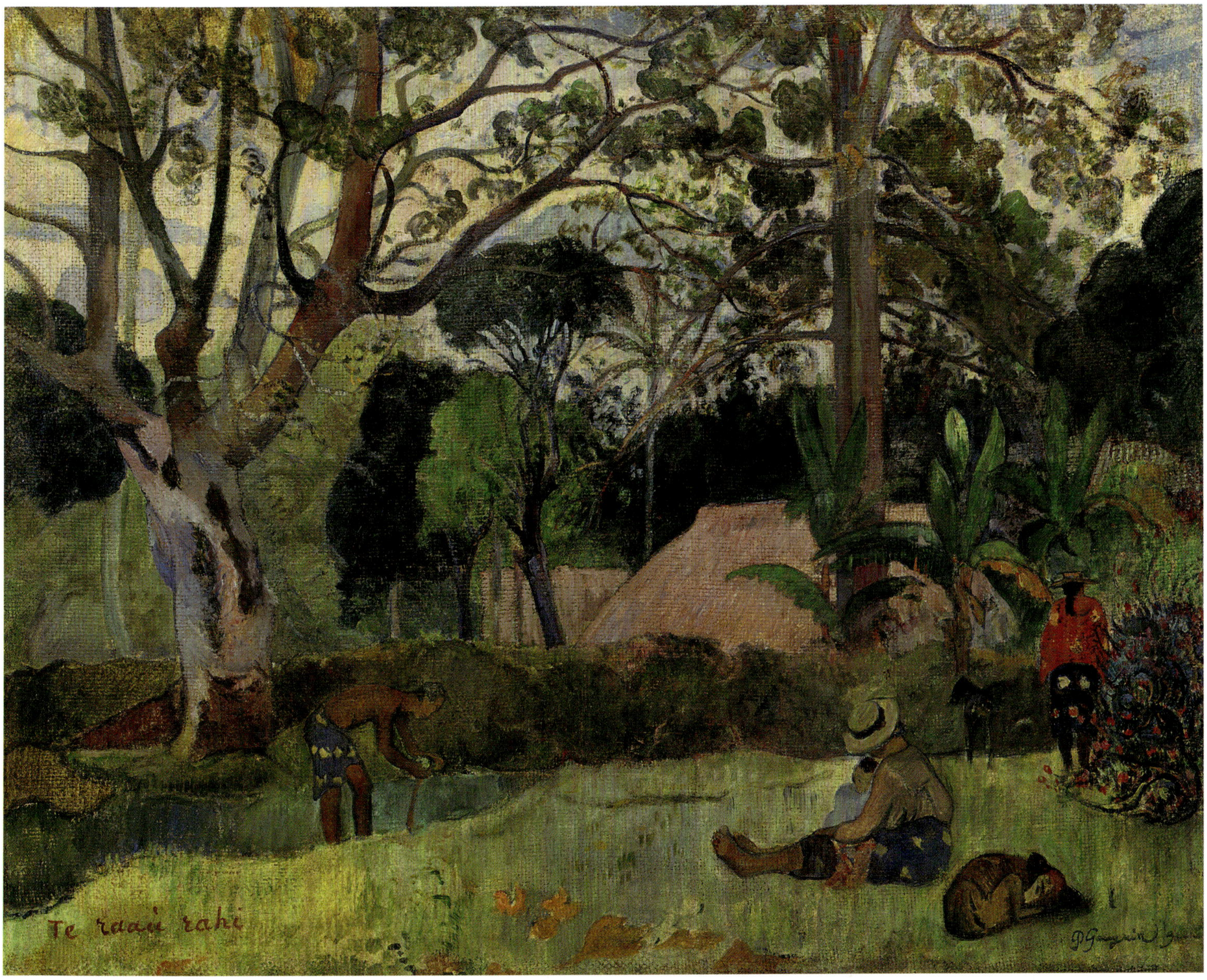

69

The Big Tree (Te raau rahi), 1891

Oil on jute; 73 x 91.5 cm (28¾ x 36 in.)
Gift of Kate L. Brewster, 1949.513
Signed lower right: *P Gauguin 91*
Inscribed lower left: *Te raaù rahi*

Paul Gauguin painted this landscape in the fall of 1891 in Tahiti, where he had arrived in June, using a coarse jute support and a range of paint applications, from thin washes of color to low impasto in the sky and foliage. The picture grew out of the artist's initial period of study of local flora and fauna, which is reflected in his drawings and echoed in his early reports home. Rather than painting, he explained, he was carrying out "a pile of research that will bear fruit, many documents that will serve me for a long time." Such research informs *The Big Tree*, which, though picturesque, reveals Gauguin's attention to local nature and practices. It features, at left, a violet-trunked *hotu* tree and, between the huts, a tall, thin mango tree and an even taller spindly coconut (*haari*); large green leaves of banana (*tunu maia*) trees form a screen at the right, behind which rises a majestic tropical almond (*auteraa*); at the right edge, the red blossoms of a peacock-like hibiscus shrub add a note of color, and breadfruit (*uru*) leaves dot the foreground. A native man husks a coconut, and one woman looks after a child while another performs chores in the background. *Te raau rahi*, the Tahitian title that Gauguin inscribed at the lower left, means "the big tree"—the translation that the artist supplied to his wife, Mette. It also refers to the use of plants for medicinal purposes, suggesting the artist's awareness of the role of the natural setting in the Tahitian domestic narrative: how the indigenous people used the nuts and leaves of the *auteraa* tree and the pods and flowers of the *hotu* tree as remedies. Here Gauguin rendered both varieties with an exactitude that is remarkable given his parallel interest in overall decorative effect.

Late Monet: The Series Paintings

GIVERNY

OUTSIDE FRANCE

WATER LILIES

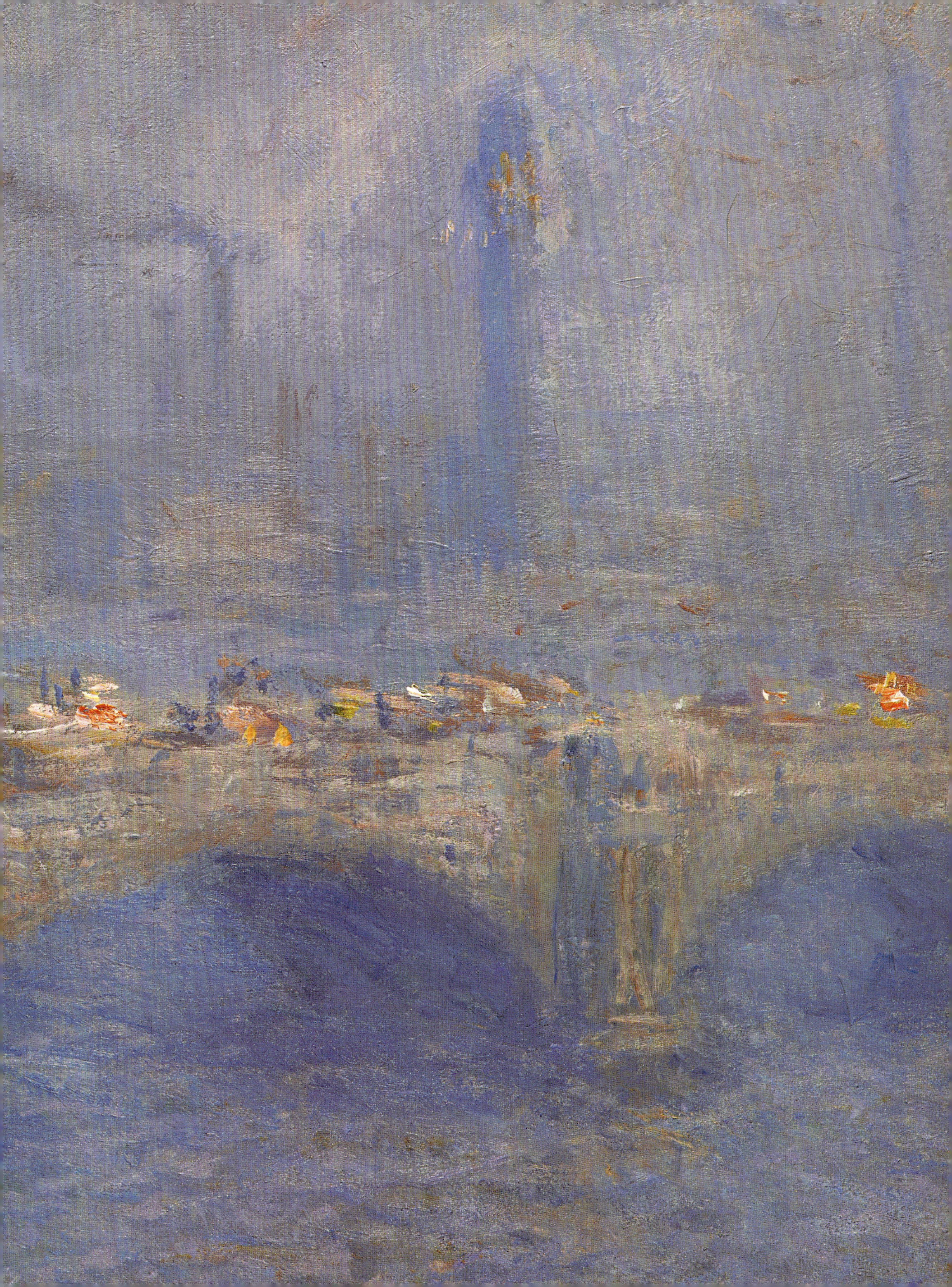

GIVERNY

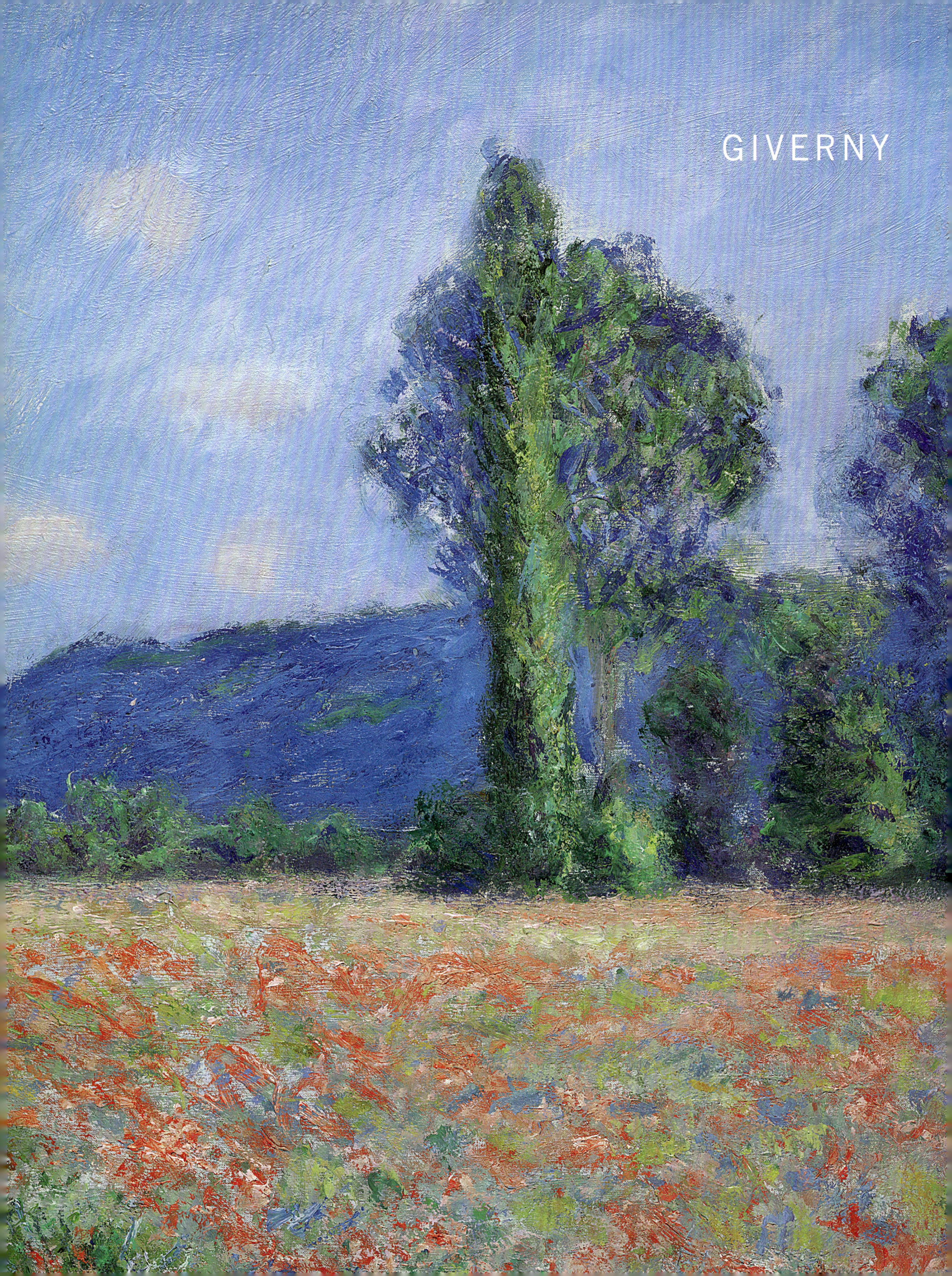

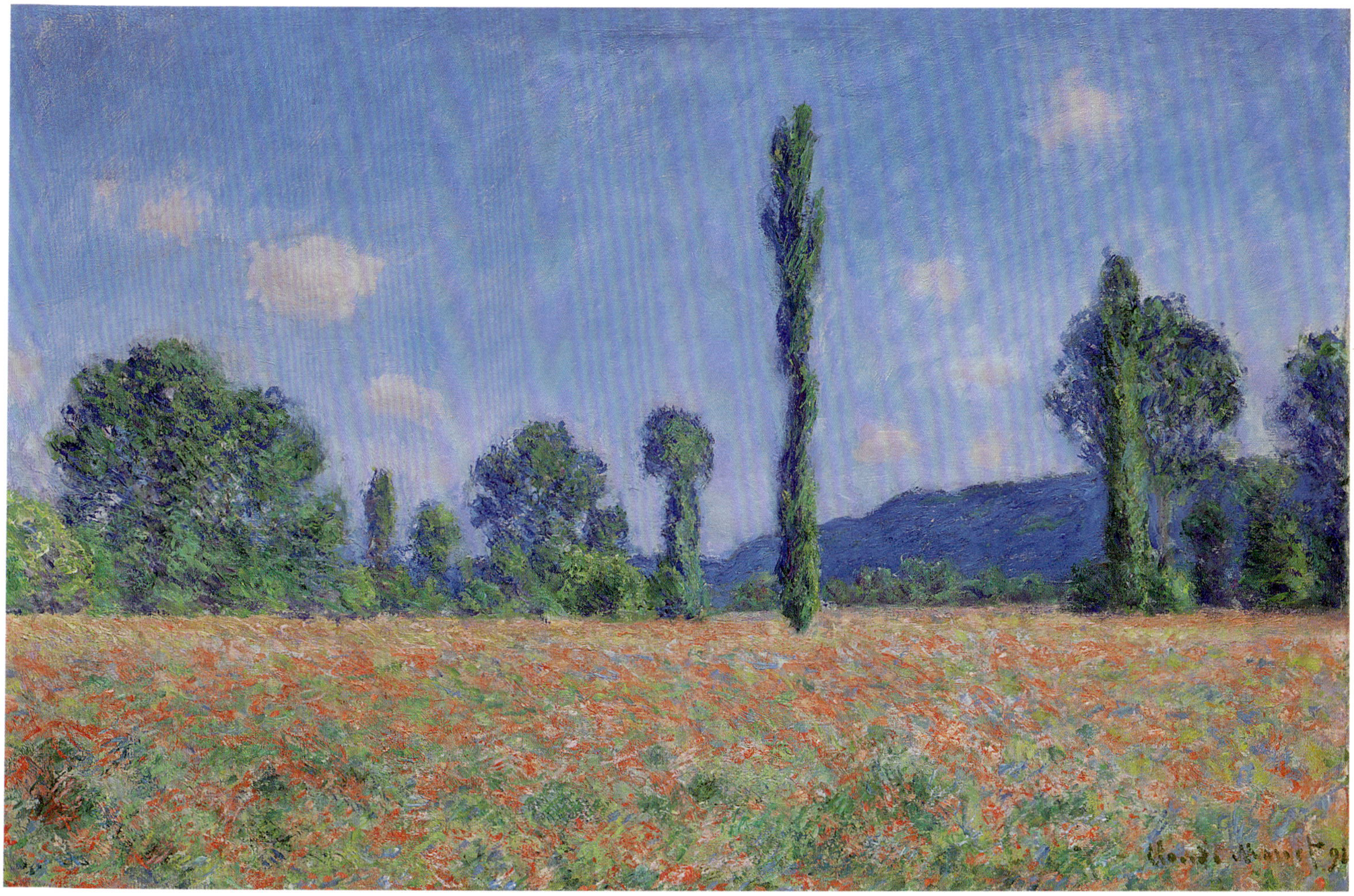

74

Poppy Field (Giverny), 1890–91

Oil on canvas; 61.2 x 93.1 cm (24 1/16 x 36 5/8 in.)
Mr. and Mrs. W. W. Kimball Collection, 1922.4465
Signed lower right: *Claude Monet 91*

In 1887 Claude Monet began painting subjects that were visible from his backyard in Giverny. These included a few stacks of wheat (1888–89), a pond (1887–89), and poppy fields, which he depicted in four almost identically scaled canvases undertaken in July 1890. Although they are compositionally and chromatically similar, the artist did not consider the poppy-field pictures serial works in the same way as the twenty-five paintings of stacks of wheat that he began shortly after the harvest that same summer. What this miniseries did reveal, however, was his growing interest in expressing nature using relatively homogenous touches and developing several canvases at once. Monet's future biographer, the politician and journalist Georges Clemenceau, who visited the artist while he was at work on these canvases, believed that they constituted "a new way of seeing, of feeling, of expression—a revolution."

Monet was now not just painting variants of a subject but rather the same motif from the same viewpoint, its differences nuanced only by changes in light. Here the varied light effects color the poppies orange, orange-yellow, and fiery red, contrasting them with the green trees fringing the horizon and the blue hills at the right. Conceived to translate a particular temporal condition, this painting bears little resemblance to Monet's sketchlike and more freely brushed landscapes of the 1870s. Instead, the surface has a tapestry-like materiality that recalls Georges Seurat's use of divided color in his canvases from the mid-1880s (see cats. 50–51). *Poppy Field*'s dense and reworked surface, along with the fact that the artist dated it 1891, suggests a long gestation period. This is typical of his later major series, in which he explored the possibilities of painting a simple motif from the same viewpoint with varying degrees of surface complexity.

OUTSIDE FRANCE

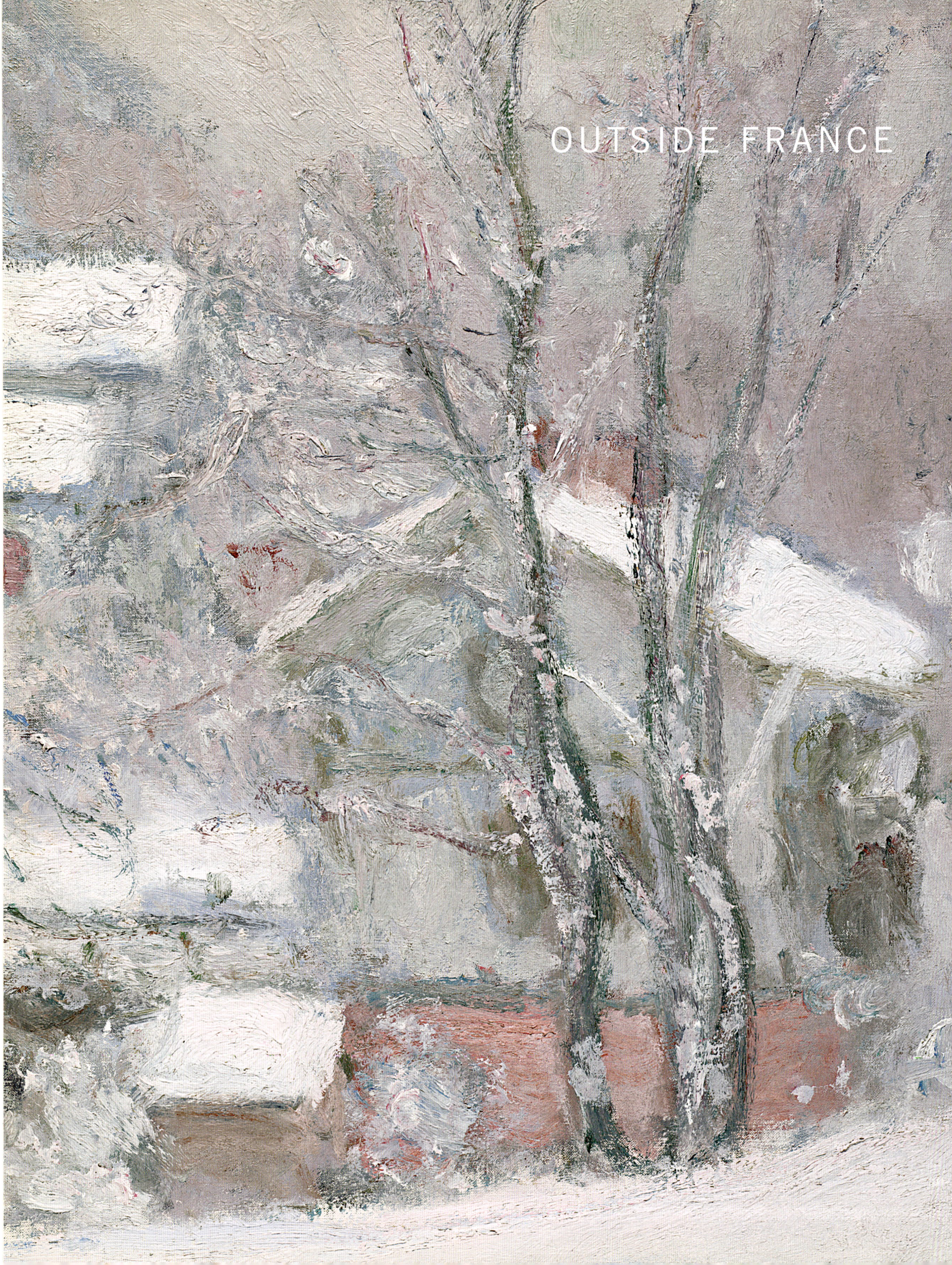

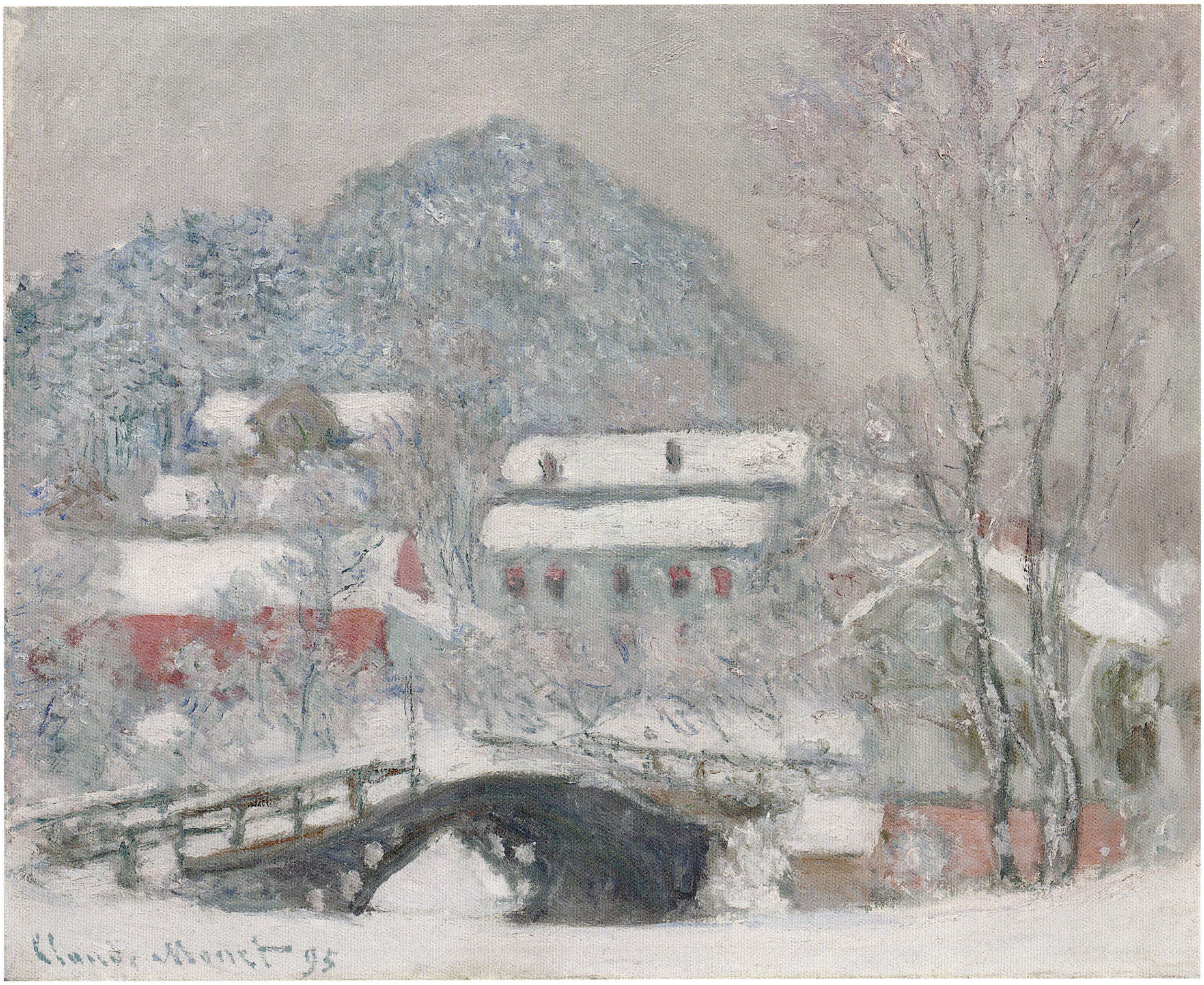

84

Sandvika, Norway, 1895

Oil on canvas; 73.4 x 92.5 cm (28⅞ x 36⅜ in.)
Gift of Bruce Borland, 1961.790
Signed lower left: *Claude Monet 95*

Among Claude Monet's most physically taxing and unusual painting campaigns was his trip to Norway. Over two months, he painted twenty-nine canvases, including at least six views of the village of Sandvika. With his stepson Jacques Hoschedé, who had resided in Christiania (now Oslo) since June 1894, as cicerone, Monet toured the snowbound landcapes, awe-struck and then frustrated in his struggle to find a theme amid the snow. He finally settled in Sandvika, a village less than an hour from Christiania, and painted the blue and red houses with snow-covered roofs and the iron bridge of Lokken—the latter reminiscent of the Japanese-style bridge on his property at Giverny, which he had depicted covered in snow a few weeks before departing for Norway.

The Art Institute's canvas, dominated by pinks and whites, was probably sufficiently finished before the inevitable thaw, which Monet dreaded because of how it would transform his snowy motifs. Returning to Giverny at the beginning of April, the artist bypassed his customary studio reworking and allowed eight canvases—six views of Mount Kolsaas and two of Sandvika (including this one)—to be shown a month later with scenes from Normandy and his views of Rouen Cathedral. Although Monet would insist that his Norwegian subjects were unfinished, *Sandvika* is signed, dated, and solidly painted. It is possible that he continued to work on it, but by 1899 Monet considered the painting "the best thing" he owned and donated it to an auction benefiting the family of Alfred Sisley, who had died that year. The rest of the works from this series remained with the artist: indeed, *Sandvika*, given to the Art Institute in 1961, was the first of Monet's Norwegian paintings to enter a public institution.

CLAUDE MONET French, 1840–1926

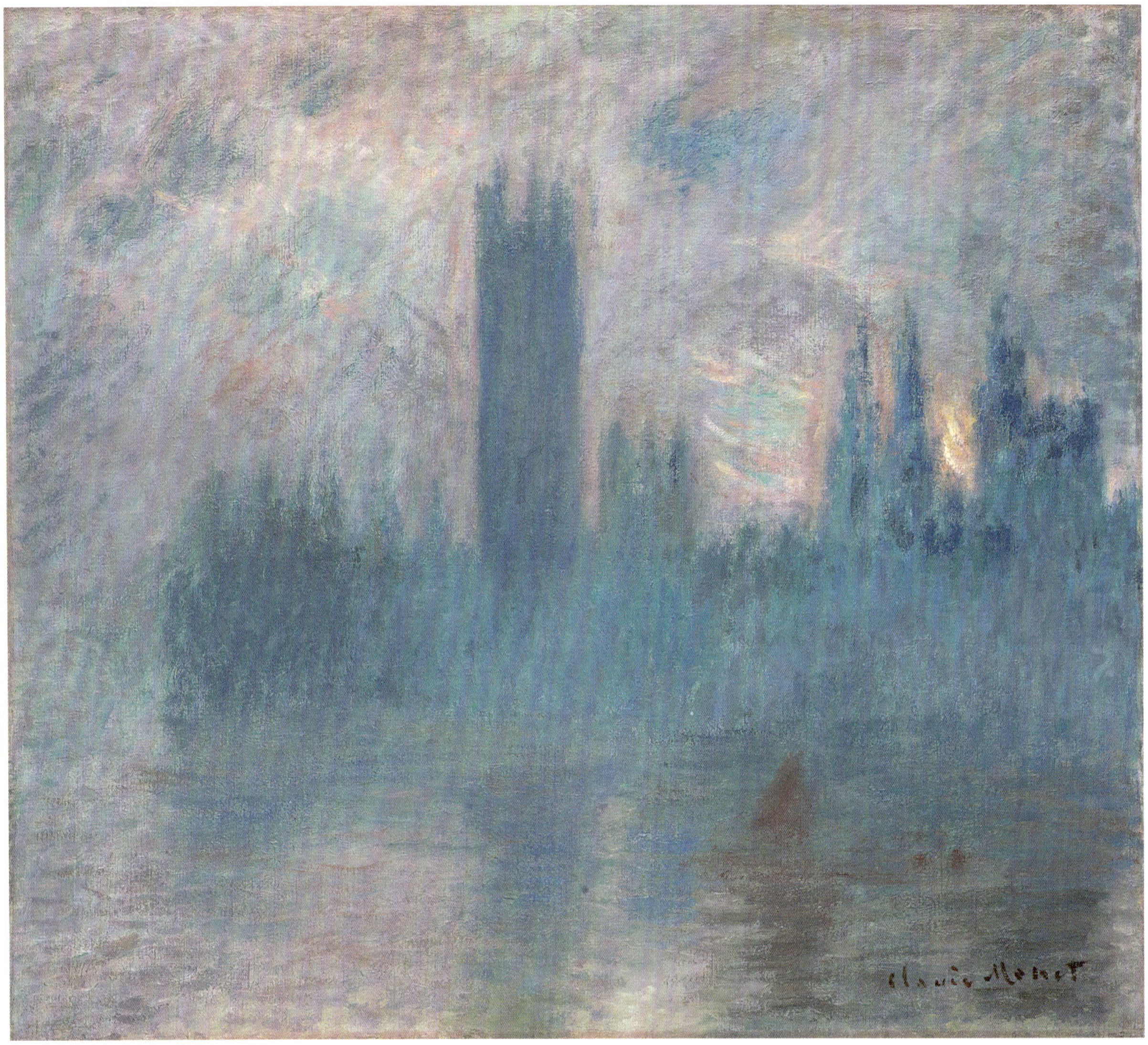

88

Houses of Parliament, London, 1900–01

Oil on canvas; 81 x 92 cm (31 ⅞ x 36 ¼ in.)
Mr. and Mrs. Martin A. Ryerson Collection, 1933.1164
Signed lower right: *Claude Monet*

Claude Monet began his series on the fantastical Neo-Gothic Houses of Parliament at the beginning of his second trip to London. On February 14, 1900, he reported to his wife, Alice, that he "had started work at the hospital. If only you could see how beautiful it was." The hospital he referred to was St. Thomas, where, thanks to Mary Hunter—the English collector whom he had met through the American painter John Singer Sargent—and her friend Dr. Joseph Payne, he had access to a large room and terrace on the opposite bank of the river Thames from the Savoy Hotel, close to Westminster Bridge. As always, Monet's excitement about this new prospect was mitigated by anticipated difficulties, but in actuality these paintings seem to have caused him few problems and were apparently the most satisfactory of all his London series. Not only did he exhibit a larger proportion of these canvases at the Durand-Ruel Gallery in 1904, but he also asked 20,000 francs for them rather than the 15,000 francs at which the other works in the exhibition were priced. The Art Institute's *Houses of Parliament* was not shown among these, although it displays no signs of having been reworked at a later stage. Monet painted all the *Parliament* canvases in the late afternoon or at sunset, so that the backlit pinnacles and towers convey an immutable, iconic quality in contrast to the rushing trains and carriages that animate and modernize his depictions of bridges. The artist was undoubtedly thinking of the poetic *Nocturnes* of James McNeill Whistler, as well as the famous *Parliament Houses* of Joseph Mallord William Turner, both of which dissolved objective references with sweeping chromatic harmonies. But the apparitional quality of Monet's Neo-Gothic buildings, which he painted in closely ranged hues that make them appear to loom out of the fog, also shows his assimilation of contemporary Symbolist aesthetics, which championed mood, mystery, and emotional expression over description.

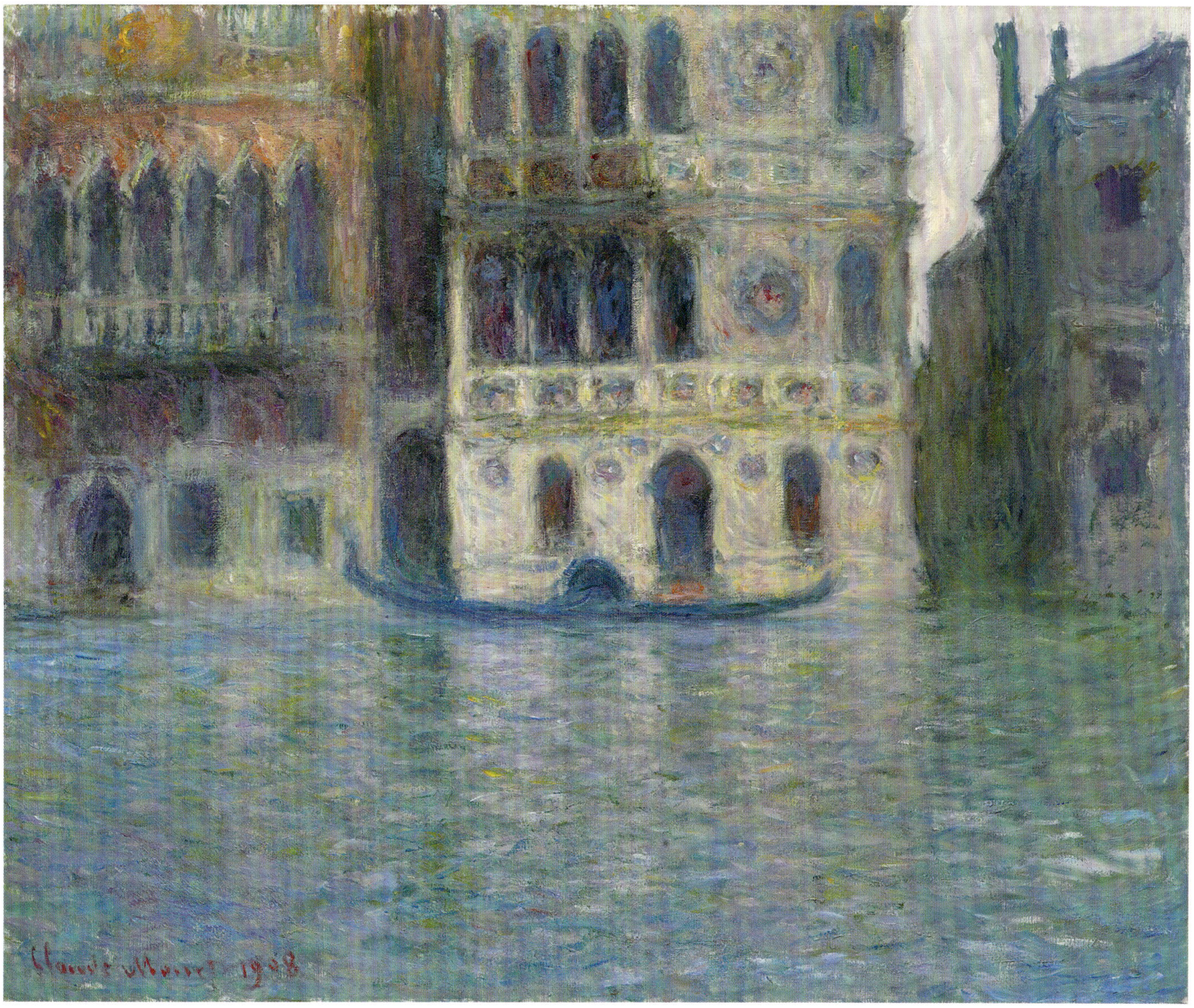

89

Venice, Palazzo Dario, 1908

Oil on canvas; 64.8 x 78.8 cm (25½ x 31 in.)
Mr. and Mrs. Lewis Larned Coburn Memorial Collection, 1933.446
Signed lower left: *Claude Monet 1908*

Claude Monet's final major thematic series of easel paintings was the result of his trip to Venice, where he and his wife, Alice, had been invited by Mary Hunter, who eight years earlier had helped arrange for the artist's use of a terrace at St. Thomas Hospital in London (see cat. 88). Although Monet visited London several times before his 1899–1901 campaigns, in Venice he was a tourist, following in the footsteps of John Singer Sargent, Joseph Mallord William Turner, and James McNeill Whistler, who had already painted its architecture, water, and brilliant light. Perhaps because he was exploring Venice while painting it, the artist chose ten different motifs for which he realized a total of thirty-seven paintings. Among these are the palazzi along the Grand Canal, including that of Giovanni Dario, secretary of the Venetian Senate, whose richly decorative fifteenth-century residence is the subject of this and three other canvases. Although Monet's painting of the palace shares with the London series similar elements of architecture, water, and mist, his aims were quite different here. Instead of dissolving the stone with broad directional strokes, he used smaller brushes and thicker pigments to highlight the prismatic marble facing that was the structure's distinguishing feature. While placing the palazzo off center, he put a gondola directly in front of its entryway. Like a gentle smile articulating the water's edge, the boat's bulbous cabin echoes the curved windows, whose deep shadows prevent any glimpse into the building's interior. Monet showed this and twenty-eight other Venetian scenes at the Bernheim-Jeune Gallery, Paris, in May 1912, but he remained dissatisfied with the series, in part because Alice's long illness (and death in May 1911) made it impossible for him to return to Venice and to the subject. He would freely admit, however, that his Venice paintings provided an important breakthrough for an entirely new kind of series: *Water Lilies*.

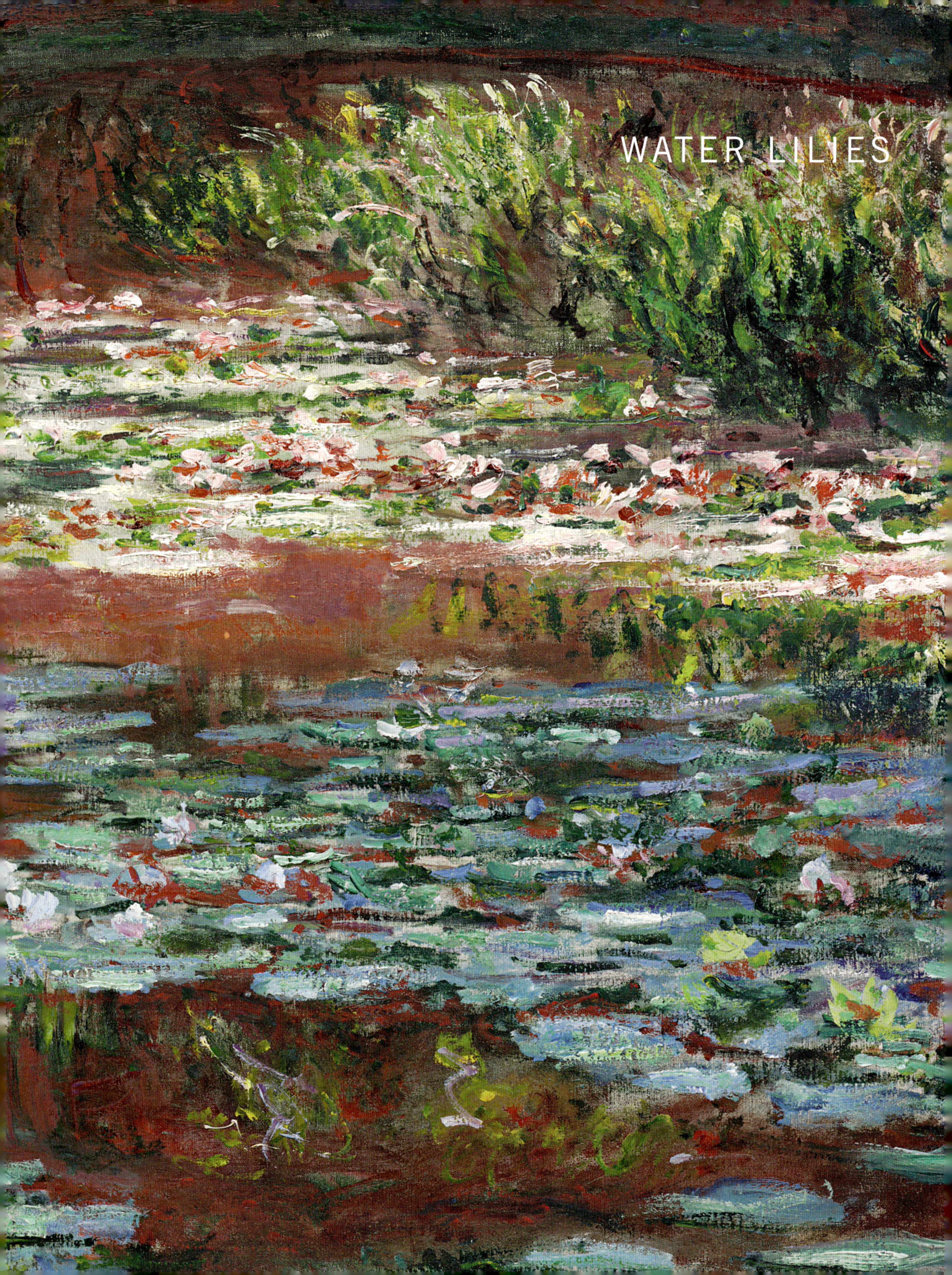
WATER LILIES

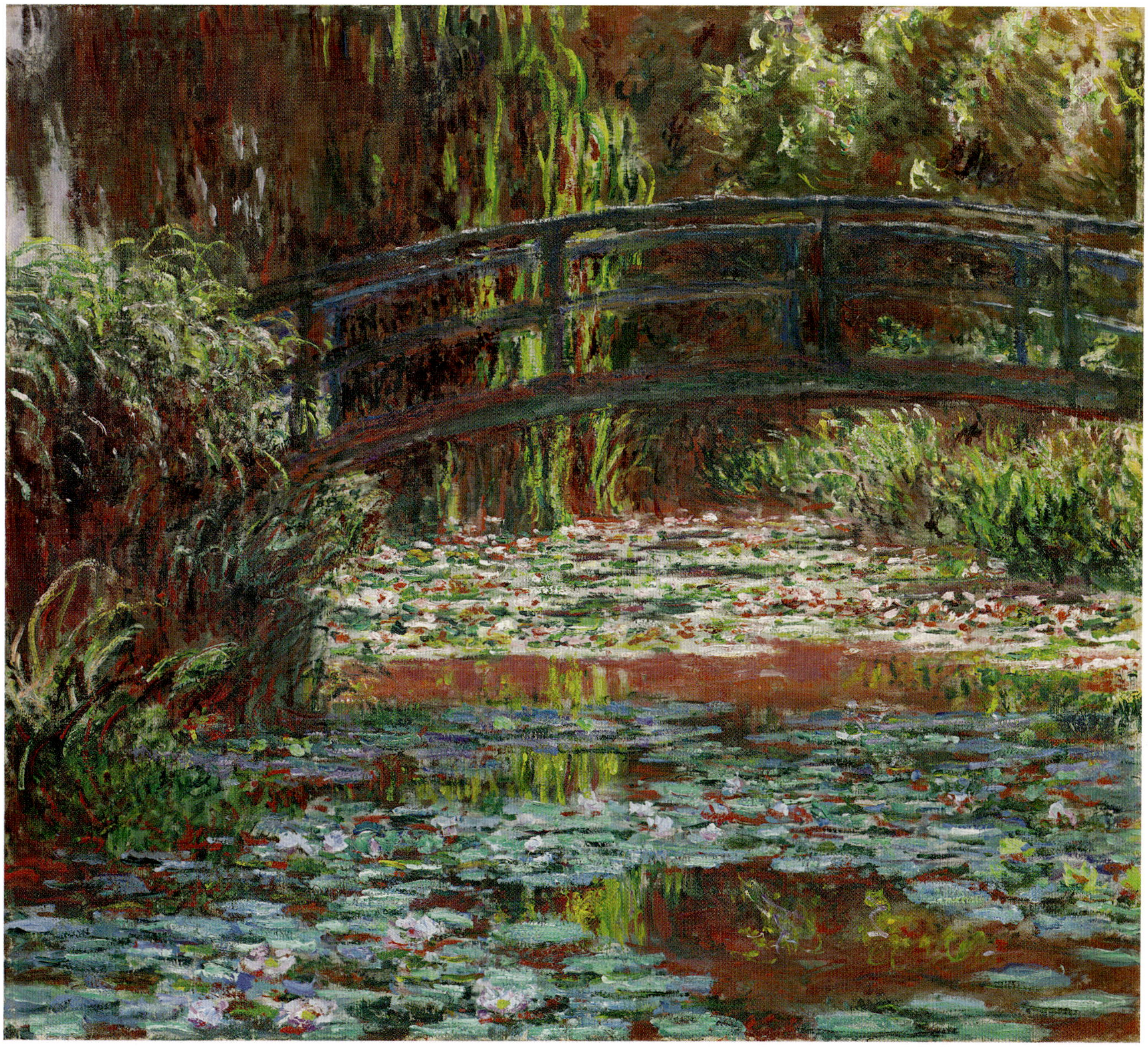

90

Water Lily Pond, 1900

Oil on canvas; 89.8 x 101 cm (35⅜ x 39¾ in.)
Mr. and Mrs. Lewis Larned Coburn Memorial Collection, 1933.441
Signed upper left: *Claude Monet / 1900*

In 1893, three years after buying property at Giverny, Claude Monet began transforming the marshy ground behind his home into a pond, on the narrow end of which he built a Japanese-style, arched wooden bridge. Adding both exotic and domestic plantings, including his famous water lilies, he set out to create the ideal garden, which would be among his principal subjects until his death in 1926. The Art Institute's *Water Lily Pond*, showing the green-painted bridge cut off at the right so that it seems to float across the pool of lilies, was among eighteen similar versions of the subject that the artist made between 1899 and 1900, twelve of which he showed in November–December 1900 at the Durand-Ruel Gallery. Although not included in this exhibition, the painting was signed, dated, and sold in December 1900, suggesting that Monet considered it complete and simply chose not to exhibit it. By 1900 he had added more plants to his pond, swelling the vegetation that hung over the water along the embankments, so that its reflection is confused with those of the aquatic plants that surge up toward the surface. It was this seamless continuum of surface and depth that the Belgian Symbolist poet Émile Verhaeren noted upon seeing the *Water Lilies* canvases. For him, Monet had created an alterative universe: "One senses the subterranean life at the bottom of the pool, the thick growth of roots; the intertwining of the stems, of which the flowers, massed on the surface, are only the continuation." In 1901 Monet enlarged the pond but abandoned the bridge motif (which he only took up again in 1918) to focus on the water lilies and their reflections.

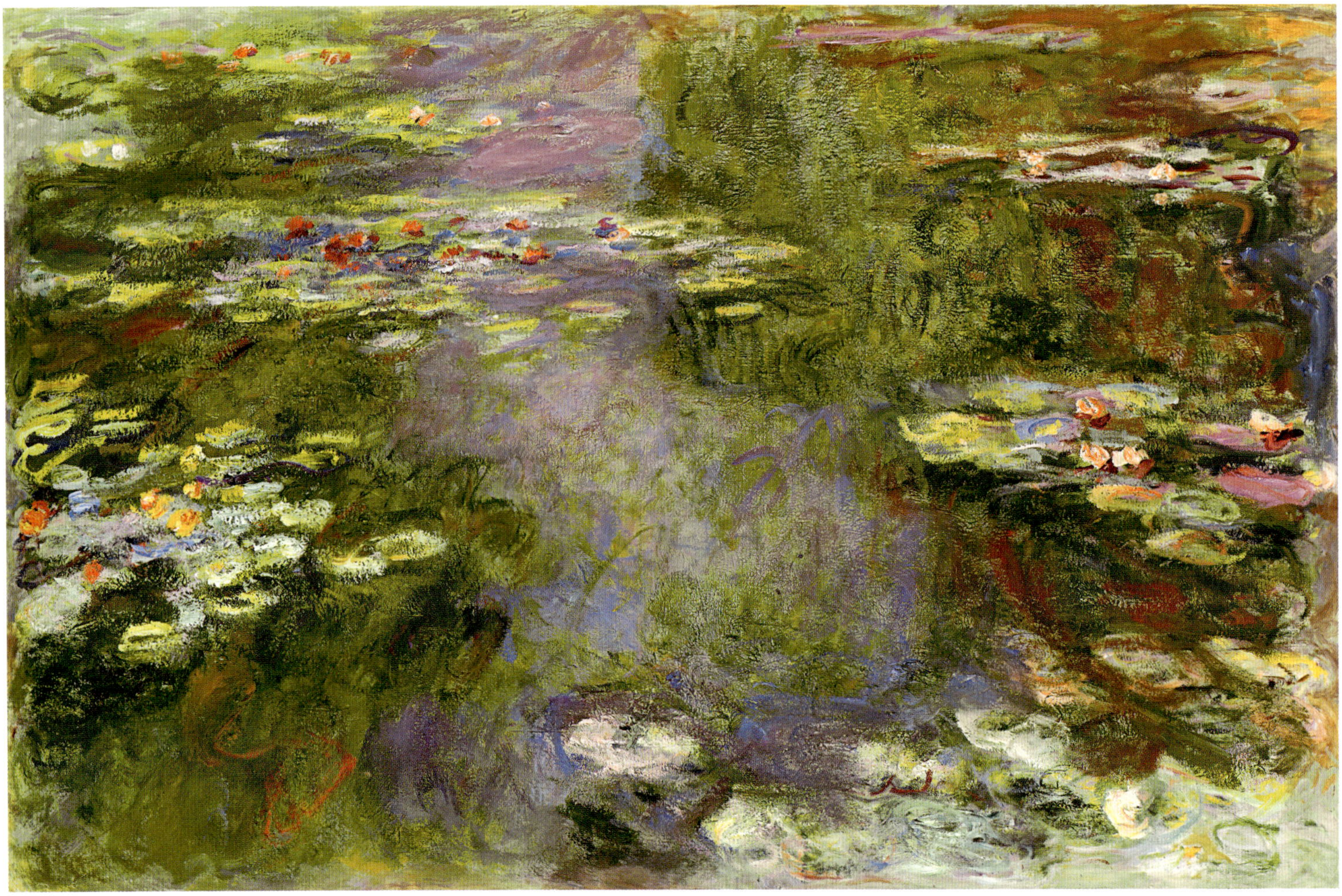

92

Water Lily Pond, 1917–22

Oil on canvas; 130.2 x 201.9 cm (51 ½ x 79 ½ in.)
Gift of Mrs. Harvey Kaplan, 1982.825

Following the outbreak of World War I, Claude Monet, who had not been able to work for several years because of his deteriorating health and his grief over the death of his wife, Alice, became immensely productive. Building a large studio and improving his garden, he entered an intense period of work focused on the monumental water-lilies cycle that he would later offer to the French state. Over the next twelve years, these canvases were extensively documented by journalists, photographers, collectors, and celebrities who paid homage to the Giverny master. Less well known are the nineteen smaller canvases that he painted between 1917 and 1922. These works, including the Art Institute's *Water Lily Pond*, occupy a pivotal role between the easel paintings that he completed by 1909 (see cat. 91) and the enormous murals on which he would embark in 1914. Monet envisioned the latter exhibited in elliptical rooms, an installation realized only in 1927 at the Orangerie in the Tuileries Gardens, Paris.

Although Monet worked on the Art Institute's painting and other canvases from this series while he was also making pictures double and triple them in size, the smaller compositions are not directly preparatory to his larger ones. In the smaller works, the artist moved from depicting single water lilies, willows, clouds, and their reflections to more personal, decorative compositions, in which the water-lily reflections are densely rendered and repeated rather than made to fit coloristically and compositionally with one another. There is evidence—including a few photographs that show Monet working by the pond—that these independent paintings were conceived out of doors and then reworked in the studio. In all of them, the sense of light, shade, and subaqueous vegetation surging upward seems as closely observed as in the earlier *Water Lilies* paintings, which are known to have been executed in part outside.

In the Art Institute's canvas, the fluid surface of the underlying water is interrupted with broad swirls of scumbled pigments similar to those found in other works in this series, such as *Water Lilies* (1919), in the Metropolitan Museum of Art, New York. It is as if the artist used this series of easel paintings to experiment with ways of transforming a carefully studied fragment of nature into a large artistic statement. Perhaps because of their personal nature and significance as an experimental detour from his larger mural project, Monet was reluctant to release them to dealers and collectors, allowing only five of the nineteen works to leave his studio during his lifetime. Signed and dated, the five attest to the artist's habit of personalizing his paintings as he sold or gave them away. At this time, Monet also "finished" (filled in) the compositions' edges (usually the bottom right) as an authorial sign-off, which, according to the artist, made no difference to the artwork but was expected by the buyer. The Art Institute's unsigned and undated *Water Lily Pond* has an unfinished edge, as do other canvases remaining in his possession at his death.

Only in the 1950s were these works eagerly pursued, at the moment when their large-scale, gestural brushwork would have appealed to collectors and curators who saw them as precursors to Abstract Expressionism. Unlike those post–World War II artists, whose aim was to express the subconscious through abstraction, Monet's final pictorial testaments—his water-lilies paintings and murals—were based entirely in nature. However, the distinction between indoors and outdoors, between observation and memory, had become meaningless for the artist in the last, inspired decade of his life.

SELECTED BIBLIOGRAPHY

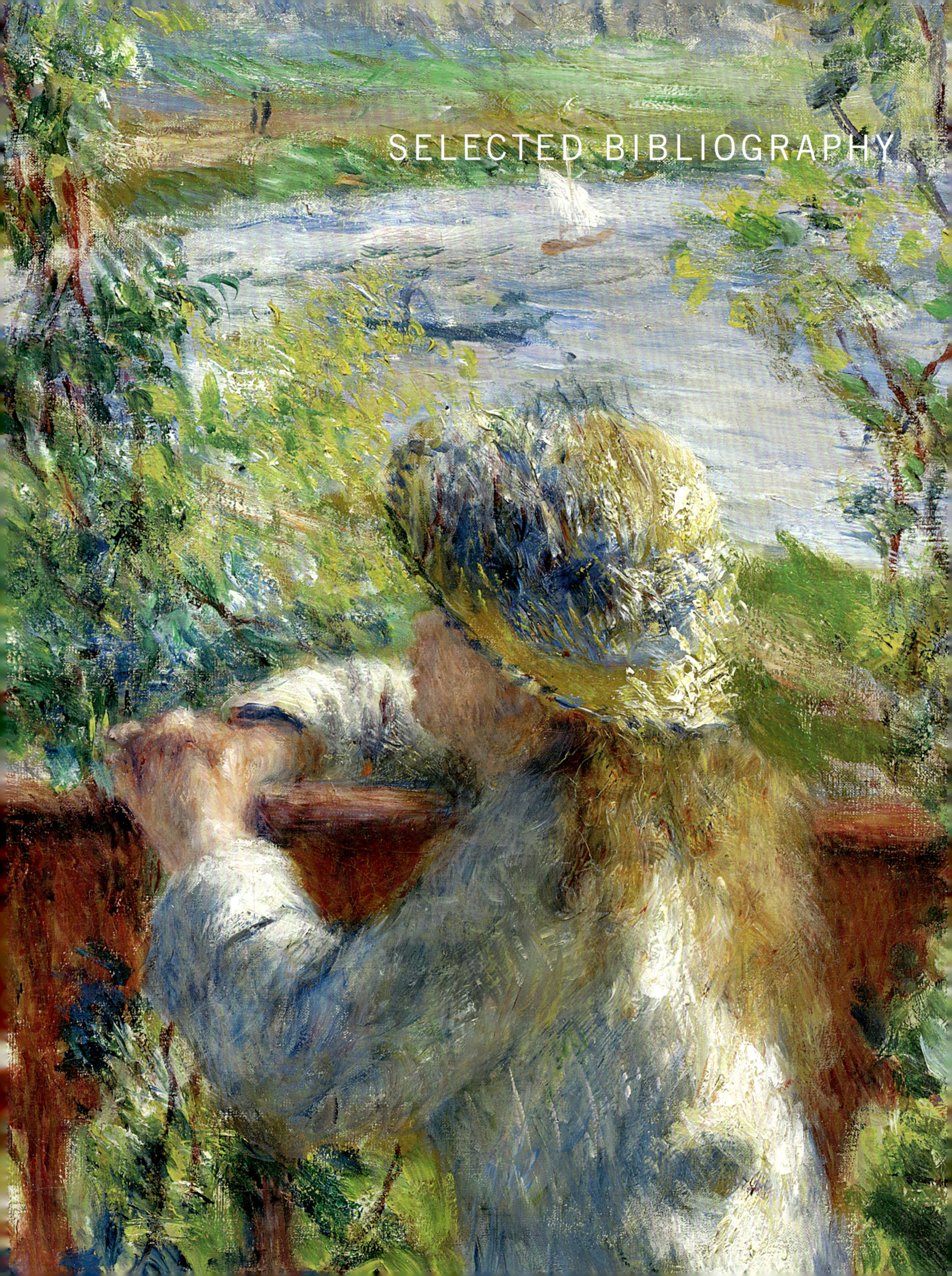

All references to the Art Institute as publisher are listed below as AIC.

BOOKS ON THE ART INSTITUTE'S HISTORY AND COLLECTION

Art Institute of Chicago. 1986. *The Helen Birch Bartlett Memorial Collection*. *Museum Studies* 12, 2.

———. 1986. *The Joseph Winterbotham Collection: A Living Tradition*. AIC.

———. 1988. *The Architecture of the Art Institute of Chicago*. *Museum Studies* 14, 1.

———. 1993. *One Hundred Years at the Art Institute: A Centennial Celebration*. *Museum Studies* 19, 1.

———. 2000. *Impressionism and Post-Impressionism in the Art Institute of Chicago*. AIC/Hudson Hills Press, Inc.

———. 2003. *Graphic Modernism: Selections from the Francey and Dr. Martin L. Gecht Collection at the Art Institute of Chicago*. Exh. cat. AIC/Hudson Hills Press, Inc.

———. 2006. *Master Paintings in the Art Institute of Chicago*. AIC/Yale University Press.

Boggs, Jean Sutherland. 1996. *Artists in Focus: Degas*. AIC/Harry N. Abrams, Inc.

Brettell, Richard R. 1987. *French Impressionists*. AIC/Harry N. Abrams, Inc.

———. 1987. *Post-Impressionists*. AIC/Harry N. Abrams, Inc.

Brettell, Richard R., and Suzanne Folds McCullagh. 1984. *Degas in The Art Institute of Chicago*. Exh. cat. AIC/Harry N. Abrams, Inc.

Druick, Douglas W. 1997. *Artists in Focus: Renoir*. AIC/Harry N. Abrams, Inc.

Forge, Andrew. 1995. *Artists in Focus: Monet*. AIC/Harry N. Abrams, Inc.

McCullagh, Suzanne Folds, ed. 2006. *Drawings in Dialogue: Old Master through Modern, the Harry B. and Bessie K. Braude Memorial Collection*. AIC/Yale University Press.

Rich, Daniel Catton. 1938. *Catalogue of the Charles H. and Mary F. S. Worcester Collection of Paintings, Sculpture, and Drawings*. Lakeside Press.

Salvesen, Britt, et al. 2001. *Artists in Focus: Gauguin*. AIC/Harry N. Abrams, Inc.

Thomson, Belinda. 2001. *Artists in Focus: Van Gogh*. AIC/Harry N. Abrams, Inc.

GENERAL BOOKS ON THE PERIOD

Brettell, Richard R., et al. 1984. *A Day in the Country: Impressionism and the French Landscape*. Exh. cat. Los Angeles County Museum of Art/Harry N. Abrams, Inc.

———. 2000. *Impression: Painting Quickly in France, 1860–1890*. Exh. cat. Sterling and Francine Clark Art Institute/Yale University Press.

Brettell, Richard R., with Natalie H. Lee. 1999. *Monet to Moore: The Millennium Gift of Sara Lee Corporation*. Yale University Press.

Gamboni, Dario. 2002. *Potential Images: Ambiguity and Indeterminacy in Modern Art*. Reaktion Books.

Herbert, Robert L. 1968. *Neo-Impressionism*. Exh. cat. Solomon R. Guggenheim Museum.

———. 1988. *Impressionism: Art, Leisure, and Parisian Society*. Yale University Press.

Johnston, Sona, ed. 1999. *The Faces of Impressionism: Portraits from American Collections*. Exh. cat. Baltimore Museum of Art, Museum of Art, Houston, and Cleveland Museum of Art/Rizzoli.

Moffett, Charles, et al. 1986. *The New Painting: Impressionism, 1874–1886*. Exh. cat. National Gallery of Art and Fine Arts Museums of San Francisco.

Rabinow, Rebecca A., ed. 2006. *Cézanne to Picasso: Ambroise Vollard, Patron of the Avant-Garde*. Exh. cat. Metropolitan Museum of Art/Yale University Press.

Schapiro, Meyer. 1997. *Impressionism: Reflections and Perceptions*. George Braziller.

Smith, Edward Lucie. 1989. *Impressionist Women*. Weidenfeld and Nicolson.

Smith, Paul. 1995. *Impressionism: Beneath the Surface*. Harry N. Abrams, Inc.

Sondergaard, Sidsel Maria, ed. 2006. *Women in Impressionism: From Mythical Feminine to Modern Woman*. Exh. cat. Ny Carlsberg Glyptotek/Skira.

Sturgis, Alexander, et al. 2006. *Rebels and Martyrs: The Image of the Artist in the Nineteenth Century*. Exh. cat. National Gallery Company Ltd./Yale University Press.

Tinterow, Gary, and Henri Loyrette. 1994. *Origins of Impressionism*. Exh. cat. Metropolitan Museum of Art/Harrry N. Abrams, Inc.

Torsten, Gunnarsson, et al. 2003. *Impressionism and the North: Late 19th-Century French Avant-Garde Art and Art in the Nordic Countries, 1870–1920*. Exh. cat. Nationalmuseum Stockholm.

BOOKS ON THE ARTISTS

BAZILLE

Jourdan, Aleth. 1992. *Frédéric Bazille: Prophet of Impressionism*. Exh. cat. Translated by John Goodman. Brooklyn Museum.

Pitman, Diane W. 1998. *Bazille: Purity, Pose and Paintings in the 1860s*. Pennsylvania State University Press.

BOUDIN

Hamilton, Vivien. 1992. *Boudin at Trouville*. Exh. cat. Glasgow Museums and Courtauld Institute Galleries/John Murray.

CAILLEBOTTE

Distel, Anne, et al. 1995. *Gustave Caillebotte: Urban Impressionist*. Exh. cat. Musée d'Orsay and AIC/Abbeville Press.

Varnedoe, Kirk. 1987. *Gustave Caillebotte*. Yale University Press.

CÉZANNE

Adriani, Götz. 1995. *Cézanne Paintings*. Translated by Russell Stockman. Harry N. Abrams, Inc.

Buren, Ann H. van. 1966. "Mme Cézanne's Fashions and the Dates of Her Portraits." *Art Quarterly* 9, 2, pp. 111–27.

Cachin, Françoise. 1996. *Cézanne*. Exh. cat. Harry N. Abrams, Inc., in association with Philadelphia Museum of Art.

Conisbee, Philip, et al. 2006. *Cézanne in Provence*. Exh. cat. National Gallery of Art/Yale University Press.

Howard, Michael. 1990. *Cézanne.* Bison Group.

Reff, Theodore. 1977. "Cézanne's Late Bather Paintings." *Arts Magazine* 52, 2 (October), pp. 116–19.

Rewald, John, Walter Feilchenfeldt, and Jayne Warman. 1996. *The Paintings of Paul Cézanne: A Catalogue Raisonné*. Harry N. Abrams, Inc.

R. M. F. 1926. "Cézanne, Rousseau, Picasso." *Art Institute of Chicago Bulletin* 20, 5 (May), pp. 61–64.

Shiff, Richard. 1978. "Seeing Cézanne." *Critical Inquiry* 4, 4 (Summer), pp. 769–808.

Verdi, Richard. 1990. *Cézanne and Poussin: The Classical Vision of Landscape*. Exh. cat. National Galleries of Scotland.

———. 1992. *Cézanne*. Thames and Hudson.

CROSS

Compin, Isabelle. 1964. *H. E. Cross*. Quatre Chemins-Editart.

Rewald, John. 1951. *Henri-Edmond Cross*. Exh. cat. Fine Arts Associates.

DEGAS

Baumann, Felix, and Marianne Karabelnik, eds. 1994. *Degas Portraits.* Exh. cat. Kunsthaus Zurich/Merrell Holberton Publishers.

Boggs, Jean Sutherland, et al. 1988. *Degas*. Exh. cat. Metropolitan Museum of Art and National Gallery of Canada.

Bomford, David, et al. 2004. *Art in the Making: Degas*. Exh. cat. National Gallery Company Ltd./Yale University Press.

DeVonyar, Jill, and Richard Kendall. 2002. *Degas and the Dance*. Exh. cat. American Federation of Arts/Harry N. Abrams, Inc.

Dumas, Ann, et al. 1997. *The Private Collection of Edgar Degas*. Exh. cat. Metropolitan Museum of Art/Harry N. Abrams, Inc.

———. 2002. "Degas: Sculptor/Painter." In *Degas Sculptures: Catalogue Raisonné of the Bronzes*, by Joseph S. Czestochowski and Anne Pingeot, pp. 39–47. International Arts/Torch Press.

Kendall, Richard. 1996. *Degas: Beyond Impressionism*. Exh. cat. National Gallery Publications in association with AIC.

Reff, Theodore. 1968. "Some Unpublished Letters of Degas." *Art Bulletin* 50, 1 (March), pp. 87–94.

Robins, Anna Gruetzner, and Richard Thomson. 2005. *Degas, Sickert, and Toulouse-Lautrec: London and Paris, 1870–1910*. Exh. cat. Tate Publishing.

FANTIN-LATOUR

Druick, Douglas, and Michel Hoog. 1983. *Fantin-Latour*. Exh. cat. National Gallery of Canada/National Museums of Canada.

GAUGUIN

Brettell, Richard R., et al. 1988. *The Art of Paul Gauguin*. Exh. cat. National Gallery of Art.

Druick, Douglas W., and Peter Kort Zegers, et al. 2001. *Van Gogh and Gauguin: The Studio of the South*. Exh. cat. AIC/Thames and Hudson.

Laudon, Paule. 2003. *Tahiti-Gauguin: Mythe et vérités*. Adam Biro.

Shackelford, George T. M., and Claire Frèches-Thory, et al. 2004. *Gauguin Tahiti*. Exh. cat. Museum of Fine Arts, Boston.

Wildenstein, Daniel, et al. 2001. *Gauguin: Premier itinéraire d'un sauvage, catalogue de l'oeuvre peint (1873–1888)*. 2 vols. Skira/Wildenstein Institute.

Wildenstein, Georges. 1964. *Gauguin*. Beaux-Arts.

VAN GOGH

Cachin, Françoise, and Bogomila Welsh-Ovcharov. 1988. *Van Gogh à Paris*. Exh. cat. Éditions de la Réunion des Musées Nationaux.

Dorn, Roland, George S. Keyes, and Joseph J. Rishel, et al. 2000. *Van Gogh Face to Face: The Portraits*. Exh. cat. Detroit Institute of Arts/Thames and Hudson.

Druick and Zegers, et al. 2001. *Van Gogh and Gauguin* (see Gauguin).

Hendriks, Ella, and Louis van Tilborgh. 2006. "New Views on Van Gogh's Development in Antwerp and Paris: An Integrated Art Historical and Technical Study of His Paintings in the Van Gogh Museum." 2 vols. Dissertation Universiteit van Amsterdam.

Hulsker, Jan. 1996. *The New Complete Van Gogh: Paintings, Drawings, Sketches; Revised and Enlarged Edition of the Catalogue Raisonné of the Works of Vincent van Gogh*. J. M. Meulenhoff/John Benjamins.

Pickvance, Ronald. 2000. *Van Gogh*. Exh. cat. Fondation Pierre Gianadda.

Uitert, Evert van, Louis van Tilborgh, Sjraar van Heugten. 1990. *Vincent van Gogh: Paintings*. Exh. cat. Rijksmuseum Vincent van Gogh/Rizzoli.

GONZALÈS

Grant, Carol Jane. 1994. "Eva Gonzalès (1849–1883): An Examination of the Artist's Style and Subject Matter." 2 vols. Ph.D. diss., Ohio State University.

JONGKIND

Sillevis, John, et al. 2003–04. *Johan Barthold Jongkind*. Exh. cat. Haags Gemeentemuseum, Wallraf-Richartz Museum—Fondation Corboud, and Musée d'Orsay.

MANET

Armstrong, Carol. 2002. *Manet Manette*. Yale University Press.

Hanson, Anne Coffin. 1966/67. *Édouard Manet, 1832–1883*. Exh. cat. Philadelphia Museum of Art and AIC.

Reff, Theodore. 1982. *Manet and Modern Paris*. Exh. cat. National Gallery of Art.

Tinterow, Gary, and Geneviève Lacambre, eds. 2003. *Manet/Velázquez: The French Taste for Spanish Painting*. Exh. cat. Metropolitan Museum of Art/Yale University Press.

Wilson-Bareau, Juliet. 1998. *Manet, Monet, and the Gare Saint-Lazare*. Exh. cat. Réunion des Musées Nationaux/Yale University Press.

Wilson-Bareau, Juliet, and David Degener. 2003. *Manet and the Sea*. Exh. cat. Philadelphia Museum of Art.

MONET

Baillio, Joseph, ed. 2007. *Claude Monet (1840–1926): A Tribute to Daniel Wildenstein and Katia Granoff*. Exh. cat. Wildenstein.

Clarke, Michael, and Richard Thomson. 2003. *Monet: The Seine and the Sea, 1878–1883*. Exh. cat. National Galleries of Scotland.

Hellandsjø, Karin, et al. 1995. *Monet in Norway: Exhibition to Mark the Centenary of Claude Monet's Visit to Norway During the Winter of 1895*. Exh. cat. Rogaland Kunstmuseum and Musée Rodin.

House, John. 1986. *Monet: Nature into Art*. Yale University Press.

———, et al. 2005. *Monet's London: Artists' Reflections on the Thames, 1859–1914*. Exh. cat. Museum of Fine Arts, St. Petersburg, Florida/Snoeck.

Isaacson, Joel. 1978. *Claude Monet: Observation and Reflection*. Phaidon.

Kendall, Richard, ed. 1989. *Monet by Himself*. Mcdonald Orbis.

Koja, Stephan. 1996. *Claude Monet*. Exh cat. Translated by John Brownjohn. Österreichische Galerie/Prestel.

Lemonedes, Heather, Lynn Federle Orr, David Steel, et al. 2006. *Monet in Normandy*. Exh. cat. Fine Arts Museums of San Francisco/Rizzoli.

Moffett, Charles. 1981. "Monet's Haystacks." In *Aspects of Monet: A Symposium on the Artist's Life and Times*, edited by John Rewald and Frances Weitzenhoffer, pp. 142–59. Harry N. Abrams, Inc.

Pissarro, Joachim. 1997. *Monet and the Mediterranean*. Exh. cat. Kimbell Art Museum/Rizzoli.

Seiberling, Grace. 1976. "Monet's Series." Ph.D. diss., Yale University.

Stuckey, Charles F., ed. 1985. *Monet: A Retrospective*. Hugh Lauter Levin Associates.

———. 1995. *Claude Monet, 1840–1926*. Exh. cat. AIC/Thames and Hudson.

Tucker, Paul Hayes. 1989. *Monet in the '90s: The Series Paintings*. Exh. cat. Museum of Fine Arts, Boston/Yale University Press.

———. 1996. *Monet in Norway*. Exh. cat. Ordrupgaard.

———, et al. 1998. *Monet in the 20th Century*. Exh. cat. Yale University Press.

Wildenstein, Daniel. 1996. *Monet*. 4 vols. Taschen.

Wilson-Bareau. 1998. *Manet, Monet, and the Gare Saint-Lazare* (see Manet).

MORISOT

Higonnet, Anne. 1992. *Berthe Morisot's Images of Women.* Harvard University Press.

Patry, Sylvie, et al. 2002. *Berthe Morisot, 1841–1895*. Exh. cat. Palais des Beaux-Arts/Éditions de la Réunion des Musées Nationaux.

Rouart, Denis. 1986. *The Correspondence of Berthe Morisot with Her Family and Her Friends*. Camden Press.

PISSARRO

Adler, Kathy. 1986. "Camille Pissarro: City and Country in the 1890s." In *Studies on Camille Pissarro*, edited by Christopher Lloyd, pp. 99–116. Routledge and Kegan Paul.

Bailly-Herzberg, Janine, ed. 1988. *Correspondance de Camille Pissarro*. Vol. 3. Presses Universitaires de France.

Brettell, Richard R. 1990. *Pissarro and Pontoise: The Painter in a Landscape*. Yale University Press.

Brettell, Richard R., and Joachim Pissarro. 1992. *The Impressionist and the City: Pissarro's Series Paintings*. Exh. cat. Dallas Museum of Art/Yale University Press.

Pissarro, Joachim. 1992. *Camille Pissarro*. Rizzoli.

Rewald, John, ed. 2002. *Camille Pissarro: Letters to His Son Lucien*. Translated by Lionel Abel. Artworks.

Thomson, Richard. 1990. *Camille Pissarro: Impressionism, Landscape, and Rural Labour*. Exh. cat. City Museum and Art Gallery, Birmingham, and Burrell Collection/South Bank Centre.

Ward, Martha. 1996. *Pissarro, Neo-Impressionism, and the Spaces of the Avant-Garde*. University of Chicago Press.

RENOIR

Bailey, Colin B., et al. 1997. *Renoir's Portraits: Impressions of an Age*. Exh. cat. Yale University Press in association with National Gallery of Canada.

———, et al. 2007. *Renoir Landscapes, 1865–1883*. Exh. cat. National Gallery Company Ltd.

SEURAT

Herbert, Robert L., et al. 2004. *Seurat and the Making of "La Grande Jatte."* Exh. cat. AIC/University of California Press.

SIGNAC

Bocquillon-Ferretti, Marina. 2001. *Signac, 1863–1935*. Exh. cat. Metropolitan Museum of Art/Yale University Press.

Cachin, Françoise, et al. 2003. *P. Signac*. Exh. cat. Fondation Pierre Gianadda.

SISLEY

Stevens, Mary Anne, ed. 1992. *Alfred Sisley*. Exh. cat. Royal Academy of Arts/Yale University Press.

TOULOUSE-LAUTREC

Murray, Gale B. 1991. *Toulouse-Lautrec: The Formative Years, 1878–1891*. Clarendon Press.

Robins and Thomson. 2005. *Degas, Sickert, and Toulouse-Lautrec* (see Degas).

Stuckey, Charles F. 1979. *Toulouse Lautrec: Paintings*. Exh. cat. AIC.

Sweetman, David. 1999. *Explosive Acts: Toulouse-Lautrec, Oscar Wilde, Felix Féneon, and the Art and Anarchy of the Fin de Siècle*. Simon and Schuster.

Thomson, Richard, et al. 2005. *Toulouse-Lautrec and Montmartre*. Exh. cat. National Gallery of Art/Princeton University Press.

INDEX OF ARTISTS

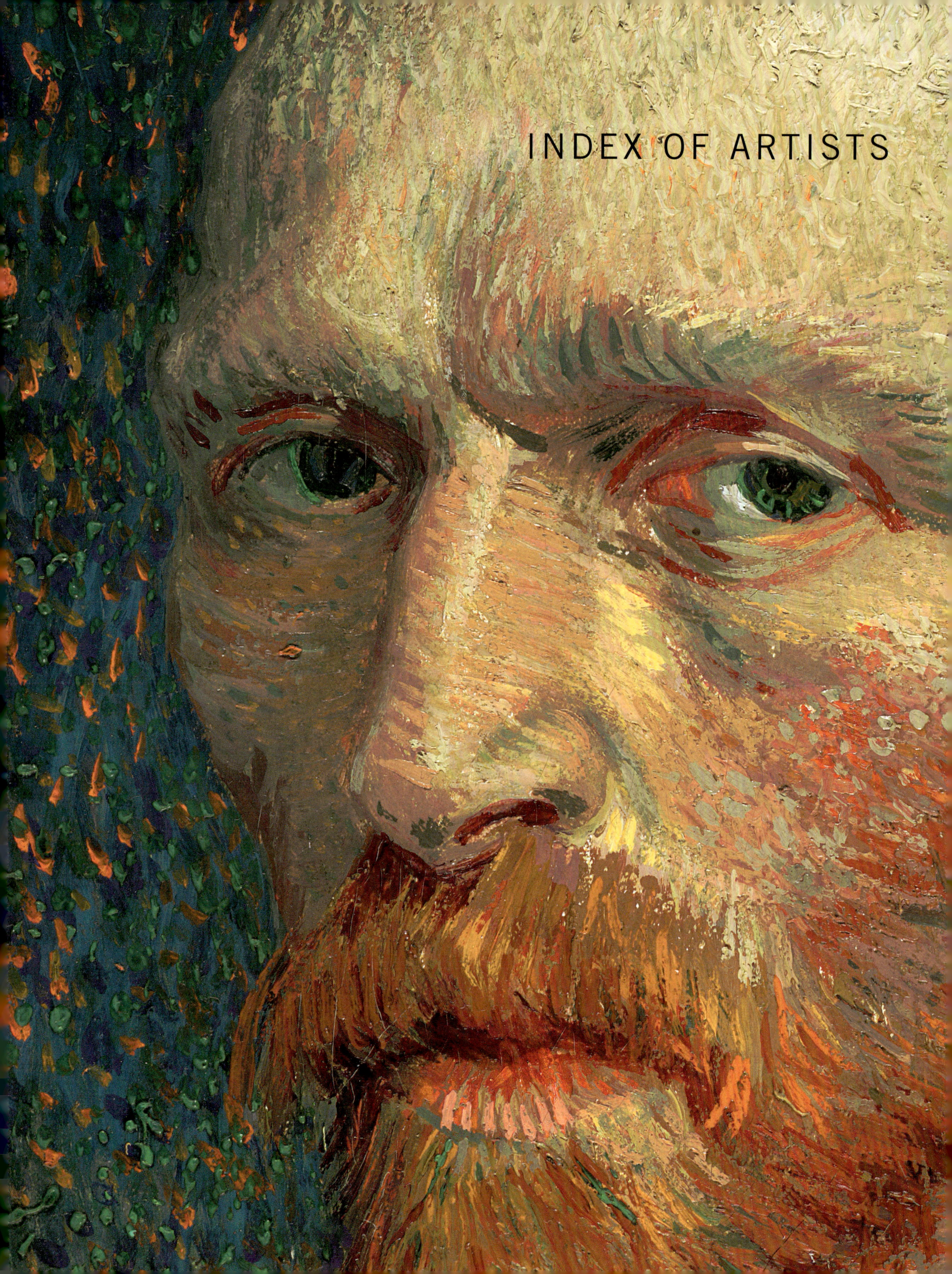

PHOTOGRAPHY CREDITS

Unless otherwise noted, all photographs of the works in the catalogue were made by the Department of Imaging of the Art Institute of Chicago, Christopher Gallagher, Associate Director, and are copyrighted by the Art Institute of Chicago.

Unless otherwise noted, photographs in the chronology are courtesy of the Art Institute of Chicago.

Every effort has been made to contact and acknowledge copyright holders for all reproductions; additional rights holders are encouraged to contact the Art Institute of Chicago. The following credits apply to all images in this catalogue for which separate acknowledgment is due.

Page 12 (upper right): Collection of the Union League Club of Chicago.

Page 15 (upper left): Courtesy of Libby Bartlett Sturges.

Page 16 (lower right): Courtesy of Colonel Robert R. McCormick Research Center.

Page 17 (upper center): © 2008 Artists Rights Society (ARS), New York/ADAGP, Paris.

Page 17 (lower center): Koehne Photo.

Page 19 (upper left): AP/Wide World Photos.

Page 19 (lower right): Courtesy of Chicago American.

Page 21 (lower center): Photograph by Karen Engstrom.

Page 21 (lower right): Paul Hansen Photography.

Page 22 (left): Photograph by Faye Wrubel.

Page 23 (lower left): Photograph by Robert Lifson, Department of Imaging, Art Institute of Chicago.

Page 24 (upper left): Photograph by Gloria Groom.

Page 24 (upper right): Photograph by Susan Huang, Department of Imaging, Art Institute of Chicago.

Page 24 (lower left): © Robert Carl.

Page 25 (upper left): © Kurt Gerber.

Page 25 (lower left): Photograph by Susan Huang, Department of Imaging, Art Institute of Chicago.